World War II Resources on the Internet

World War II Resources on the Internet

by ROLAND H. WORTH, JR.

McFarland & Company, Inc., Publishers
Jefferson, North Carolina, and London

Library of Congress Cataloguing-in-Publication Data

Worth, Roland H. Jr., 1943-
    World War II resources on the Internet / by Roland H. Worth, Jr.
      p.   cm.
    Includes index.

    ISBN 0-7864-1436-7 (softcover : 50# alkaline paper)

    1. World War, 1939–1945—Computer network resources.
2. Web sites—Directories.   I. Title: World War Two resources
on the Internet.   II. Title: World War 2 resources on the Internet.
III. Title.
D743.W675   2002
025.06'94053—dc21   2002008471

British Library cataloguing data are available

Cover art ©2002 Corbis Images and PhotoSpin

Manufactured in the United States of America

McFarland & Company, Inc., Publishers
  Box 611, Jefferson, North Carolina 28640
    www.mcfarlandpub.com

Contents

Section Two: The World Aflame

Section Three: Wartime Leaders

Preface

Every researcher needs a place to start. Finding that place is sometimes the most difficult step in the entire research endeavor. Once the first door opens, more doors appear, and one begins to breathe a little easier as it becomes clear that productive research is possible.

To provide Internet users with a jumping-off place for World War II research is the purpose of this book. Not only does it offer many possible starting points, it promotes efficient research by leading the user to the best Internet sites available.

The book covers the years 1939–1945 as well as those immediately preceding crises and diplomatically related events necessary to an adequate understanding of how the war erupted. Section One deals with diplomacy. The first chapter in this section lists sites having to do with the diplomatic relations of the western powers with the Axis and related crises that occurred during the 1930s and before formal war resulted. The second chapter centers on U.S.–Allied diplomacy after the war began—dated for our purposes as 1939 in Europe and 1941 in Asia.

Section Two is titled "The World Aflame," for this (many times more than the preceding "world" war) was truly one that encompassed in sacrifice and blood virtually the entire planet. Even nations that did not see combat and did not furnish troops still experienced economic, political, and social dislocations. The section begins with an overview of the war, which deals with those themes and subjects that go beyond the narrow confines of one theater of action. A chapter each is then devoted to the European War, the Mediterranean War (including the Near East and North Africa), the Pacific Island War, and the mainland Asian War (which still does not receive the attention it deserves in the West). Within each of these chapters, sites focusing on major battles, campaigns and controversies are listed.

Finally, Section Three focuses on wartime leadership, providing data on significant civilian and military leaders of the various wartime powers.

This list, of course, could have been far more lengthy, but that would have stretched the work beyond a practical limit.

Altogether, these hundreds of separate resources provide a wealth of information: diplomatic correspondence, personal memoirs, and scholarly interpretation of world-changing events. A small minority of these are available at multi-sites, which are listed as well.

The "home page" of a site often provides the user the key information as to what is at the site. On the other hand, the home page is, at times, the *least* useful information for the user of this book. For example, some sites have a number of *first hand narratives* of events but nothing in the home page title to suggest that. Even if the home page mentions the narratives, that does one no good if one is interested in only a specific battle and must wade through a lengthy list—perhaps only to discover that *that* battle is not mentioned at all. Especially in such cases, I have felt free to list the lead-in page under the appropriate title and to provide separate entries for the most intriguing autobiographical accounts. This way the user will immediately find the best research leads, rather than coming across them by chance.

OMISSIONS

No work can exist without borders. To keep this volume within manageable limits, a number of omissions and choices were appropriate and even essential. For example, World War Two in the Pacific actually began in the *early* thirties, but concerns of brevity meant that only modest consideration could be given to events before the Japanese attack on Pearl Harbor.

Certain subjects and themes did not fit comfortably within the confines of this work. For example, fascism and other ideologies of the thirties provided the ideological underpinning for the actions of numerous major and secondary powers. Yet such an obvious and dominant element of "political thought" (in contrast to "war action") did not seem an easy fit in the present work.

Related to this are the multitude of cultural, economic, and social events of the inter-war years and how they set the stage for the Second World War by wrecking established patterns of behavior, destroying economic security, and inflaming national hatreds. For example, the Second World War—at least in anything like its actual form—would be unimaginable without the Great Depression wrecking the socio-economic order of the day. Yet any but the most glancing discussion of that fact would take this work too far afield.

Internal German religious and secular opposition to the excesses (or even the existence) of the Nazi regime represents yet another area that would have been intriguing to include, but space considerations seemed to require the omission of this as well. (As with the Holocaust, a very few entries touch on the subject, but these represent a mere fragment of the attention full consideration would provide.) For similar reason the Nuremberg War Trials and their Pacific equivalent have had to be omitted from the work.

Although I mention it last, the Holocaust is the most obvious omission. The systematic slaughter of millions of Jews and a huge number from other ethnic groups is a topic that would have taken the book too far afield from its central emphases on the broad pattern of battles and leaders of the war. Equaled only by the massacres of Stalin's purges, these blots on humanity's collective claim to a conscience have been amply documented in a multitude of printed volumes. Hopefully a work aimed at the Internet materials will one day appear to supplement the available print resources.

AUTHORSHIP AND STYLE OF NOTATION

Where available, I have noted the authorship of particular materials. When materials are the result of the work of unidentified individuals (and this is not uncommon in the military historian composed narratives) I have typically listed them as "Unidentified" in origin. When a concise identification of the responsible military history unit was available I included it.

An unfortunate Internet phenomenon is the number of otherwise first class sites—first class from the standpoint of both physical layout and appearance and the material included—that lack clear attribution to an individual or organization. When sites do not clearly or inferentially attribute the material to a specific individual or organization, I have simply placed them in the "Unidentified" category.

If an individually named "web master" (rather than a company) is identified I have often used his or her name as the one responsible for the content of the site on the assumption that the two could easily be one and the same. Following a site's links to other places dealing with the same subject has provided the identifications for some additional sites. Many sites seem to work on the assumption that you began at their home page and ultimately worked your way to the page of interest. And even *that* doesn't always provide the information.

Some identifications have clearly been missed. I often went back a link or two in an attempt to identify the author. If the information was available further back than that, all I can do is to apologize for the omission of the name.

A word as to dates: typical civilian usage then and today in the United

States speaks, for example, of September 26, 1943. Official military usage writes 26 September 1943. When it comes to such matters I have attempted to preserve the usage—not always consistent—of the sources as given on the individual Internet sites.

Most entries include brief parenthetical notes. These are used for several overlapping purposes: to describe the central thrust of the material, to provide additional information as to the source of the material (commonly indicating what series of publications a given work is part of), and to explain what makes this site different from other sites that may have a similar name. In short, the goal is to provide a description that will permit the user to quickly evaluate the possible significance of the material to his or her own research.

There are more than a few cases where an entry doesn't quite fit under any specific heading. In such cases I have attempted to locate it under the one that seemed conceptually closest. For example, Italy's embarrassing imperial "conquest" of Ethiopia is discussed under the Mediterranean War even though that division of the book is centered on the events that began in 1939. Likewise "Homefront" sections have been taken in their broadest sense to include not only strictly domestic matters (such as social policy and industrial output) but also things that might be militarily related that were taking place in the particular homeland being discussed rather than abroad.

Some of these decisions might well have been handled differently by someone else. Since Chiang Kai-shek was present at the Cairo Conference, should I list that meeting in a section uniquely reflecting Pacific affairs, or one that predominantly concerned the European power brokers? I have chosen the former since Chiang's presence obviously shifted the concerns of those attending. On the other hand, the Chinese leader was looked down upon as a secondary figure and had minimal impact, so one could just as reasonably have chosen to simply consider all the diplomatic conferences together. It is only a judgment call.

Similarly, should the scattered materials on the Seabees appear under "naval forces" or "infantry and other land forces"? Although the Seabees functioned as part of the Navy, the *building* was on land and in support of land operations—to a great extent Marine. Hence placement of these entries is based on *where* the work was done, rather than *for whom*.

Yes, the Coast Guard *is* separate from the Navy but, for organizational purposes, it is a "naval force"—at least in time of war. Likewise Marine aviators aren't about to let you forget they are *Marines*; on the other hand they normally operated from *ground* bases like the Air Force and, for that reason, I have typically included their exploits in with those of the "air forces." Service purists please have mercy!

Some materials are "composite" works, approved by several nations.

In those cases the individual countries concerned are listed. In some cases there are fine distinctions that are useful: for example, describing a decree as from the "Reich Government" is a means of noting laws passed independent of Reichstag action.

When it comes to spelling, I have attempted to follow that of the source being cited. Whether a document uses "Adolph" or "Adolf" Hitler, I have let the spelling stand. If you are an American you speak of an "armored" division; if British, of an "armoured" division. The site's choice is the determining factor. Likewise I have referred to "World War II," "World War Two," and "World War 2"—again according to the site's preferences.

Throughout the text I have utilized brackets for several reasons. In some cases there is no clear title for a site and it has been necessary to provide one in brackets. In some cases, only the first or last name of the site's author is given and, hence, for the uncited part I provide: [?]. In certain cases brackets are utilized within a site title to clarify a point of potential confusion: If we are dealing, for example, with a *German* POW and there is nothing in the title to make that clear, you will find "[German]," bracketed for the sake of clarity.

Doubtless in a work as varied and widespread as this one, some errors will have sailed over my head. If the reader would like to share these with me, they can be sent care of the publisher. Likewise I would enjoy receiving information about any interesting sites the reader comes across that he or she believes would be useful in future editions.

Roland H. Worth, Jr.

Section One

Diplomacy

1

Prewar International Diplomacy and Crises

Europe

OVERVIEW

1. Bauer, Jim. *Belligerent Acts Prior to U.S. Entry into World War II* (traces German/Japan acts against U.S. and vice versa)
http://www.ww2pacific.com/bellacts.html

2. Bobadilla, Michael. *Britain and France: A Deadly Appeasement*
http://www.omnibusol.com/wcessay2.html

3. Cheney, Alexis. *An Appeasement History*
http://www.omnibusol.com/wcessay6.html

4. Coates, Jennifer. *Interwar Appeasement as Naivete: Why Did Only Churchill See It?*
http://www.omnibusol.com/wcessay1.html

5. Doody, Richard. *Europe in an Age of Autocracy: A Chronology of Dictatorial Regimes between the World Wars* (includes lesser known powers)
http://worldatwar.net/article/autocracy/index.html

6. [French Government.] *Diplomatic Documents, 1938-1939;* a/k/a *The French Yellow Book*
http://www.ibiblio.org/pha/fyb/fyb-preface.html

7. Frose, Donna. *Treaty of Versailles/League of Nations* (primarily dealing with successes and failures of latter)
http://www.west-teq.net/~dmf/vers.htm#jap

8. Secretary of State for Foreign Affairs. *The British War Blue Book: Documents Concerning German-Polish Relations and the Outbreak of Hostilities between Great Britain and Germany on September 3, 1939* (1939)
http://ibiblio.org/pha/bb/bb-preface.html

9. [Signatory Powers.] *The Versailles Treaty (June 28, 1919)* (for better and worse all western powers reacted to and against this treaty until the next war broke out)
http://history.sandiego.edu/gen/text/versaillestreaty/vercontents.html

10. Sontag, Raymond J., and James S. Beddie, editors. *Nazi-Soviet Relations, 1939-1941* (from the Archives of the German Foreign Office; published by U.S. Department of State, 1948)
http://www.ibiblio.org/pha/nsr/nsr-preface.html
http://www.yale.edu/lawweb/avalon/nazsov/nazsov.htm

11. [Unidentified.] *How the End of World War I Led to World War II*
http://www.ww2pacific.com/ww1end.html

12. [Unidentified.] *Pre-U.S. Entry in World War II* (unofficial and official acts of war)
http://www.ww2pacific.com/prewar.html

13. [Unidentified.] *Racial [Ethnic] Map of Europe* (as published in 1923)
http://www.anesi.com/rmap.htm

14. [Unidentified.] *Versailles Treaty to Polish Blitzkrieg, 1919-1939* (political and naval related diplomatic matters in parallel columns)
http://www.naval-history.net/WW2CampaignPreWar.htm

15. U.S. State Department. *Chronology of International Events: March 1938 to December 1941* (published December 1941)
http://www.ibiblio.org/pha/events/events.html

16. White, Matthew. *Historical Atlas of the Twentieth Century* (tracks many different aspects)
http://users.erols.com/mwhite28/20centry.htm

PREWAR NAZI REGIME

16. Barth, Karl. *Barmen Declaration* (1934; traditional Christian manifesto rejecting the often successful Nazi effort to Nazify German Protestantism)
http://www.ucc.org/faith/barmen.htm

17. Day, Nigel. *Did Artur Seyss-Inquart Receive a Fair Trial?*
http://www.waikato.ac.nz/wfass/subjects/
history/waimilhist/1999/warcrimes.htm

18. [German Reichstag.] *Enabling Act* (March 23, 1933; permitting government to enact legislation independent of action by the Reichstag)
http://www.csustan.edu/History/Weikart/enabling.htm

19. Goebbels, Joseph. *German Women* (March 18, 1933; speech to women about their anticipated role in the new Nazi regime)
http://www.calvin.edu/academic/cas/gpa/goeb55.htm

20. Gonzalez, Servando. *The Swastika and the Nazis: A Study on the Origins of the Adoption of the Swastika by Adolf Hitler as a Symbol of the Nazi Movement*
http://www.intelinet.org/swastika/

21. Hitler, Adolf. *On National Socialism and World Relations* (January 30, 1937 before the Reichstag)
http://www.calvin.edu/academic/cas/gpa/hitler1.htm

22. Hossbach [Colonel]. *Hossbach Memorandum* (November 10, 1937; summary of Hitler's 4-1/4 hour conference with his top military men as to long and short term prospects for Germany in Europe)
http://www.yale.edu/lawweb/avalon/imt/document/hossbach.htm

23. [Joint Statement.] *The Italo-German Alliance* (May 22, 1939; text)
http://www.ibiblio.org/pha/policy/pre-war/390522a.html

24. Marriott Library Exhibition. *The Nazi Olympics: Berlin, 1936*
http://www.ushmm.org/olympics/

25. [Reich Government.] *Law for the Protection of Hereditary Health* (July 14, 1933; permitting involuntary sterilization to be ordered)
http://www.mtsu.edu/~baustin/nurmlaw1.html

26. [Reich Government.] *Law for the Restoration of the Professional Civil Service* (April 7, 1933; banning non-Aryans from government employment)
http://www.yadvashem.org/about_holocaust/documents/part1/doc10.html

27. Rempel, Gerhard. *Origins of Fascism*
http://mars.acnet.wnec.edu/~grempel/courses/world/lectures/fascism.html

28. Swigart, Soren. *Reichstag Fire*
http://worldatwar.net/event/reichstagsbrand/index.html

29. [Unidentified.] *"At the Heart of the Power System of Nazi Germany There Was a Confusion of Private Empires"* (intra-movement cliques as central to Nazism)
http://www.essaybank.co.uk/essays/2856.php

30. [Unidentified.] *Fall of the Weimar Republic*
http://www.barnsdle.demon.co.uk/hist/tyra.html

31. [Unidentified.] *Germany during World War Two* (begins study with the pre-war, pre-takeover years)
http://www.geocities.com/Athens/Rhodes/6916/ww2.htm

32. [Unidentified.] *The Nazi Olympics*
http://www.us-israel.org/jsource/Holocaust/olympics.html

33. [Unidentified.] *The Reichstag Fire*
http://www.barnsdle.demon.co.uk/hist/fire.html

34. [Unidentified.] *"Triumph of the Will"* (information on the film and links to film clips from it)
http://history.sandiego.edu/gen/filmnotes/triumphB.html

35. Wilhelm, Thomas. *NDSAP Museum* (biographies, history, etc.)
http://www.nsdapmuseum.com/

36. Witte, James, and Jason Krick. *Labor Allocation during the Third Reich: The Arbeitsbuch as an Instrument of Manpower Policy* (with internal links to four sections of the study)
http://faculty-web.at.nwu.edu/sociology/witte/arbeit/ab0.html

Munich and the Czech Crisis

37. Atkinson, Becky, et al. *To War or Not to War* (factors influencing the attitude toward involvement in a war with Germany in the United States, Britain, France, and Russia)
http://saul.snu.edu/syllabi/history/s97projects/towar/

38. Chamberlain, Neville. *"Peace in Our Time"* (airport remarks of the Prime Minister, September 30, 1938)
http://www.ibiblio.org/hyperwar/ETO/Dip/peace-our-time.html
http://www.lib.byu.edu/~rdh/eurodocs/uk/peace.html

39. Finney, Patrick. *The Romance of Decline: The Historiography of Appeasement and British National Identity* (from the *Electronic Journal of International History*)
http://ihr.sas.ac.uk/publications/ejihart1.html#a1

40. [France, Germany, Great Britain, and Italy] *Munich Pact: English Translation (29 September 1938)*
http://www.yale.edu/lawweb/avalon/imt/munich1.htm
http://www.geocities.com/iturks/html/documents_1.html

41. [France, Germany, Great Britain, and Italy] *Munich Pact: Annex to the Agreement (29 September 1938)*
http://www.yale.edu/lawweb/avalon/imt/document/munich2.htm

42. Kuhlman, Kurt. *"Subject to a Humiliation:" The Military Considerations of British Czechoslovakian Policy in 1938*
http://www.warhorsesim.com/papers/MunichCrisis.htm

43. Lilly, David. *British Reaction to the Munich Crisis*
http://www.loyno.edu/history/journal/1993-4/Lilly.html

44. Martyrn, B. A. *Munich Crisis: A Personal Recollection* (how one individual in the RAF reacted to the crisis)
http://www.hillhead99.freeserve.co.uk/munich.htm

45. Rimington, John. *"The New Wolsey"—Sir Horace Wilson and the Appeasement of Hitler* (impact of his thinking on Chamberlain's policies)
http://www.sourceuk.net/indexf.html?01138

46. [Unidentified.] *Airpower during Munich* (detailed statistics of number and type of aircraft held by the opposing forces)
http://www.geocities.com/CapeCanaveral/2072/Munich.html

47. [Various Speakers.] *The British Parliamentary Debate on the Munich Agreement*
http://www.mtholyoke.edu/acad/intrel/munich.htm

TRIPARTITE PACT

48. [Germany, Italian, and Japanese governments.] *Some Documents Related to the Alliance of Germany, Japan, and Italy during World War II* (includes text of Tripartite Pact and other early agreements)
http://www.ibiblio.org/pha/policy/pre-war/361125a.html

49. [Germany, Italian and Japanese governments.] *Tripartite Pact* (26 September 1940; text)
http://www.ibiblio.org/hyperwar/PTO/Dip/Tripartite.html
http://www.danshistory.com/ww2/docs/tripartite.txt

50. Hull, Cordell. *Statement by the Secretary of State on the Tripartite Pact* (September 27, 1940)
http://www.mtholyoke.edu/acad/intrel/WorldWar2/tripartite.htm

51. Lowe, Jennifer. *Failed Coalition Warfare: The Provisions and Reality of German-Japanese Strategic Cooperation, 1940-1943*
http://www.waikato.ac.nz/wfass/subjects/history/waimilhist/1997/jl-folder/jl-p1.html

NAZI-SOVIET PACT

52. [Germany and USSR] *Nazi-Soviet Non-Aggression Pact* (August 23, 1939)

http://www.yale.edu/lawweb/avalon/nazsov/nonagres.htm
http://www.danshistory.com/ww2/docs/sov-ger_non-agression.txt
http://www.geocities.com/iturks/html/ribbentrop_molotov_pact.html

53. Molotov, V. M. *The Foreign Policy of the Government: A Report by the Chairman of the Soviet People's Commissars and People's Commissar for Foreign Affairs on March 29, 1940*
http://www.pp.clinet.fi/~pkr01/history/molotov.html

54. Raack, R. C. *Stalin's Role in the Coming of World War II* (from the Spring 1996 edition of *World Affairs*; was the agreement with Germany defensive in nature or intended as the springboard for Stalin's own attack on Germany in the future?)
http://www.mtholyoke.edu/acad/intrel/raack.htm

55. Raack, R. C. *Stalin's Role in the Coming of World War II: The International Debate Goes On* (from the Fall 1996 edition of *World Affairs*)
http://www.mtholyoke.edu/acad/intrel/raack2.htm

AMERICAN RESPONSES PRIOR TO DECEMBER 7, 1941

56. Feldmeth, Greg D. *American Foreign Policy between the World Wars*
http://home.earthlink.net/~gfeldmeth/lec.forpol.html

57. Hull, Cordell. *Destroyers for Bases Agreement (2 September 1940)* (text)
http://www.history.navy.mil/faqs/faq59-24.htm

58. Roosevelt, Franklin D. *Address Delivered to the Congress* (January 4, 1939; extract)
http://www.mtholyoke.edu/acad/intrel/WorldWar2/fdr.htm

59. Roosevelt, Franklin D. *"Arsenal of Democracy"* (fireside chat, December 1940)
http://www.tamu.edu/scom/pres/speeches/fdrarsenal.html

60. Roosevelt, Franklin D. *Message to the Congress* (January 12, 1939; extract)
http://www.mtholyoke.edu/acad/intrel/WorldWar2/fdr2.htm

61. Roosevelt, Franklin D. *Statement by President Roosevelt on the Invasions of Denmark and Norway (April 13, 1940)*
http://www.mtholyoke.edu/acad/intrel/WorldWar2/fdr12.htm

62. Roosevelt, Franklin D., and Winston Churchill. *The Atlantic Charter* (August 1941; text)
http://www.ibiblio.org/hyperwar/Dip/Atlantic.html
http://usinfo.state.gov/usa/infousa/facts/democrac/53.htm
http://www.danshistory.com/ww2/docs/atlantic_char.txt

63. Roosevelt, Franklin D. (and others). *Franklin Delano Roosevelt Library & digital Archives* (13,000 pages of Roosevelt materials and other diplomatic documents)
http://www.fdrlibrary.marist.edu/safe.html

64. Smith, Frank E. *Roosevelt and the Coming of War* (popularity of anti-intervention)
http://fsmitha.com/h2/ch22.htm

65. [Unidentified.] *Between a Rock and a Hard Place: The Moral and Political Dilemma of Franklin D. Roosevelt and the American Public Preceding WWII*
http://saul.snu.edu/syllabi/history/s97projects/towar/usa.htm

66. [Unidentified.] *List of Destroyers Transferred to Britain under the Destroyers for Bases Agreement*
http://www.history.navy.mil/faqs/faq59-24a.htm

67. [Unidentified.] *Neutrality Acts, 1935-1941* (passage; attempts to revise and apply)
http://history.sandiego.edu/gen/WW2Timeline/neutralityacts.html

68. United States Congress. *Lend-Lease Act (11 March 1941)* (text)
http://www.history.navy.mil/faqs/faq59-23.htm
http://www.danshistory.com/ww2/docs/lend-lease.act.txt

69. United States Congress. *The Neutrality Act of 1937* (text)
http://www.danshistory.com/ww2/docs/neutrality.act_37.txt

70. United States Congress. *The Neutrality Act of 1939* (text)
http://www.danshistory.com/ww2/docs/neutrality.act_39.txt

71. U. S. Department of State. *Peace and War: U.S. Foreign Policy, 1931-1941* (Washington: U.S. Government Printing Office, 1943; 271 documents included)
http://www.ibiblio.org/pha/paw/index.html

Asia

JAPANESE INTERVENTION IN MANCHURIA AND CHINA

72. Military History Section, Headquarters, Army Forces Fast East. *Political Strategy Prior to the Outbreak of War, Part I* (Japanese Monograph 144)
http://ibiblio.org/pha/monos/144/index.html

73. Military History Section, Headquarters, Army Forces Fast East. *Political Strategy Prior to the Outbreak of War, Part II* (Japanese Monograph 146)
http://ibiblio.org/pha/monos/146/index.html

74. Military History Section, Headquarters, Army Forces Fast East. *Political Strategy Prior to the Outbreak of War, Part III* (Japanese Monograph 147)
http://ibiblio.org/pha/monos/147/index.html

75. Military History Section, Headquarters, Army Forces Fast East. *Political Strategy Prior to the Outbreak of War, Part IV* (Japanese Monograph 150)
http://ibiblio.org/pha/monos/150/index.html

76. Military History Section, Headquarters, Army Forces Fast East. *Political Strategy Prior to the Outbreak of War, Part V* (Japanese Monograph 152)
http://ibiblio.org/pha/monos/152/index.html

77. [Unidentified.] *Manchuria, September 18, 1931* (factors encouraging Japanese intervention in Manchuria)
http://history.sandiego.edu/gen/WW2Timeline/step01.html

JAPAN AND RUSSIA

78. Barber, Laurie. *Checkmate at the Russian Frontier: The Russia-Japanese Conflict before Pearl Harbour*
http://www.waikato.ac.nz/wfass/subjects/history/
waimilhist/1997/lhb-folder/lhb-p1.html

79. Dando, Kris. *The Kuril Islands—The Last Battlefield of World War II*
http://www.waikato.ac.nz/wfass/subjects/history/ waimilhist/1997/
kd-folder/kd-p1.html

80. Ford, Daniel. *Japan vs. Russia, 1939* (the little noticed mini-war between the two powers when Japan attempted to expand into Russian controlled territory)
http://www.danford.net/nomonhan.htm

81. [Soviet Union.] *Soviet-Japanese Neutrality Pact and Denunciation* (includes declaration of war on Japan)
http://www.ibiblio.org/hyperwar/PTO/Dip/sov-japan-neu.html
http://www.danshistory.com/ww2/docs/soviet_neut.txt

NANKING (NANJING) MASSACRE, 1937-1938

82. Association for Advancement of Liberalist View of History. *ABC of Modern Japanese History* (strives to refute charges of Japanese military atrocities)
http://www.jiyuu-shikan.org/e/index.html

83. Kajimoto, Masato. *Nanking Atrocities (Nanjing Massacre)* (Master's thesis)
http://web.missouri.edu/~jschool/nanking/

84. Tillman, F. *Nanking Massacre* (article from the December 18, 1937 issue of the *New York Times*)
http://www.fordham.edu/halsall/mod/nanking.html

85. [Unidentified.] *Japanese Army Atrocities: Nanjing Massacre—300,000 Chinese People Killed, 20,000 Women Raped* (links to documents and sites discussing the events)
http://www.cnd.org/NJMassacre/

86. [Unidentified.] *Story of John Rabe* (westerner who organized assistance for the Chinese and obstructed the Japanese policies)
http://www.geocities.com/southbeach/channel/9643/angry3.html

87. [Unidentified.] *WWW Memorial Hall of the Victims in the Nanjing Massacre (1937-1938)* (with links to a variety of source documents and current web sites discussing the atrocity)
http://www.cnd.org/mirror/nanjing/

88. Yue, D. *History We Shall Never Forget (China, 1931-1945)*
http://www.centurychina.com/wiihist/

WESTERN ASSISTANCE FOR CHINA

89. Burgard, George. *Flying Tiger Days* (war-time diary and photographs)
http://www.flyingtigerdiary.com/

90. Chennault, Claire L. *[Letter to Widow of Killed Pilot]* (explaining circumstances of husband's death)
http://www.military.com/Content/MoreContent?file=chennault01

91. Cockfield, Jamie H. *Interview with General Robert Scott* (Scott was a member of the Flying Tigers)
http://www.military.com/Content/MoreContent?file=PRrobscott

92. Ford, Daniel. *Annals of the Brewster Buffalo* (used by several countries, including China, at beginning of war)
http://www.danford.net/buff.htm

93. Ford Daniel. *Annals of the Flying Tigers*
http://www.danford.net/avg.htm

94. Ford, Daniel. *The Sorry Saga of the Brewster Buffalo*
http://www.airspacemag.com/ASM/Mag/Index/1996/JJ/ssbb.html

95. Frisbee, John L. *China Bomber*
http://www.afa.org/magazine/valor/0488valor.html

96. Public Broadcasting System. *Flying Tigers: The Film* (includes downloadable text of the film script)
http://www.flyingtigersvideo.com/photogallery.htm

97. Rossi, Dick. *A Flying Tiger's Story*
(part 1:) http://home.att.net/~C.C.Jordan/Rossi-AVG.html
(part 2:) http://home.att.net/~C.C.Jordan/Rossi-AVG2.html
(part 3:) http://home.att.net/~C.C.Jordan/Rossi-AVG3.html
For the same account with different introductory material and differences in text narrative:
(intro:) http://www.elknet.pl/acestory/rossi/rossi.htm
(part 1:) http://www.elknet.pl/acestory/rossi/rossi1.htm
(part 3:) http://www.elknet.pl/acestory/rossi/rossi2.htm

98. Sherman, Stephen. *The Flying Tigers: Claire Cheannault and the American Volunteer Group Flew Curtis P-40 Warhawks in China and Burma against the Japanese*
http://www.acepilots.com/misc_tigers.html

99. Smith, Robert T. *Tale of a Tiger: From the Diary of Robert T. Smith, Flying Tiger*
(part 1:) http://home.att.net/~ww2aircraft/RTSmith1.html
(part 2:) http://home.att.net/~ww2aircraft/RTSmith2.html
(part 3:) http://home.att.net/~ww2aircraft/RTSmith3.html
(part 4:) http://home.att.net/~ww2aircraft/RTSmith4.html

100. Suzuki, [? .] *Mr. Suzuki's Interview* (interview with a Japanese pilot who fought against the Flying Tigers)
http://www.danford.net/suzuki.htm

101. [Unidentified.] *American Volunteer Group: Flying Tigers*
http://www.flyingtigersavg.com/

102. [Unidentified.] *B-10s to Stratojets: The Amazing Aviation Odyssey of Chuck Baisden* (served as gunner and armorer with the Flying Tigers—man responsible for assuring that all weapons systems were functional)
http://home.att.net/~C.C.Jordan/Baisden.html

103. [Unidentified.] *China Days, 1944-1945* (pictures and information on 14th Air Force)
http://community-2.webtv.net/HaoBooHao/doc25/

104. [Unidentified.] *Erik Shilling: Flying Tiger*
(part 1:) http://home.att.net/~C.C.Jordan/Shilling.html
(part 2:) http://home.att.net/~C.C.Jordan/Shilling2.html

105. [Unidentified.] *The Flying Tigers: Claire Chennault and the American Volunteer Group*
http://www.acepilots.com/misc_tigers.html

U.S.-JAPANESE NEGOTIATIONS

106. Ballantine, Joseph W. *Memorandum Regarding a Conversation between the Secretary of State, the Japanese Ambassador [Nomura], and Mr. Kurusu (18 November 1941)*
http://www.mtholyoke.edu/acad/intrel/WorldWar2/ballan.htm

107. Dower, John W. *Japan Addresses Its War Responsibility*
http://www.umich.edu/~iinet/journal/vol3no1/jpnwar.html

108. Hull, Cordell. *The Secretary of State to the Japanese Ambassador [Horinouchi] Terminating the 1911 Treaty of Commerce and Navigation between the U.S. and Japan (26 July 1939)]*
http://www.mtholyoke.edu/acad/intrel/WorldWar2/hull5.htm

109. Hull, Cordell. *Memorandum by the Secretary of State Regarding a Conversation with the Japanese Ambassador [Horinouchi] (August 26, 1939)* (U.S. annoyance at Japan's interference with U.S. commercial interests in occupied parts of China)
http://www.mtholyoke.edu/acad/intrel/WorldWar2/hull6.htm

110. Hull, Cordell. *Memorandum by the Secretary of State Regarding a Conversation with the Japanese Ambassador [Horinouchi] (April 20, 1940)* (Far Eastern issues, especially the Philippines and Dutch East Indies)
http://www.mtholyoke.edu/acad/intrel/WorldWar2/hull8.htm

111. Hull, Cordell. *The Four Principles* (underlying U.S.-Japanese negotiations)
http://www.ibiblio.org/hyperwar/PTO/Dip/4Principles.html

112. [Japanese Government.] *Japanese Embassy to the Department of State Protesting the Ban on Exports of Iron and Steel Scrap (October 7, 1940)*
http://www.mtholyoke.edu/acad/intrel/WorldWar2/scrap.htm

113. [Japanese Government.] *Japanese 14-Part Message of December 7, 1941*
http://www.ibiblio.org/hyperwar/PTO/Dip/Fourteen.html

114. [Japanese and U.S. Governments.] *Japanese Proposal "B" of November 20, 1941, and U.S. Counterproposal of November 26, 1941* (text)
http://www.ibiblio.org/hyperwar/PTO/Dip/PlanB.html

115. [Japanese Government.] *Policy Adopted at Imperial Conference, 2 July 1941* (accepting the possibility of war with the U.S.)
http://www.ibiblio.org/hyperwar/PTO/Dip/IR-410702.html

116. Konoye, Fumimaro. *Address of Prince Fumimaro Konoye, Prime Minister of Japan, Delivered before the 76th Session of the Imperial Diet (Tokyo, Japan, January 21, 1941)*
http://www.ibiblio.org/pha/policy/1941/410121a.html

117. Matsuoka, Yosuke. *Address by Foreign Minister of Japan, Yosuke Matsuoka, Delivered before the 76th Session of the Imperial Diet (Tokyo, Japan, January 21, 1941)*
http://www.ibiblio.org/pha/policy/1941/410121b.html

118. Stevens, Neal. *The Japanese Motivation [for War]*
http://www.subsim.com/ssr/edit10_98.html

119. [Unidentified.] *A Chronological Collection of Documents Relating to the U.S. Entry into World War II*
http://www.ibiblio.org/pha/timeline/

2

U.S. and Allied
Wartime Diplomacy

Europe

OVERVIEW

120. Kudryashov, Sergei. *Stalin and the Allies: Who Deceived Whom?* (from the May 1995 issue of *History Today*; an examination of Stalin's philosophy of negotiation with wartime confederates)
http://www.mtholyoke.edu/acad/intrel/kudrya.htm

121. [Multi-nations.] *The United Nations Pact* (January 1, 1942; declaration of war aims and intents of Allied nations)
http://www.ibiblio.org/hyperwar/Dip/UNPact.html

122. Roosevelt, Franklin D. *FDR's Statement on North Africa (17 November 1942)* (Roosevelt backs General Eisenhower's decisions concerning the French role in North Africa)
http://www.ibiblio.org/hyperwar/ETO/Dip/fdr-nafrica.html
http://members.aol.com/forcountry/ww2/fdr9.htm

123. [Unidentified.] *Conferences of the Allied Grand Strategy*
http://history.acusd.edu/gen/WW2Timeline/confer.html

124. Wolfe, L. *The Other War: FDR's Battle against Churchill and the British Empire*
http://members.tripod.com/~american_almanac/FDRlw95.htm

CASABLANCA CONFERENCE

125. [Allied Governments.] *Casablanca Conference Communique*
http://www.ibiblio.org/pha/policy/1943/430124a.html

126. Roosevelt, Franklin D. *Casablanca Conference* (Presidential radio
address, February 12, 1943)
http://www.ibiblio.org/hyperwar/Dip/casablanca-cnf.html
http://historicaltextarchive.com/sections.php?op=viewarticle&artid=198
http://www.danshistory.com/ww2/docs/casablanca_conf.txt
http://members.aol.com/forcountry/ww2/fdr2.htm

127. Timmins, David B. *[Excluding General de Gaulle]* (no title; explaining how Colonel Alfred Grunther was assigned the duty by the President of assuring that de Gaulle was unable to attend the meeting he
insisted upon attending)
http://homepage.mac.com/brownsteve/timmins/misc/005.html

QUEBEC CONFERENCE

128. Roosevelt, Franklin D., and Winston S. Churchill. *Joint Statement*
(August 1943)
http://www.yale.edu/lawweb/avalon/decade/decade06.htm

129. Simon Wisenthal Center. *Strategic Clash at Quebec Conference*
http://motlc.wiesenthal.com/text/x20/xm2067.html

MOSCOW CONFERENCE

130. Joint Four Nation Declaration. *Moscow Conference Statement (October 1943)* (demanding unconditional surrender)
http://www.ibiblio.org/hyperwar/Dip/moscow-cnf.html
http://history.vif2.ru/library/archives/speeches/speech2.html

TEHERAN CONFERENCE

131. Roosevelt, Franklin D., and Joseph Stalin. *Roosevelt and Stalin Dis-
cuss the Future of French Rule in Indochina: Tehran Conference (November
28, 1943)*
http://www.mtholyoke.edu/acad/intrel/fdrjs.htm

132. Roosevelt, Franklin D., Winston Churchill, and Joseph Stalin. *Declaration of the Three Powers*
http://www.ibiblio.org/pha/policy/1943/431201c.html

133. Roosevelt, Franklin D., Winston Churchill, and Joseph Stalin. *The Tehran Round Table Sitting* (excerpts from the transcripts)
http://humanities.uwe.ac.uk/corehistorians/powers/text/s24teher.htm# Title

134. [Unidentified.] *Big Three at Teheran—Europe 1943*
http://history.acusd.edu/gen/WW2Timeline/Europe04a.html

Yalta Conference

135. Churchill, Winston. *Address in Commons on the Crimea Conference (February 27, 1945)*
http://www.sunsite.unc.edu/pha/policy/1945/450227a.html

136. Mantenieks, Maris A. *Yalta and the Baltic Countries*
http://www.bafl.com/yalta.htm

137. Roosevelt, Franklin D. *President Roosevelt's Report to Congress on the Crimea Conference (March 1, 1945)*
http://www.sunsite.unc.edu/pha/policy/1945/450301a.html

138. Stalin, Joseph, Franklin D. Roosevelt, and Winston Churchill. *Protocol of Proceedings* (February 1945; statement of Allied policy)
http://www.ibiblio.org/hyperwar/Dip/yalta-cnf.html
http://www.yale.edu/lawweb/avalon/wwii/yalta.htm
http://www.danshistory.com/ww2/docs/yalta_conf.txt

139. Wesserle, A. R. *Yalta: Fact or Fate? A Brief Characterization* (from the *Journal of Historical Review*)
http://vho.org/GB/Journals/JHR/3/4/Wesserle359-370.html

Potsdam Conference

140. Britain, China, and the United States. *Potsdam Declaration* (July 26, 1945; demanding immediate and unconditional surrender by Japan)
http://www.ibiblio.org/hyperwar/PTO/Dip/Potsdam.html

141. Britain, U.S., USSR *Potsdam: Protocol of the Proceedings* (August 1, 1945; on future division of Europe and joint post-war policy goals)
http://www.yale.edu/lawweb/avalon/decade/decade17.htm

142. LaFeber, Walter. *Potsdam Conference* (with emphasis on Truman as a new President having to deal personally with the other major heads of state)
http://www.pbs.org/wgbh/amex/presidents/nf/featured/truman/potsdam.html

DECLARATIONS OF WAR AND SURRENDER: EUROPE

143. Churchill, Winston. *Announcement in Parliament of Germany's Unconditional Surrender (May 8, 1945)*
http://www.sunsite.unc.edu/pha/policy/1945/450508e.html

144. Doenitz, Karl. *Grand Admiral Karl Doenitz' Broadcast Informing the German People of Their Unconditional Surrender (May 8, 1945)*
http://www.sunsite.unc.edu/pha/policy/1945/450508b.html

145. Ellis, Gena. *Victory in Europe*
http://www.dtic.mil/soldiers/may95/p50.html

146. [France and Germany.] *Franco-German Armistice* (25 June 1940, English translation)
http://www.yale.edu/lawweb/avalon/wwii/frgearm.htm

147. [Germany.] *German Declaration of War with the United States: December 11, 1941*
http://www.yale.edu/lawweb/avalon/wwii/gerdec41.htm
http://fcit.coedu.usf.edu/holocaust/resource/document/DECWAR.htm

148. [German and Allied powers.] *German Surrender Documents* (May 1945; texts)
http://www.ibiblio.org/hyperwar/ETO/Dip/german-surr.html
http://www.law.ou.edu/hist/germsurr.html
http://www.danshistory.com/ww2/docs/german_surrender.txt
http://www.geocities.com/iturks/html/german_surrender_documents.html

149. Hallstead, William F. *Flight to Surrender* (how a British plane with an American crew landed up flying the German surrender delegation to the place where documents would be signed)
http://www.military.com/Content/MoreContent?file=PRreich

150. Hitler, Adolf. *Hitler Announced to the Reichstag the Declaration of War against the United States* (December 11, 1941)
http://metalab.unc.edu/pha/policy/1941/411211b.html

151. Hitler, Adolf. *Radio Report: Germany Invades Poland* (audio of speech)
http://www.rjgeib.com/thoughts/hitler/hitler.html

152. Hitler, Adolf. *Speech by Herr Hitler to the Reichstag on September 1, 1939* (justifying the war with Poland)
http://www.geocities.com/iturks/html/hitlerspeech1.html

153. [Italy and Western Powers.] *Armistice with Italy—September 3-*

November 17, 1943 (includes armistice related documents and the surrender)
http://www.yale.edu/lawweb/avalon/wwii/italy.htm

154. [Multiple Governments.] *U.S.- British-U.S.S.R. Armistice with Hungary*
http://www.sunsite.unc.edu/pha/policy/1945/450120b.html

155. Truman, Harry. *President Truman's Broadcast on Surrender of Germany (May 8, 1945)*
http://www.sunsite.unc.edu/pha/policy/1945/450508c.html

156. U.S. Congress. *U.S. Declaration of War on Germany (December 11, 1941)* (includes Roosevelt's formal notification of Congress that Germany had declared war)
http://www.ibiblio.org/hyperwar/ETO/Dip/DecWar-G.html
http://www.law.ou.edu/hist/germwar.html
http://www.danshistory.com/ww2/docs/us_dec_germany.txt

Asia

CAIRO CONFERENCE

157. [Unidentified.] *Cairo Conference* (under "all documents" has several items related to the wartime conferences)
http://www.taiwandocuments.org/cairo.htm

158. [Unidentified.] *Cairo Declaration* (December 1, 1943; policy statement by Allies)
http://www.ibiblio.org/hyperwar/Dip/cairo-cnf.html

DIPLOMATIC AND LEGAL MATERIALS IMPACTING BOTH EUROPEAN AND PACIFIC/ASIAN THEATERS OF WAR

159. Avalon Project at the Yale Law School. *World War II: Documents* (over 60 treaties, agreements, surrenders and other materials)
http://www.yale.edu/lawweb/avalon/wwii/wwii.htm

160. Canadians in the World. *History of Canada's International Relations: 1921-1939—Between Two World Wars*
http://www.canschool.org/relation/history/4betwe-e.asp

161. Canadians in the World. *History of Canada's International Relations: 1939-1945—The World at War*
http://www.canschool.org/relation/history/5world-e.asp

162. Legislative Reference Service. *Events Leading Up to World War II: Chronological List of Certain Major International Events Leading Up to and during World War II with the Ostensible Reasons Advanced for Their Concurrence, 1931-1944* (Washington: U.S. Government Printing Office, 1944; 421 pages)
http://www.ibiblio.org/pha/events/index.html

163. [Unidentified.] *Words of Peace/Words of War: Treaties, Declarations, Instruments of Surrender, etc.* (large collection, divided into periods of time)
http://www.ibiblio.org/pha/policy/index.html

164. University of Minnesota Human Rights Library. *Law of Armed Conflict* (text of treaties and agreements since the 1800s)
http://www1.umn.edu/humanrts/instree/auoy.htm

DECLARATIONS OF WAR AND SURRENDER: PACIFIC

165. Churchill, Winston. *Winston Churchill Declares War on Japan* (audio)
http://history.acusd.edu/gen/projects/RADIO.html

166. Commander in Chief, Pacific Fleet. *The Formal Surrender of the Empire of Japan* (extract from *Report on Surrender and Occupation of Japan*)
http://www.history.navy.mil/faqs/faq69-1.htm

167. Hirohito, Emperor. *Imperial Respect of 15 August 1945—Hirohito Surrenders* (text of Emperor's radio broadcast to the nation)
http://www.ibiblio.org/hyperwar/PTO/Dip/Crane.html

168. [Multi-Authors.] *Japanese Surrender Documents* (Instrument of Surrender and documents from the emperor authorizing them to be signed)
http://www.ibiblio.org/hyperwar/PTO/Dip/Japan-Surrender.html
http://www.law.ou.edu/hist/japsurr.html
http://www.danshistory.com/ww2/docs/japan_surrender.txt
http://www.geocities.com/iturks/html/japanese_surrender_documents.html

169. Roosevelt, Franklin D. *"A Date Which Will Live in Infamy:" The First Typed Draft of Franklin D. Roosevelt's War Address*
http://www.nara.gov/education/teaching/fdr/infamy.html

170. Roosevelt, Franklin D. *FDR's "Day of Infamy" Speech (December 8, 1941)*
http://www.ibiblio.org/hyperwar/PTO/EastWind/Infamy.html (text)
http://history.acusd.edu/gen/projects/RADIO.html (audio)

171. Soviet Union. *Soviet Declaration of War on Japan, 8 August 1945* (text)
http://www.ibiblio.org/hyperwar/PTO/Dip/USSR-Jap-DoW.html

172. Tojo. *Tojo Declares War on the Allies* (audio)
http://history.acusd.edu/gen/projects/RADIO.html

173. U.S. Government. *The End of the War in the Pacific: Surrender Documents in Facsimile* (1945)
http://worldwar2.smu.edu/cgi-bin/Pwebrecon.cgi?v1=150&ti=101,150&
CNT=50&Search_Arg=world+war&Search_Code=GKEY&x=29&y=8&
y=8&PID=3767&SEQ=20020105201341&SID=1

174. U.S. Congress. *U.S. Declaration of War on Japan (December 8, 1941)*
http://www.ibiblio.org/hyperwar/PTO/Dip/DecWar-J.html
http://www.danshistory.com/ww2/docs/us_dec_japan.txt

Section Two

The World Aflame

3

Overview of the War

European and Mediterranean War

AIRBORNE FORCES

175. Bando, Mark. *Trigger Time* (101st Airborne: unit histories and individual stories)
http://www.101airborneww2.com/

176. Cull, Jack. *Signalman Jack Linder Cull, Army No. 2575857* (served in the British 8th Army parachute regiment in North Africa, Italy, and Yugoslavia)
http://www.warlinks.com/jackcull/index.shtml

177. [Unidentified.] *First Allied Airborne Army* (orientated toward re-enactors)
http://www.geocities.com/Pentagon/Bunker/1944/

178. [Unidentified.] *1st Canadian Parachute Battalion* (includes photos and official reports of training and combat)
http://www.geocities.com/can_para_btn/main.html

179. [Various German officers in a collaborative endeavor.] *Airborne Operations: A German Appraisal* (CMH Publication 104-13; includes evaluation of both German and Allied operations)
http://www.army.mil/cmh-pg/books/wwii/104-13/104-13.HTM

AIR FORCES

180. Andrew, Norman K. *A Navigator's Diary*
http://www.geocities.com/CapeCanaveral/1393/andy.html

181. Ankey, Jr., Harold. *Combat Diary, 1944* (Ankey was a P-52 pilot)
http://cpcug.org/user/billb/hankeny/index.html

182. Barnes, Robert T. *War on Their Minds* (trained as an aviator; main emphasis on stateside training: got to Europe shortly before war ended)
http://www.whshistoryproject.org/ww2/Interviews/mr_barnes.html

183. Bates, Martin. *Holton Airfield* (East Anglia, England)
http://www.batesuk.cwc.net/holton/halesworth.html

184. Chetwyn, Kim. *East Anglia: The Air War*
http://www.stable.demon.co.uk/

185. Cleaver, Thomas M. *"American Eagles:" The 4th Fighter Group in World War II*
(introduction:) http://www.elknet.pl/acestory/eagles/eagles.htm
(in RAF service:) http://www.elknet.pl/acestory/eagles/eagle1.htm
(as part of USAAF:) http://www.elknet.pl/acestory/eagles/eagle2.htm

186. Crawford, Alex. *Gloster Gladiator Homepage* (a biplane that survived into World War Two usage)
http://www.geocities.com/acrawford0/index.html

187. Crump, John. *Urban Drew's Two Me 262 Victories* (had distinction of bringing down two German jets)
http://www.elknet.pl/acestory/drew/drew.htm

188. Farley, Patricia B. *Birds of a Feather: A Wren's Memoirs*
http://home.nc.rr.com/ww2memories/memoirs_farley.txt

189. Ferwerda, C. Arthur. *C. Arthur Ferwerda's Home Page* (photographs of bombers and crews)
http://www.graphics.cornell.edu/~jaf/caf.html

190. Graham, James H. *English East Anglia Aerial Lighthouse: The Caravan Role in World War II, the "Gypsy Wagons"* (these were large trucks with communication equipment parked at the end of runways to help guided wounded planes into a landing)
http://www.geocities.com/oralbio/caravan.html

191. Grolier On-line. *Air Combat Films* (three; downloadable)
http://gi.grolier.com/wwii/movies/movies.html

192. Hamilton, Jim. *The Writing 69th Home Page* (journalists attached to the 8th Air Force)
http://www.channel1.com/users/jimham/

193. Heleno, Joao C. *Spitfire and Messerschmitt BF109* (history of both, pictures, flying characteristics, etc.)
http://www.geocities.com/capecanaveral/hangar/9378/

194. Jennings, William K. *The Private Diary of Staff Sergeant William K. Jennings* (8th USAAF)
http://home.talkcity.com/homepopup.html?url=/LibertySt/bjenningsdiary/index.html

195. Johnson, Robert. *B-17 Combat Crewmen and Wingmen* (including recollections of those who flew them)
http://www.b-17combatcrewmen.org/

196. Kortas, Matthew P. *Spitfire* (pictures, aircrew slang, etc.)
http://www.acm.cps.msu.edu/~kortasma/spitfire.html

197. Landberg, Christer. *Hawker Tempest* (engines, armaments, markings, etc.)
http://user.tninet.se/~ytm843e/tempest.htm

198. Long, Jason. *Sturmvogel (Axis and Neutral Air Forces)*
http://www.geocities.com/CapeCanaveral/2072/index.html

199. MacDowell, Kenneth. *War on Their Minds* (served with the 404th Fighter Group)
http://www.whshistoryproject.org/ww2/Interviews/mr_macdowell.html

200. Manninen, Tony. *Tony's B-17 Page* (location on plane of each crew member and other details)
http://www.ratol.fi/~tmannine/b-17/

201. Mathieu, Marc. *Hommage aux Equipages de B-24* (French and English material)
http://users.skynet.be/sky72940/

202. McNeill, Ross. *RAF Commandos, 1939-1945* (by type of command and aircraft)
http://www.rafcommands.currantbun.com/home.html

203. Mears, Dwight S. *1Lt. George W. Mears* (discusses 351 Bombardment Group with this participant as the focus)
http://www.geocities.com/Pentagon/7185/AV1.html

204. Military History Group & Antique Militaria Net. *U.S. Army Air Forces in World War II*
http://collectorsnet.com/milhist/

205. Patrick, Bethanne K. *Brig. Gen. Lester J. Maitland* (Army Air Force pioneer)
http://www.military.com/Content/MoreContent?file=ML_maitland_bkp

206. Patrick, Bethanne K. *Sgt. Andy Rooney* (later a television journalist, during the war he served as an Army Air Force reporter for *Stars and Stripes*)
http://www.military.com/Content/MoreContent?file=ML_rooney_bkp

207. Patrick, Bethanne K. *Sgt. Maynard H. Smith, Jr.* (B-17 ball-turret gunner; Medal of Honor winner)
http://www.military.com/Content/MoreContent?file=ML_snuffy_bkp

208. Pepin, Roland. *War Memoirs* (navigator stationed in Italy)
http://home.nc.rr.com/ww2memories/memoirs_pepin.txt

209. Pointon, Christopher. *The Royal Air Force Lichfield Association* (history and other materials concerning this RAF base through which many Commonwealth personnel—especially Australians—passed during the war)
http://www.raf-lichfield.co.uk/home.htm

210. Rarey, George. *"Dad" Rarey's Sketchbook Journals of the 379th Fighter Squadron* (with emphasis on its service in Britain)
http://www.rareybird.com/
http://idd007xs.eresmas.net/bismarck.html

211. Sherman, Stephen. *USAAF MTO [Mediterranean Theater of Operations] Aces of World War II*
http://www.westnet.com/~ssherman/usaaf_mto_aces.html

212. Swan, Philip. *Lincolnshire Heritage* (stressing the presence of war-time aviation)
http://www.pipswan.demon.co.uk/surveyremind.htm

213. 33rd Photographic Reconnaissance Squadron Online. *33rd Photographic Reconnaissance Squadron Online* (part of 9th US Air Force, 1943-1945; photographs and other data)
http://www.33rdprs.org/

214. Tyminski, Dariusz. *Joachim Muncheberg—"Spitfire" Hunter*
http://www.elknet.pl/acestory/munche/munche.htm

215. [Unidentified.] *Aces of the Eighth Air Force in World War II*
http://www.westnet.com/~ssherman/usaaf_eto_aces.html

216. [Unidentified.] *Aircraft #42-50287* (B-24 from Wendling base, shot down over France June 23, 1944; details on flight and crew)
http://www.unc.edu/~landon/clyde.html

217. [Unidentified.] *Airfields in Yorkshire* (data on original sites and current existence and status)
http://www.airfieldsinyorkshire.co.uk/

218. [Unidentified.] *Aviation in Newfoundland and Labrador* (during the War and afterwards)
http://home.thezone.net/~ainal/

219. [Unidentified.] *Cougar P-51 [Mustang] Runaway* (development and capacities of the plane)
http://www.geocities.com/Pentagon/Quarters/9696/

220. [Unidentified.] *8th Army Air Force 303rd Bombardment Group* (based at Molesworth, England; includes pictures of their missions)
http://www.megalink.net/~wejones/wwii.html

221. [Unidentified.] *Haunted Airfields in Britain* (contemporary photos and stories)
http://members.tripod.lycos.co.uk/adm/popup/targeted/roadmapcat784.shtml

222. [Unidentified.] *Heavy Bombers: B-17 Flying Fortresses* (includes history of units, illustration of tail designations of constituent units, and other materials)
http://www.heavybombers.com/tails.html

223. [Unidentified.] *Military Airfields of the East Midlands*
http://www.usaaf.8k.com/

224. [Unidentified.] *Mustang!* (large collection of data about the plane, development, and operation)
http://www.geocities.com/koala51d/links.html

225. [Unidentified.] *RAF Banff, Coastal Wing, 1943-1945*
http://www.hcs.dial.pipex.com/rafbanff.html

226. [Unidentified.] *Royal Airforce: Servicing Commandos, 1942 to 1946* (units designed to operate as close to front lines as possible)
http://geocities.com/rafscom/were.htm

227. [Unidentified.] *781st Bombardment Squadron, 465th Bombardment Group History* (based in Italy)
http://www.frankambrose.com/Pages/781.html

228. [Unidentified.] *Tales of the 316th Fighter Squadron ("Hell's Bells")* (includes photo collection)
http://www.members.home.net/gr8beyond/316thmain.htm

229. [Unidentified.] *The Air War* (in Europe)
http://history.sandiego.edu/gen/WW2Timeline/airwar.html

230. [Unidentified.] *The Glider Pilot Regiment, 1942-1945* (a study of the men and equipment)
http://home.clara.net/stevewright/GPR/index.html

231. [Unidentified.] *The Lockheed P-38 Lightning in North Africa and the MTO [Mediterranean Theater of Operations]*
http://home.att.net/~C.C.Jordan/P-38MTO.html

232. [Unidentified.] *The Martin Baltimore [Aircraft] in the North African Desert* (personal experiences)
http://www.martinbaltimore.com/

233. United States Air Force Museum. *World War II: Combat in Europe* (with links to specific subjects)
http://www.wpafb.af.mil/museum/history/wwii/combate.htm

234. United States Air Force Air Rescue Service. *Arctic Rescue: B-17E "My Gal Sal"* (crashed in Greenland in 1942)
http://www.wpafb.af.mil/museum/history/rescue/res2.htm

235. Vasicek, Radko. *Allied Airfield Behind Enemy Lines* (supplying the Slovakian rebels against Hitler in 1944)
http://www.military.com/Content/MoreContent?file=PRrevolt

236. Whitehead, Christopher. *Supermarine Spitfire: An Operational History* (from 1938 to its retirement from service)
http://www.deltaweb.co.uk/spitfire/index.htm

237. Wright, Larry, and Louise Blackah. *Larry's Bomber Command Page*
http://www.nucleus.com/~ltwright/home.htm

238. Young, Jack B. *World War II: One Airman's Story*
http://www.kmx.com/spitz/WWII/html/toc.html

239. Zorzoli, Joseph W. *Stuck in Barbed Wire as a Burning Plane Prepares to Explode* (one of his adventures as a crew chief, who had the responsibility that bombers were flight ready before taking off)
http://www.memoriesofwar.com/veterans/zorzoli.asp

INFANTRY AND OTHER LAND FORCES

240. Audinet, Patrick. *My Father and the 473rd Infantry in World War II*
http://geocities.com/Pentagon/Bunker/4325/

241. Ausland, John C. *Letters Home: A War Memoir (Europe 1944-1945)*
http://home.nc.rr.com/ww2memories/ww2_ausland.html

242. Barclay, William F. *103rd Infantry Division Signal Company Remembrances, 1918-1945* (emphasis on war-time years)
http://www.pierce-evans.org/remembrancesa.htm

243. Belmont, Larry. *Skylighters: The Official Web Site of the 225th AA* (searchlight battalion; from Omaha Beach to Germany)
http://www.skylighters.org/

244. Colley, David P. *The Red Ball Express* (moving supplies from the ports to the front lines)
http://www.military.com/Content/MoreContent?file=PRredball

245. Dracass, Stanley. *2187987—"Sapper:" Royal Engineers, 1939-1945* (Dracass served in both the Middle East and Europe)
http://www.geocities.com/sapper_dracuss/

246. Evans, Pierce. *Papa's War* (arrived in France in 1944 after Normandy)
http://www.pierce-evans.org/papaswar.htm

247. Farley, John. *High Life in the ETO [European Theater of Operations]* (actually a collection of his letters from combat in Europe)
http://home.nc.rr.com/ww2memories/wren_letters.txt

248. Felhofer, Mark. *Wayne William Felhofer: Life and Times in the U.S. Army during World War II*
http://www.felhofer.com/wayne.htm

249. Freeman, Benjamin F. *War on Their Minds* (fought in Torch and on the edge of the Battle of the Bulge)
http://www.whshistoryproject.org/ww2/Interviews/mr_freeman.html

250. Furukawa, Michael. *100th Battalion/442 Regimental Combat Team* (Japanese-American unit that fought in Europe)
http://www.katonk.com/442nd/442nd.htm

251. Govan, Thomas P. *History of the Tenth Light Division (Alpine)* (1946; Army Ground Forces Study No. 28; analysis of creation and early training of the Division)
http://www.army.mil/cmh-pg/books/agf/agf28.htm

252. Hanaway, Charles. *A March to Manhood* (at top of screen click on "H-L;" pick this person's name from list on left screen; text appears to right)
http://www.warlinks.com/memories/index.html

253. Harris, Kevin. *The 83rd Infantry Division: Through the Eyes of a Thunderbolt*
http://users.1st.net/bharris/83rdDivision.htm

254. Heller, Rich. *3rd Infantry Division: World War II Memoirs and Photos*
http://www.enteract.com/~rheller/ww2/webrings.htm

255. Heller, William. *World War II Memoirs, 1942-1945* (from Casablanca to the Rhine)
http://www.warfoto.com/

256. Holmes, D. *A Tribute to Arthur F. Holmes, Sr.* (summary history of division; war-time incidents noted)
http://people.ne.mediaone.net/debdav/AFH.htm

257. Houser, John R. *I Never Had It so Good: or the Private War of John R. Houser 33873307* (based on his scrapbook of notes taken during the war and photographs)
http://www.nb.net/~jrh/ww2scrap.htm

258. Kreipke, Herman. *World War 2 ETO Logbook* (Kreipke served in the 26th Ordnance M.M.)
http://www.indyrad.iupui.edu/public/dkreipke/ww2_log.html

259. Lundgren, Merrill H. *Almost at the Front: The Wartime Letters of Corporal Merrill H. Lundgren* (covers 1944-1945, with additional material on what was happening in other parts of the war at the time the letters were written)
http://home.nc.rr.com/ww2memories/almost_at_the_front.html

260. Mason, Eric and Olive Mason. *Eric and Olive Website* (wartime letters of both which they served in North Africa and Italy)
http://www.west-london.freeserve.co.uk/OliveandEric/index.html

261. Molnar, Jr., Alexander. *Marines in the Atlantic, Europe, and Africa* (in the "World War II Fact Sheet, USMC" series)
http://www.usmc.mil/history.nsf/Table+of+Contents/77f992b2acb682eb852564d70059c642?OpenDocument&ExpandSection=5

262. North, George E. *Oral History of a World War II Veteran*
http://tec.uno.edu/George/myBestWork/oralHistory2.html

263. Patrick, Bethanne K. *2nd Lieutenant Audie Murphy* (most decorated combat soldier in the war)
http://www.military.com/Content/MoreContent?file=ML_murphy_bkp

264. Pitts, Rick. *150th Combat Engineer Battalion of World War II* (stories, photos)
http://www.150th.com/index1.htm

265. Pranger, Arthur. *Private Art, 86th Chemical Mortar Battalion: A Collection of World War II Letters to and from the Front*
http://www.private-art.com/

266. Rayment, Alan. *It Happened to Me* (service in the Royal Artillery anti-aircraft)
http://raymenta.tripod.com/contents.htm

267. Ricci, John F. *War on Their Minds* (interview)
http://www.whshistoryproject.org/ww2/Interviews/mr_ricci.html

268. Rose, Ben L. *Letters Home while a Chaplain in the U.S. Army in the European Theater of Operations during World War II, 1944-45*
http://home.nc.rr.com/ww2memories/memoirs_rose.html

269. Sands, Richard. *Keep 'em Moving: Dedicated to all Highland Division Soldiers and the Queen's Own Cameron Highlanders in Particular (1939-1946)* (served in Sicily, France, and Holland)
http://homepage.ntlworld.com/richard.sands/

270. Schmidt, Vern. *Interview* (rifle company replacement)
http://www.tankbooks.com/intviews/schmidt/schmidt1.htm

271. Sherman, Jr., Hugh J. *Yankee Division: Letters from the Front* (with commentary)
http://www.mmpro.org/YD/dad's%20story.htm

272. Slawsby, Norman. *War on Their Minds* (interview; in field artillery)
http://www.whshistoryproject.org/ww2/Interviews/mr_slawsby.html

273. Texas Military Forces Museum. *36th Division in World War II: A Pictorial History*
http://www.kwanah.com/txmilmus/36division/archives.htm

274. [Unidentified.] *Audie L. Murphy Memorial Web Site* (most decorated U.S. soldier of the war)
http://www.audiemurphy.com/

275. [Unidentified.] *Eighth [British] Army: Deeds and Dates*
http://www.warlinks.com/pages/8thdeeds.html

276. [Unidentified.] *488th Engineers* (bridge builders)
http://humber.northnet.org/488thengineers/

277. [Unidentified.] *Gerhard H. Tanning* (a medic in North Africa and Europe)
http://ww-iiheroes.com/gerard.html

278. [Unidentified.] *History 133rd Infantry, 34th Infantry Division*
http://www.milhist.net/34/133hist.shtml

279. [Unidentified.] *913th Field Artillery Battalion [88th Infantry Division]: World War II Narrative* (text partially available on line)
http://www.milhist.net/deep/913narrhist.shtmlJanuary 1, 1990

280. [Unidentified.] *One of Many: British Army, 1942-1946* (with emphasis on British 46th Infantry Division)
http://www.btinternet.com/~oneofmany/

281. [Unidentified.] *103rd Cactus Division* (European service in 1944-1945)
http://www.eastmill.com/103rd/index.htm

282. [Unidentified.] *133rd Infantry Regiment [34th Infantry Division]: World War II Narrative* (partially on line)
http://www.milhist.net/deep/133narrhist.shtml

283. [Unidentified.] *Order of Battle of the U.S. Army, World War II: European Theater of Operations* (1945; reprinted from manuscript prepared at end of war)
http://www.army.mil/cmh-pg/documents/eto-ob/etoob-toc.htm

284. [Unidentified.] *720th Railway Operating Battalion* (American soldier-railroaders)
http://rwy720th.home.att.net/

285. [Unidentified.] *Skylighters: 225th AA Searchlight Battalion*
http://www.skylighters.org/

286. Wilson, Monfrey. *My Life* (concisely describes service in North Africa, Sicily, and Europe)
http://www.tankbooks.com/stories/story103/monfrey1.htm

287. Wise, Edward. *Combat Diary (September 1944-May 1945)*
http://www.thewarpage.com/diary.html

288. Yascarage, Albert J. *Your World War II Buddy* (his account, with photos, of service at Omaha Beach, the Battle of the Bulge and contact with the Russians at the end of the war)
http://www.wwiibuddy.com/

NAVAL FORCES

289. Allen, Tonya. *Sinking of the "S.S. Leopoldville"*
http://uboat.net/history/leopoldville.htm

290. Bauer, Jim. *Escort Carriers [Provided] to Britain: Lend-Lease, 1941-1944*
http://www.ww2pacific.com/brcve.html

291. Benvenuto, Bob. *I Join the Navy—The Reality & the Realization*
http://members.aol.com/famjustin/LST7.html

292. Dailey, Jr., Franklyn E. *Joining the War at Sea, 1939-1945* (the view from the U.S. destroyer *Edison*; book length)
http://www.daileyint.com/seawar/index.htm

293. Edel, Matthias. *Power at Sea* (German language site comparing the German and British navies)
http://www.geocities.com/Pentagon/Quarters/5768/index.htm

294. Forsman, Mats. *War at Sea* (1939-1945, in Europe, of all combatant nations)
http://www.geocities.com/waratsea/

295. Gray, Edwyn. *The Arks at War* (a survey of British warships named *Ark Royal*, with the overwhelming emphasis on twentieth century ones)
http://www.military.com/Content/MoreContent?file=PR1000arksf

296. Guttman, John. *Specialist in Diversion* (interview with the actor Douglas Fairbanks, Jr., who served in the Navy)
http://www.military.com/Content/MoreContent?file=PRdoug

297. Hickman, N. J. *H.M.S. Illustrious* (aircraft carrier)
http://world.std.com/~Ted7/Illus.htm

298. Historic Naval Ships Association. *H.M.S. Belfast*
http://www.maritime.org/hnsa-belfast.htm

299. History Channel. *Sinking of the "S.S. Leopoldville:" Survivor Interview* (sunk December 24, 1944; nearly 800 American dead)
http://www.historychannel.com/exhibits/leopoldville/

300. H.M.S. Hood Association. *Battle Cruiser* (dedicated to preserving the memory of the *Hood*)
http://www.hmshood.com/

301. Johns, [? .] *The Naval Ships of Victor Johns* (wartime activities of several British warships tracked due to the service of Johns on board)
http://home1.swipnet.se/~w-11578/dads_ships.htm

302. Kipling, S. H. *The Royal Naval Commandos*
http://ourworld.compuserve.com/homepages/Keith_Oakley/rnhist.htm

303. Patrick, Bethanne K. *Chaplain George L. Fox* (he and three other chaplains gave up their life vests to others on a sinking ship)
http://www.military.com/Content/MoreContent?file=ML_gfox_bkp

304. Phipps, Norman M. *Royal Navy Carrier in World War Two* (centers on pictures and data concerning the lend-lease carrier *H.M.S. Arbiter*)
http://uk.geocities.com/nmptwentyone/index.html

305. Price, Scott T. *The Coast Guard and the North Atlantic Campaign in World War II*
http://www.uscg.mil/hq/g-cp/history/h_AtlWar.html

306. Senate Committee on Naval Affairs. *Investigation of Charges that American Naval Vessels Are Conveying Ships or Have Destroyed German Naval Vessels* (July 29, 1941)
http://www.ibiblio.org/pha/USN/77-1s617.html

307. Tilley, John A. *The Coast Guard and the Greenland Patrol*
http://www.uscg.mil/hq/g-cp/history/h_greenld.html

308. [Unidentified.] *Undeclared Naval War in the Atlantic 1941*
http://history.sandiego.edu/gen/WW2Timeline/Prelude18.html

309. Wynen, James C. *My Coast Guard Life during World War II*
http://www.jacksjoint.com/mycglife.htm

TANK AND ARMORED FORCES

310. Albee, Dale. *Interview* (712th Tank Battalion; received a battlefield promotion)
http://www.tankbooks.com/intviews/albee/albee1.htm

311. Bell, Bryan. *An Infantry Platoon Leader in Patton's Army*
http://www.bbll.com/army/

312. Bevis, Mark. *World War II: American Armoured Division, 1944-1945: Europe*
http://www.magweb.com/sample/smicroma/smma1aad.htm

313. Blumenson, Martin. *Examples of Employment of Tanks in Night Fighting on the European Land Mass during World War II*
http://www.army.mil/cmh-pg/documents/237ACY.htm

314. Bussell, George. *Interview* (tank driver)
http://www.tankbooks.com/intviews/bussell/bussell1.htm

315. Johnston, Wesley. *U.S. 7th Armored Division* (including detailed chronology and losses per constituent units)
http://members.aol.com/dadswar/7ada.htm

316. Krenn, Arthur E. *Personal War Diary: A Living History of the 1st Armored Division's Actions in North Africa and Italy*
http://www.angelfire.com/wi2/krennpapers

317. Liew, Francis. *Track and Armor* (on tracked and armored units in the various combatant nations)
http://www.geocities.com/MotorCity/8418/index.html

318. 2nd Armored Association. *Official U.S. Army 2nd Armored "Hell on Wheels" Division*
http://www.2ndarmoredhellonwheels.com/

319. [Unidentified.] *419th Field Artillery Battalion, 10th Armored Division* (includes such items as a 1944 series of articles on the unit in combat in Europe)
http://www.419th.com/

320. [Unidentified.] *Mechanized Cavalry in World War II* (organizational structure, unit histories, etc.)
http://www.geocities.com/Pentagon/Quarters/9517/

321. [Unidentified.] *Second Armored Division: It's a Fact Page*
http://www.2ndarmoredhellonwheels.com/itsafact.html

CANADIAN FORCES

322. Copp, Terry. *Examining a [Canadian] General's Dismissal* (the forced "retirement" of General Andrew McNaughton)
http://www.legionmagazine.com/features/canadianmilitaryhistory/97-05.asp

323. Copp, Terry. *The Early Days of World War [for the Canadian Army]*
http://www.legionmagazine.com/features/canadianmilitaryhistory/96-04.asp

324. Dorosch, Michael, and Kevin Winfield. *Calgary Highlanders Heritage Section* (Canadian)
http://members.home.net/calgaryhighlanders/

325. Maple Leaf Up. *The Canadian Army Overseas in WW2*
http://www.mapleleafup.org/

326. [Unidentified.] *History of the SSR [South Saskatchewan Regiment, Canada: 1939-1945]* (from the *Weyburn Review*, May 8, 1985)
http://cap.estevan.sk.ca/SSR/nominal/history.html

MAPS AND PHOTOGRAPHS

327. Department of History, U.S. Military Academy. *Maps of World War II: European Theater*
http://www.dean.usma.edu/history/dhistorymaps/WWIIPages/WWII Europe/WWIIEToC.htm

328. Doody, Richard. *"This Is London"—A Tour of World War II Memorials & Museums*
http://worldatwar.net/article/thisislondon/index.html

329. Heineman, John L. *Maps Concerning World War II* (1919-Spring 1940, stressing German expansionism)
http://www.bc.edu/bc_org/avp/cas/his/CoreArt/maps/hs220maps.html

330. O'Connor, [? .] *Harry G. O'Connor's World War II Photo Album* (covers his photographs from Omaha Beach to the end of the war)
http://members.tripod.com/~BMWR50S/wwii.html

331. [Unidentified.] *A Selection of Maps for Rise of Modern Germany (1914-1945)*
http://www2.bc.edu/~heineman/hs442maps.html

332. [Unidentified.] *Historic Photos Online* (searchable data bank of public domain materials)
http://carlisle-www.army.mil/usamhi/HPOL.html

333. [Unidentified.] *Lost Images of World War II* (mainly pictures taken by Jerry Pinkowski, 347th O.D.C., U.S. Army)
http://geocities.yahoo.com/toto?s=76000015

334. [Unidentified.] *Photo Gallery of World War Two* (photos of tanks, aircraft, and ships of the combatants; German language site with English version under construction)
http://www.warlinks.com/cgi-bin/links/jump.cgi?ID=434

335. [Unidentified.] *Photographs & Artwork: 10th Mountain Division*
http://www.army.mil/cmh-pg/matrix/10MD/10MD-Photos.htm

OTHER MATERIALS

336. Allinson, Sidney. *Undercover: Ernest Hemingway* (his role as an amateur spy in Cuba during the war)
http://www.military.com/Content/MoreContent?file=PRhemingway

337. Barnard, Douglas B., and Caroline Barnard. *War on Their Minds* (he served in the ETO)
http://www.whshistoryproject.org/ww2/Interviews/mr_mrs_bernard.html

338. Bugnion, Francois. *ICRC Action during the Second World War* (Red Cross investigation of accusations its neutrality had been violated)
http://www.icrc.org/icrceng.nsf/c1256212004ce24e
4125621200524882/e211c6776680270a412564ae00506a9a?Open
Document

339. Center for Military History. *U.S. Army in Northern Ireland, 1941-1945* (a collection of raw material for researchers)
http://www.army.mil/cmh-pg/reference/ireland/readme.htm

340. Cienciala, Anna M. *Select, Annotated Bibliography of English Language Works on the History of East Central Europe and the Balkans; part II: From the Outbreak of the First World War to the End of the Second, 1914 through 1945*
http://www.ukans.edu/~ibetext/texts/cienciala3/

341. Coleman, Cleo, and Doug Coleman. *Interview* (discussing the similarities and differences between World War II, that Cleo served in, and Vietnam, in which Doug saw duty)
http://www.tankbooks.com/intviews/colemans/colemans1.htm

342. Cope, Arthur. *War Diaries* (stories of North Africa and Italy)
http://www.beyondthedoor.co.uk/wardiaries/index.htm

343. Dorsey, Mason H. *Cavalry Reconnaissance Armored Car Model M-8* (description of the equipment and danger involved in reconnaissance missions)
http://members.aol.com/famjustin/Dorsey4.html

344. Eisenhower, Dwight D. *Instructions to German Troops and to Foreign Workers, in Preparation for Defeat of Germany (March 31, 1945)*
http://www.sunsite.unc.edu/pha/policy/1945/450331b.html

345. Eisenhower, Dwight D. *Letter to President Roosevelt on the Possibility of a German Surrender (March 31, 1945)*
http://www.sunsite.unc.edu/pha/policy/1945/450331a.html

346. Faeth, Harald. *Tunnel and Shelter Researching* (studies such facilities utilized during the war both on the Continent and in Britain)
http://www.geocities.com/cgi-bin-local/GeoAD?pageID=/gpf/CapeCanaveral

347. Heaton, Colin D. *Wolfpack Ace Robert S. Johnson* (interview with)
http://www.military.com/Content/MoreContent?file=PRrsjohnson

348. Historical Sub-Section, Office of Secretary, General Staff, Supreme Headquarters Allied Expeditionary Force. *History of COSSACK, 1943-1944* (May 1944)
http://www.army.mil/cmh-pg/documents/cossac/cossac.htm

349. History Place. *World War II In Europe* (dates of key events, 1918-1945)
http://www.historyplace.com/worldwar2/timeline/ww2time.htm

350. Leniart, Brandon. *World War II in Europe* (summaries, statistics and other data)
http://www.angelfire.com/ct/ww2europe/

351. MacDonald, Charles B., et. al. *Information about Operations in Southern France, Rear Area Security in Russia 1941-1944, North Africa, and Korea*
http://www.army.mil/cmh-pg/documents/237adt.htm

352. MacDonald, Charles B. *The War against Germany and Italy.* (Chapter 22 of *American Military History*)
http://www.army.mil/cmh-pg/BOOKS/amh/amh-22.htm

353. Smith, Ron. *Refusal of Orders [in the British Army]: The Case of William Douglas Home*
http://www.waikato.ac.nz/wfass/subjects/history/waimilhist/1998/wdhome.html

354. Swartz, Gerald E. *Poetry* (based on his experiences as an artillery loader in 1944-1945)
http://www.angelfire.com/ct/ww2europe/swartz.html

355. [Unidentified.] *Casualty Notification—World War II* (reproduction of telegrams and postcards concerning a GI wounded in France)
http://carlisle-www.army.mil/usamhi/Sampler/miller/index.htm

356. [Unidentified.] *C'est La Guerre—My War, World War II*
http://www.geocities.com/Athens/Forum/4840/H.htm

357. [Unidentified.] *Congressional Medal of Honor Recipients: Mediterranean Theater of Operations, World War II*
http://www.milhist.net/mto/moh.shtml

358. [Unidentified.] *Defeat of Germany—1945*
http://history.acusd.edu/gen/WW2Timeline/Europe09.html

359. [Unidentified.] *Major Campaigns of the Second World War* (covers Poland to the invasion of Russia)
http://www.thesecondworldwar.com/campaigns.html

360. [Unidentified.] *1939-1945* (French language site)
http://www.warlinks.com/cgi-bin/links/jump.cgi?ID=311

361. [Unidentified.] *Surrender Invitation—World War II* (Fifth Army's German-English "safe conduct pass" for German soldiers wishing to surrender)
http://carlisle-www.army.mil/usamhi/Sampler/surrend/index.htm
http://www.dhm.de/ausstellungen/eaintroe.html

362. [Unidentified.] *Second World War, 1939-1945* (collection of articles by various individuals)
http://www.geocities.com/pentagon/quarters/5822/

363. [Unidentified.] *The Official Lili Marleen Page* (German-English text; song itself available for listening in multiple German and English versions and in other languages)
http://ingeb.org/garb/lmarleen.html

364. [Unidentified.] *The War of Attrition*
http://history.acusd.edu/gen/WW2Timeline/Europe07b.html

365. [Unidentified.] *War Gunner: A History*
http://www.wargunner.co.uk/

366. [Unidentified.] *War Letters in the Second World War* (a site collecting war letters for scholarly and research purposes)
http://www.feldpost-archiv.de/english/index.html

367. [Unidentified.] *World War II Memoirs* (short extracts from a number of individuals of different nationalities)
http://www.angelfire.com/ct/ww2europe/diaries.html

368. U.S. Strategic Bombing Survey. *Summary Report: European War* (Washington. D.C.; 30 September 1945)
http://www.ibiblio.org/hyperwar/AAF/USSBS-ETO-Summary.html
http://www.anesi.com/ussbs02.htm
http://www.danshistory.com/ww2/docs/ussbs_euro.html

369. Williams, Donald. *106th Cavalry Group* (with information on its component parts)
http://mars.wnec.edu/~dwilliam/history/106cav.html

370. Williams, Jack A. *War on Their Minds* (interview)
http://www.whshistoryproject.org/ww2/Interviews/mr_williams.html

371. Williams, Orval. *Interview* (stress on pre-war training and life outside European combat)
http://www.tankbooks.com/intviews/williams/williams1.htm

Pacific and Asian War

Air Forces

372. Army Air Forces. *Report of the Commanding General of the Army Air Forces to the Secretary of War* (4 January 1944)
http://www.wpafb.af.mil/museum/history/wwii/aaf/aaf.htm

373. Aviation Aeroweb History. *Gregory Boyington (1912-1988)*
http://www.aero-web.org/history/aviators/boyngton.htm

374. Bauer, Jim. *Naval Aircraft 1942* (abilities and weaknesses)
http://www.ww2pacific.com/navalair.html

375. Berman, Avy. *Letters from the Pacific: Letters Written Home by a Young
World War II [B-24] Bombadier*
http://avyberman.com/

376. Broderick, Ronald F. *War on Their Minds* (interview; seaplane pilot)
http://www.whshistoryproject.org/ww2/Interviews/mr_brodrick.html

377. Carey, Alan C. *U.S. Navy Pacific-Based PB4Y Squadrons in World War
II*
http://alanc.carey.freeservers.com/

378. Cook, Jack. *Stories from the South Pacific* (flew a B-24 Liberator out
of New Guinea and the Philippines in 1943-1945; click on individual
chapters beneath the heading of "Stories")
http://www.ajcockrell.com/history/worldwar.htm

379. Dunn, Peter. *Military Airfields in Australia and the Western Pacific
Area during World War 2*
http://home.st.net.au/~dunn/airfields.htm

380. Dunn, Peter. *5th Air Force USAAF, 1942-1945*
http://home.st.net.au/~dunn/5thaf.htm

381. Guevara, Lucy. *Mexican Airmen Join the War Effort* (they served as a
squadron attached to U.S. forces in the Pacific)
http://www.utexas.edu/projects/latinoarchives/narratives/
vol1no2/ESCUADRON_201/ESCUADRON_201.HTML

382. Heyn, Jack, and Peter Dunn. *Jack Heyn in the South West Pacific* (member 3rd Bombardment group; saw service at Port Moresby, Hollandia,
and Philippines; includes many photographs he took)
http://home.st.net.au/~dunn/ozatwar/heynswpa.htm

383. Lawrence, Rich. *Grumman F6F-3 Hellcat* (designed as US answer to
the Japanese Zero)
http://www.cris.com/~Twist/airwar/f6f/f6f-3.shtml

384. Long, Larry E. *The Jungle Air Force of World War II: 1942-1945*
http://www.enter.net/~rocketeer/13thmain.html

385. Maxwell, David. *505th Bomb Group Tinian*
http://community-2.webtv.net/NYCB29/505BombGroupTinian/

386. Stanaway, John. *Flying Circus over the Pacific* (P-38 pilots in the Pacific)
http://www.military.com/Content/MoreContent?file=PRp38

387. Taylan, [?]. *Pacific [Warplane] Wreck Database*
http://www.pacificwrecks.com/

388. [Unidentified.] *B-26 Marauder Historical Society World War II Air War Archive*
http://www.b-26marauderarchive.org/

389. [Unidentified.] *Black Cats: U.S. Navy PBY Catalinas Fighting in the Pacific during World War II*
http://www.ixpres.com/ag1caf/blackcat/

390. [Unidentified.] *Combat Aircraft of the Pacific War*
http://www.djjp.demon.co.uk/1aircraft.htm

391. [Unidentified.] *Japan Is NOT an Air Power* (article from the January 1941 issue of *Flying and Popular Aviation,* reflecting the common opinion of the day)
http://rwebs.net/avhistory/history/japan.htm

392. [Unidentified.] *PC-1132* (a patrol craft doing duty in the Pacific)
http://www.geocities.com/kf4yno/

393. [Unidentified.] *P38 Lightning Online: "The Fork-Tailed Devil"*
http://www.p-38online.com/

394. [Unidentified.] *U.S. Marine Corps VMD-354, 1943-1945* (Aerial Photo Reconnaissance Squadron, pulling duty at such places as Guam and Okinawa)
http://www.usmarinecorpsvmd-354.com/

395. Whitman, John W. *Aerial Reconnaissance in the Far East*
http://www.military.com/Content/MoreContent?file=PRfarf

Infantry and Other Land Forces

396. Auman, Jerome *Interview* (a Marine whose service included the invasion of the Philippines)
http://www.tankbooks.com/intviews/auman/auman1.htm

397. Bird, Roy. *Seabee in the South Pacific* (interview with Wilbur Semme: went to the Pacific for an anticipated three months work of construction and stayed three years with the Seabees)
http://www.military.com/Content/MoreContent?file=PRseabeef

398. Brooks, Harry. *Harry Remembers the 1940s* (combat memories, including continued fighting after the Japanese surrender)
http://www.angelfire.com/hi/RedArrowDivision/ww2.html

399. Duncan, Basil. *Dunc's Page* (memoirs from bootcamp to Saipan and other battles)
http://www.geocities.com/Heartland/Plains/5850/

400. Jackson, Robert. *War Memoirs* (was in the Philippines and Okinawa invasions)
http://home.nc.rr.com/ww2memories/memoirs_jackson.txt

401. Kleen, Bill. *From Cornfield to Killing Fields*
http://www.military.com/Content/MoreContent?file=PRkleen

402. Levine, Jim. *My USMC Memoirs*
http://members.aol.com/jimmemoirs/

403. Lewis, George. *War on Their Minds* (interview; construction work in the Pacific with the Marines)
http://www.whshistoryproject.org/ww2/Interviews/mr_lewis.html

404. Mansfield, Ernie. *Oral History* (served in the Seabees)
http://www-personal.umich.edu/~amnornes/alice.html

405. Marsh, Dan. *Marine Raider Page*
http://www.geocities.com/Pentagon/Quarters/3805/index.html

406. Newell, Clayton R. *The U.S. Army Campaigns of World War II: Central Pacific, 1941-1943* (CMH Publication 72-4)
http://www.army.mil/cmh-pg/brochures/72-4/72-4.htm

407. Patrick, Joe. *The Bushmasters: Arizona's Fighting Guardsmen*
http://www.military.com/Content/MoreContent?file=PRbushmasters

408. Paull, William T. *From Butte to Iwo Jima* (Marine with service in Guadalcanal and Iwo Jima)
http://www.sihope.com/~tipi/marine.html

409. [Unidentified.] *Alamo Scouts: The U.S. Sixth Army Special Reconnaissance Unit of World War II*
http://www.alamoscouts.org/

410. [Unidentified.] *Carlson's Raider's Executed: The Makin Raid—August 17 & 18, 1942* (with links to additional material on the Raiders)
http://www.angelfire.com/ca/dickg/carlsonraidersexecuted.html

411. [Unidentified.] *Gungo ho! According to Evans F. Carlson* (the original meaning of the expression)
http://expage.com/gunghousmc

412. [Unidentified.] *K-9 History: World War II, Pacific Theater of Operations*
http://community-2.webtv.net/Hahn-50thAP-K9/K9History4/

413. [Unidentified.] *96th Infantry Division* (involved in the Leyte [Philippines] and Okinawa invasions)
http://www.geocities.com/Pentagon/Barracks/4096/96th.html

414. [Unidentified.] *Private 5776807 Royal Norfolk, 4th Battalion, 18th Division* (diary extracts and letters; he worked on the "death railway")
http://www.ean.co.uk/Data/Bygones/History/Article/WW2/Private_5776807/index.htm

415. [Unidentified.] *352 AA Searchlight Battalion*
http://www.geocities.com/searchlight352/battalion.html

416. [Unidentified.] *USMC Raiders* (in the "World War II Fact Sheet, USMC" series)
http://www.usmc.mil/history.nsf/Table+of+Contents/
77f992b2acb682eb852564d70059c642?OpenDocument&Expand
Section=12

417. [Unidentified.] *War Years: in the Navy* (emphasis on one Seabee's service, with additional information on the 43rd NCB, 1942-1946)
http://www.geocities.com/Paris/Jardin/4814/waryears1.html

NAVAL FORCES

418. Ambos, John F. *Oral History Interview* (describes life on shipboard in Pacific)
http://fas-history.rutgers.edu/oralhistory/ambos.htm

419. Amburgey, Roy E. *Rambling Recollections* (landed Marines at several of their Pacific invasions)
http://www.geocities.com/Heartland/Plains/5850/amburgey.html

420. American War Library. *Number [and Type] Allied Vessels Hit by Kamikazes*
http://members.aol.com/forcountry/ww2/kam.htm

421. Bauer, Jim. *Japanese Suicide Attacks at Sea* (includes description of type of craft used)
http://www.ww2pacific.com/suicide.html

422. Bell, Jr., Alexander. *Oral History Interview* (served as pharmacist on multiple trips across Pacific bringing sick and injured stateside)
http://fas-history.rutgers.edu/oralhistory/bell.html

423. Brehm, H. Paul. *Navy Helldivers Strike "Hyuga"* (the *Hyuga* was a Japanese hybrid carrier and battleship combination; Brehem participated in the attack)
http://www.military.com/Content/MoreContent?file=PRhyuga

424. Browning, Jr., Robert M. *The Coast Guard and the Pacific War in World War II*
http://www.uscg.mil/hq/g-cp/history/h_pacwar.html

425. Daly, Paul. *War on Their Minds* (interview; electrician on an LST)
http://www.whshistoryproject.org/ww2/Interviews/mr_daly.html

426. Davis, Scott. *At Close Quarters* (PT boats; emphasis on Philippines, Guadalcanal, and New Guinea)
http://www.geocities.com/Pentagon/5133/acqpt.htm

427. Davis, Scott. *AVR's* (= Air Sea Rescue Boats)
http://nobadlie.tripod.com/index.html

428. Enterpise CV-6 Association. *USS Enterprise (CV-6): The Most Decorated Ship of the Second World War* (variety of resources including photographs and first hand accounts)
http://www.cv6.org/default.htm
http://www.cv6.org/ship/logs/default.htm (collection of action reports and logs of the vessel)

429. Fine, Sidney. *Oral History* (served in the Office of Naval Intelligence; worked with the 7th Fleet as translator and interrogator)
http://www-personal.umich.edu/~amnornes/james.html

430. Fox, Ronald E. *LCT 376 Home Port* (LCTs in the Pacific)
http://www.angelfire.com/pa/LCT376/

431. Friederich, David A. *World War II Memoirs* (Frederich was a Coxswain in the USN)
http://www.geocities.com/TheTropics/7621/navyindex.html

432. Glover, Bill. *World War II Pacific Air Battles* (Glover was a veteran of the Pacific War)
http://members.tripod.com/BilGlo/pacific.html

433. Green, Daniel. *War in the Pacific* (air campaigns waged by the opposing sides)
http://www.danshistory.com/ww2/pacific.html

434. Guttman, Jon. *Free-For-All over Rabaul*
http://www.military.com/Content/MoreContent?file=PRrabaul

435. Halterman, Gerald. *War on Their Minds* (interview; served at Pearl Harbor immediately after the attack)
http://www.whshistoryproject.org/ww2/Interviews/mr_halterman.html

436. Haynes, Ellsworth W. *Affidavit* (served on naval vessel carrying troops and supplies to Guadalcanal and other Pacific locations)
http://www.military.com/Content/MoreContent?file=haynes01

437. Henriott, Paul, and Shirley Lane. *U.S.S. Tucson* (took part in attacks on Japanese Home Islands just prior to surrender)
http://www.geocities.com/Pentagon/Quarters/1961/

438. Komarck, Pavel. *Naval War in Pacific, 1941-1945*
http://pacific.hyperlink.cz/

439. Lanzdendorfer, Tim. *The Pacific War: The U.S. Navy* (web site with a variety of resources)
http://www.microworks.net/pacific/January 1, 1990

440. Matusek, David. *The Pacific Air War, 1941-1942* (site with sections on Pearl Harbor, Coral Sea, and Midway)
http://www.geocities.com/Pentagon/Bunker/2206/

441. McGillicuddy, Thomas. *War on Their Minds* (served in naval intelligence)
http://www.whshistoryproject.org/ww2/Interviews/mr_mcgillicuddy.html

442. Miles, Dwayne. *U.S.S. Hornet: CV/CVA/CVS-12d ("The Gray Ghost")*
http://www.its.caltech.edu/~drmiles/hornet.html

443. Morrison, Mark. *U.S.S. Guam*
http://www.ussguam.com/

444. Office of Naval Records and Library. *U.S.S. Picking (DD-685): War Diary* (December 1, 1943-July 31, 1944)
http://www.geocities.com/Pentagon/5133/picking.htm

445. Penniston, Bradley. *Lt. John F. Kennedy* (and the destruction of his PT-109)
http://www.military.com/Content/MoreContent?file=ML_jfk_bradp

446. Reed, Chris M. *Surviving B-29 Superfortresses*
http://www.csd.uwo.ca/~pettypi/elevon/toppan/b29.html

447. Reid, Art. *Mighty Midgets* (LCS[L]: modest size vessel with an abundance of firepower, utilized in Pacific for shore bombardments)
http://www.military.com/Content/MoreContent?file=PRmidgets

448. Sherman, Stephen. *PTO [Pacific Theater of Operations] P-38 Lightning Aces of World War II*
http://www.westnet.com/~ssherman/usaaf_pto_aces.html

449. Shields, Mark. *Lt. Comdr. Butch O'Hare* (naval aviator who won the Medal of Honor)
http://www.military.com/Content/MoreContent?file=ML_ohare_shields

450. Treadwell, Terry. *Undersea Aircraft Carriers* (experiments to make it practical to launch planes from submarines)
http://www.military.com/Content/MoreContent?file=PRundersea

451. [Unidentified.] *August 1944* (carrier pilot shot down and rescued by a sub)
http://www.geocities.com/hsemerson/story1.html

452. [Unidentified.] *Bombing Squadron Nineteen, 1943-1944* (flying off the *U.S.S. Lexington*; includes personnel list and dates of various engagements)
http://www.geocities.com/hsemerson/vb19.html

453. [Unidentified.] *Charles A. Lockwood, Jr., Vice-Admiral (1890-1967)*
http://www.wardocuments.com/Lockwood.html

454. [Unidentified.] *Forrest P. Sherman,. Rear-Admiral, 1896-1951)*
http://www.wardocuments.com/Sherman.html

455. [Unidentified.] *Imperial Japanese Navy Page* (with many links to pictures, information on specific vessels, etc.)
http://www.combinedfleet.com/kaigun.htm

456. [Unidentified.] *John A. Towers, Vice-Admiral (1885-1955)*
http://www.wardocuments.com/Towers.html

457. [Unidentified.] *Kamikaze: Tribute of Memory*
http://www1.itnet.com.pl/~wojmos/KAMIKAZE/

458. [Unidentified.] *Pacific Naval Battles in World War II* (includes map, list of battles)
http://www.combinedfleet.com/map.htm

459. [Unidentified.] *Robert B. Carney, Rear Admiral (1895-1990)*
http://www.wardocuments.com/Carney.html

460. [Unidentified.] *U.S. Navy Fleet and Task Force Organizations in World*

War II: Asiatic Fleet, 8 December 1941-23 February 1942 (includes listing of all warcraft assigned to it)
http://www.ibiblio.org/hyperwar/USN/TF/AsiaticFlt-1.html

461. [Unidentified.] *U.S.S. Atlanta, CL-104* (served at Okinawa and near Japan for remainder of war)
http://www.meditype-ts.com/Atlanta/

462. [Unidentified.] *U.S.S. Ganter DE-60/APD-42* (destroyer escort; served in Pacific; has short crew stories)
http://gantner.webhouse.cc/

463. [Unidentified.] *U.S.S. Indianapolis*
http://members.home.net/jrolette/indy.htm

464. Uranaka, Taiga. *Kamikaze Diaries Reveal Pilots' Human Side*
http://www.asiamedia.ucla.edu/Weekly/01.12.2000/Japan3.htm

465. Vaughn, Ron. *Two Years before the Mast* (served two years on a "pocket carrier," including at Leyte Gulf)
http://www.memoriesofwar.com/veterans/vaughn.asp

Tank and Armored Forces

466. Donaldson, Graham. *Australian Tank Deployment in the Pacific Theatre of War*
http://worldatwar.net/article/australiantank/index.html

Maps and Photographs

467. Dunn, Peter. *South West Pacific Area* (good map of boundary lines between the regions the U.S. military divided the Pacific-Asia region into)
http://home.st.net.au/~dunn/swpa.htm

468. Hanson, Dave. *Naval Air War in the Pacific* (photographs)
http://www.ixpres.com/ag1caf/navalwar/frames.htm

469. [Unidentified.] *Photographs & Artwork: 25th Infantry Division* (small collection of photographs from World War II, Korea, and Vietnam)
http://www.army.mil/cmh-pg/matrix/25id/25ID-Photos.htm

470. West Point History Department. *Maps of World War II: Asian Theater* (50 maps)
http://www.dean.usma.edu/history/dhistorymaps/WWIIPages/
WWIIPacific/WWIIAToC.htm

OTHER MATERIALS

471. Allmon, William B. *Gilbert Islands Campaign: Takin' Makin*
http://www.military.com/Content/MoreContent?file=PRmakin

472. Antoine, L. W. *Ulithi Atoll* (abandoned by Japanese prior to invasion; used as a ship staging ground for major assaults)
http://www.geocities.com/Pentagon/Barracks/2436/anaccount.html

473. Ballendorf, Dirk. *Exigencies of Two American Campaigns* (Ballendorf is professor of History and Micronesian Studies at the University of Guam)
http://www.uog.edu/faculty/ballendo/exigencies.htm

474. Ballendorf, Dirk. *Holding the Pacific Front* (against Japanese expansion)
http://www.uog.edu/faculty/ballendo/pfront.htm

475. Ballendorf, Dirk. *Problems of Supply in World War II with Special Reference for the Pacific*
http://www.uog.edu/faculty/ballendo/SUPPLY.htm

476. Ballendorf, Dirk. *The American Counteroffensive in the Pacific in World War II*
http://www.uog.edu/faculty/ballendo/counter.htm

477. Ballendorf, Dirk. *Timeline of World War II Events in the Pacific, 1941-1945*
http://www.uog.edu/faculty/ballendo/counter.htm

478. Ballendorf, Dirk. *World War II in Micronesia*
http://www.uog.edu/faculty/ballendo/WWII&.htm

479. Barber, Laurie. *Willard Price: Uncle Sam's Spy [against the Japanese]?*
http://www.waikato.ac.nz/wfass/subjects/history/waimilhist/1999/willardprice.htm

480. Braun, Harold. *Taking Noemfoor Island* (Braun was a member of the 158th Regimental Combat Team, which drew the assignment)
http://www.military.com/Content/MoreContent?file=PRnoemfoor

481. Casey, Gavan. *Some Voices from the Pacific Battle Zone, World War II*
http://home.vicnet.net.au/~gcasey/voices.html

482. Coppersmith, Morris D. *When Victory Is Ours: Letters Home from the South Pacific, 1943-1945*
http://www.topshot.com/dh/Victory.html

483. Dunn, Peter. *Command Structure in the South West Pacific Area* (an evolving web site on both organization and individuals involved)
http://home.st.net.au/~dunn/ozatwar/commandstructure.htm

484. Ford, Dan. *Japan at War, 1931-1945* (large collection of articles by a variety of individuals)
http://www.danford.net/japan.htm

485. Frankel, Stanley A. *Frankel-y Speaking: About World War II in the Pacific* (autobiography)
http://www.frankel-y.com/

486. Hough, Frank O., Verle E. Ludwig, and Henry J. Shaw. *From Pearl Harbor to Guadalcanal;* volume 1 of *History of U.S. Marine Corps Operations in World War II*
http://www.ibiblio.org/hyperwar/USMC/USMC-I.html

487. MacMeekin, Dan. *Northern Marianas Chronology, 1931-1950*
http://www.macmeekin.com/Library/NMIchron/1931.htm

488. Patrick, Behtanne K. *Lt. J.G. George H. W. Bush*
http://www.military.com/Content/MoreContent?file=ML_bush_bkp

489. Schapiro, Ben. *The Great Pacific War Naval Aviation Bibliography, 1936-1945* (annotated briefly)
http://www.ameritech.net/users/bschapiro/NABhtxt.htm

490. [Unidentified.] *Rabaul: History, Paradise, Fortress, Inferno*
http://www.milart.com.au/rabaul/default.htm

491. [Unidentified.] *Ulithi Atoll in World War II*
http://geocities.com/Pentagon/Barracks/2436/ulithi.html

492. United States Air Force Museum. *World War II: Combat in the Pacific* (with links to specific battles of the war)
http://www.wpafb.af.mil/museum/history/wwii/combatp.htm

493. U.S. Strategic Bombing Survey. *Summary Report: Pacific War* (Washington, D.C., 1 July 1946)
http://www.ibiblio.org/hyperwar/AAF/USSBS-PTO-Summary.html
http://www.anesi.com/ussbs01.htm
http://www.danshistory.com/ww2/docs/ussbs_pac.html

494. Youngkirst, Gus. *A Damn Fine Gesture* (tribute to an influential and wealthy Southerner who voluntarily endured the hazards of combat in the Pacific)
http://members.aol.com/famjustin/Youngkrist2.html

Overlapping Theaters of War

AIRBORNE FORCES

495. [Unidentified.] *Airborne Troops in Ground Operations* (primarily a listing of what units were involved in different specific assaults)
http://www.army.mil/cmh-pg/documents/abnops/tabb.htm

496. [Unidentified.] *Drop Zone Virtual Museum* (paratrooper photos, articles, and sound clips)
http://www.thedropzone.org/

497. [Unidentified.] *Tracing American Airborne's German Heritage*
http://www.geocities.com/mvea/airborne.htm

498. [Unidentified.] *U.S. Airborne Combat Jumps* (from World War II through Desert Storm)
http://www.dropzonepress.com/usjumps.htm

AIR FORCES

499. Air Force Historical Research Agency. *Air Force Statistical Digest: World War II* (Adobe Acrobat Reader required)
http://www.au.af.mil/au/afhra/wwwroot/aafsd/aafsd_index_table.html

500. Arnold, Ken. *World War II Memories* (first hand narratives from airmen and support personnel in the air forces of the various combatants)
http://www.geocities.com/CapeCanaveral/Runway/9601/

501. Bauer, Jim. *Jet Aircraft Development during World War II* (developers and number produced)
http://www.ww2pacific.com/jethist.html

502. Baugher, Joe. *Encyclopedia of American Military Aircraft* (past and present)
http://www.csd.uwo.ca/~pettypi/elevon/baugher_us/

503. Baugher, Joe. *USAAS-USAAC-USAAF-USAF Aircraft Serial Numbers—1908 to Present*
http://home.att.net/~jbaugher/usafserials.html

504. Birnn, Roland. *Where Is Our Air Power* (from the June 1942 *Flying and Population Aviation* magazine, attempting to explain why American airpower had not yet made major dents in the enemy)
http://rwebs.net/avhistory/history/where.htm

505. Bowen, Al, and David Lednicer. *Fighter Pilot "Ace" List* (all nations; twentieth century wars)
http://www.csd.uwo.ca/~pettypi/elevon/aces.html

506. DC-3 Aviation Museum. *The DC-3 Aviation Museum* (in addition to other materials, heavy on book reviews of aircraft)
http://www.centercomp.com/cgi-bin/dc3/books?2000

507. Directorate of Flying Safety, United States Army Air Force. *Lessons that Live as Told by Army Air Force Pilots* (1942 or 1943 edition; personal experiences to help new pilots stay alive)
http://rwebs.net/avhistory/history/lessons.html

508. Futrell, Robert F. *Developments in Airwarfare*
http://gi.grolier.com/wwii/wwii_13.html

509. Gustin, Emmanuel. *Aircraft Strength and Losses* (by combatant nations)
http://www.csd.uwo.ca/~pettypi/elevon/gustin_military/strength.html

510. Gustin, Emmanuel. *Gustin's Military Aircraft Database* (treats from World War I to Vietnam)
http://www.csd.uwo.ca/~pettypi/elevon/gustin_military/

511. Hanson, Don. *"Grand Old Lady:" The DC-3*
http://www.centercomp.com/cgi-bin/dc3/stories?1902

512. Hogg, John E. *Is Aerial Warfare Doomed?* (from the November 1934 *Modern Mechanic and Inventions* magazine, predicting the complete failure of warplanes as offensive weapons in any future conflict)
http://rwebs.net/avhistory/history/doomed.htm

513. Jordan Publishing. *Planes and Pilots of World War Two* (includes detailed studies of plane manufacturers)
http://home.att.net/~C.C.Jordan/index.html

514. Keller, Cindy. *Air Museum Planes of Fame*
http://www.planesoffame.org/

515. Lawrence, Rich. *North American P51 Mustang*
http://www.cris.com/~Twist/airwar/p51/p51d.shtml

516. Lawrence, Rich. *Republic P-47D Thunderbolt*
http://www.cris.com/~Twist/airwar/p47/p47d.shtml

517. Lee, Jeremy. *Aircraft of the Second World War*
http://www.btinternet.com/~lee_mail/

518. Mersky, Peter B. *Marine Corps Aces* (in the "World War II Fact Sheet, USMC" series)
http://www.usmc.mil/history.nsf/Table+of+Contents/
77f992b2acb682eb852564d70059c642?OpenDocument&Expand
Section=4

519. Nanney, James S. *Armed Air Forces Medical Service in World War II* (1998)
http://www.airforcehistory.hq.af.mil/online/nanney.pdf

520. Naval Historical Center. *U.S. Navy and Marine Corps Aces*
http://www.history.navy.mil/branches/aces.htm

521. Oates, Carl C. *Douglas A-26 Invader: Bringing the Ghost to Life* (aircraft introduced too late in war to have made a major impact on war memories)
http://www.military.com/Content/MoreContent?file=PRghost

522. Pixler, Dennis R. *United States Army Air Force in World War II* (photographs of aircraft and historical information)
http://www.geocities.com/cgi-bin-local/GeoAD?pageID=/
gp/CapeCanaveral/Hangar/1956/

523. [Unidentified.] *Aircraft Types Operated by the Combatant Nations in World War Two*
http://www.senet.com.au/~mhyde/ww2_aircraft_title.htm
http://sfstation.members.easyspace.com/allyx.htm

524. [Unidentified.] *Air Group 4: "Casablanca to Tokyo"*
http://www.airgroup4.com/index.htm

525. [Unidentified.] *Allies' X Planes* (various western planes in developmental stage when the war ended)

526. [Unidentified.] *American Aircraft of World War II* (divided by types of plane)
http://www.ixpres.com/ag1caf/usplanes/american.htm

527. [Unidentified.] *An Unofficial History of 879, Fleet Air Arm (Royal Navy), 1942-1946*
http://www.gavinbull.pwp.blueyonder.co.uk/879.html

528. [Unidentified.] *Biplane Fighter Aces from the Second World War* (country studies and video clips)
http://www.dalnet.se/~surfcity/index.html

529. [Unidentified.] *Boeing B-17G Flying Fortress*
http://freepages.military.rootsweb.com/~josephkennedy/Default.htm

530. [Unidentified.] *British Military Airfield Histories in Brief* (claims to have 790 of them in its records and will provide, by e-mail, data on the one requested)
http://www.airfieldhistoriesuk.fsnet.co.uk/

531. [Unidentified.] *Hawker Hurricane: "Defender of the Empire"* (history of the plane's development)
http://www3.mistral.co.uk/k5083/

532. [Unidentified.] *Heavy and Very Heavy Bombardment Groups of the Army Air Force*
http://www.heavybombers.com/default.asp

533. [Unidentified.] *Historic Air* (available in French or English)
http://www.multimania.com/historicair/index.htm

534. [Unidentified.] *Marine Corps Aces of World War II: Wildcat and Cosair Pilots at Guadalcanal and the Solomons*
http://www.acepilots.com/usmc_aces.html

535. [Unidentified.] *Royal Air Force Veterans' Organizations* (list)
http://www.raf-war-veterans.co.uk/

536. [Unidentified.] *211 Squadron RAF 1938-1942* (these years were service in the Middle East; link takes you to discussion of 1942-1945 and the unit's service in the Far East)
http://users.bigpond.com/clardo/

537. [Unidentified.] *United States Army Air Force Resource Center* (includes plane specifications and other data)
http://www.warbirdsresourcegroup.org/URG/index.html

538. [Unidentified.] *U.S. Naval Air Operations, World War II* (day by day chronology)
http://home.att.net/~ww2aviation/USNair.html

539. [Unidentified.] *U.S. Navy Aces of World War Two*
http://www.acepilots.com/usn_aces.html

540. [Unidentified.] *War Memoirs* (anonymous tale of how *not* to succeed in pilot's school and how to spend the war years as a plane mechanic; great detail on practical problems of plane maintenance and life in off-hours)
http://home.nc.rr.com/ww2memories/soldiers_story.txt

541. [Unidentified.] *World War II Air Power* (with special studies of night combat, the eastern front, etc.)
http://www.danshistory.com/ww2/index.html

542. [Unidentified.] *Zeno's Warbird Video Drive-In* (includes eighteen World War II pilot training films)
http://www.zenoswarbirdvideos.com/

543. United States Naval Flight Preparatory Schools. *A Message to Aviation Cadets* (pamphlet; 1943)
http://rwebs.net/avhistory/history/nacpam.html

544. U.S. Air Force Museum. *A Push for Performance* (concise summary of efforts to develop ultra-effective aircraft during the war)
http://www.wpafb.af.mil/museum/history/wwii/push.htm

545. U.S. Air Force Museum. *Glider Pilots* (with links)
http://www.wpafb.af.mil/museum/history/wwii/gp.htm

546. U.S. Air Force Museum. *World War II Training [of Pilots]* (follow links through several connected sections)
http://www.wpafb.af.mil/museum/history/wwii/trng.htm

547. Warbirds Resource Group. *Warbirds Resource Group* (data on aircraft of the warring powers)
http://www.warbirdsresourcegroup.org/

548. Wilson, Randy. *World War II Aircraft Designations and Names* (Allied and Axis)
http://rwebs.net/avhistory/designations.htm

INFANTRY AND OTHER LAND FORCES

549. Adamcyzk, Richard D., and Morris J. MacGregor. *United States Army in World War II: Reader's Guide* (concise summary of all volumes in the series)
http://www.ibiblio.org/hyperwar/USA/USA-Guide/index.html
http://www.army.mil/cmh-pg/books/wwii/11-9/11-9c.htm

550. Anders, Steven E. *A Brief History of the Quartermaster Corps*
http://www.quartermaster.army.mil/oqmg/Professional_Bulletin/
2001/Spring01/A_Brief_History_of_the_QM_Corps.htm

551. Anders, Steven D. *Quartermaster Supply in the Pacific during World War II*
http://www.quartermaster.army.mil/oqmg/Professional_Bulletin/1999/
spring1999/QM%20Supply%20in%20the%20Pacific%20During%20W
WII.htm

552. Armfeld, Blanche B. *Medical Department U.S. Army in World War II: Organization and Administration in World War II* (1963; CMH 80-4)
http://www.armymedicine.army.mil/history/booksdocs/wwii/orgadmin/

553. Bourdeau, William H. *Army Bugle Calls* (recorded for computer use)
http://www.metronet.com/~harryb/cgi_perl/dateline/1st_team.cgi

554. Carpenter, Eric. *Excerpts from Letters of Eric Carpenter, Gunner, Royal Artillery: England 1940-Burma 1946*
http://homepage.ntlworld.com/the.carpenters/earlyday.htm

555. Dzwonchyk, Wayne M., and John R. Skates. *The U.S. Army Campaigns of World War II: A Brief History of the U.S. Army in World War II* (1992)
http://www.ibiblio.org/hyperwar/USA/USA-C-USA-WWII.html
http://www.army.mil/cmh-pg/brochures/brief/overview.htm

556. Dzwonchyk, Wayne M., and John R. Skates. *A Brief History of the U.S. Army in World War II.*
http://www.army.mil/cmh-pg/brochures/brief/overview.htm

557. Evans, Nigel F. *British Field Artillery in World War 2*
http://members.tripod.com/~nigelef/index.htm

558. Foster, Renita. *The Army's Best Invention* (the P-38; used to open C-rations and many other purposes)
http://www.dtic.mil/soldiers/august94/p45.html

559. Govan, Thomas P. *Training for Mountain and Winter Warfare* (Army Ground Forces Study Number 23; 1946)
http://www.army.mil/cmh-pg/books/agf/agf23.htm

560. Hogan, David W., Jr. *U. S. Army Special Operations in World War II* (1992)
http://www.army.mil/cmh-pg/books/wwii/70-42/70-42c.htm

561. Juckett, Daniel P. *Lynn K. Juckett: My Dad Goes to War* (served in both Europe and Pacific; documents and photographs included)
http://www.thejucketts.com/ww2.htm

562. Kirkpatrick, Charles E. *The U.S. Army Campaigns of World War II: Defense of the Americas*
http://www.ibiblio.org/hyperwar/USA/USA-C-Americas.html
http://www.army.mil/cmh-pg/brochures/DOA/DOA.htm

563. Mills, T. F. *Land Forces of Britain, the Empire and Commonwealth* (includes those involved in combat in the last several centuries)
http://regiments.org/

564. Rodriquez, Juan E. *Laundry and Shower Quartermasters through Two World Wars*
http://www.quartermaster.army.mil/oqmg/Professional_Bulletin/1996/W inter/shower.html

565. Shaw, Henry I. *Opening Moves: Marines Gear Up for War* (1991; in the "Marines in World War II Commemorative Series")
http://www.ibiblio.org/hyperwar/USMC/USMC-C-Opening.html

566. Steinert, David. *World War II Combat Medic* (source of information on varied aspects of their work)
http://home.att.net/~steinert/index.html
http://home.att.net/~steinert/newpage3.htm (accounts by individual medics)

567. [Unidentified.] *Amphibious Operations, Staff Officers' Manual* (November 1944)
http://carlisle-www.army.mil/cgi-bin/usamhi/DL/showdoc.pl?docnum=718

568. [Unidentified.] *Inventory of Army Facilities, December 1945*
http://carlisle-www.army.mil/cgi-bin/usamhi/DL/showdoc.pl?
docnum=448

569. [Unidentified.] *Medical Department U.S. Army in World War II: Medical Training in World War II* (1974; compiled from the research of a number of military historians)
http://www.armymedicine.army.mil/history/booksdocs/
wwii/medtrain/default.htm

570. [Unidentified.] *U. S. Army Divisions in World War II: Activation and Participation* (treats date called into service and campaigns involved in; includes additional bibliographical leads)
http://www.ibiblio.org/hyperwar/USA/USA-Div.html

571. U.S. Armed Forces. *Loose Lips Sink Ships* (pamphlet given to GIs about what was needed to be omitted from letters home because of national security)
http://www.ibiscom.com/lslips.htm

572. [Various authors]. *United States Army in World War II* series (bibliographical listing)
http://www.ibiblio.org/hyperwar/USA/index.html#usa

573. Vittur, Robert. *Mulvaney on Bomb Disposal* (Supplement to Intelligence Bulletin 85, 15 September 1945; contains cartoons by Vittur on bomb disposal)
http://www.multicians.org/thvv/mulvaney.html

574. Wigginton, F. Peter. "A Soldier's Song" (history of the official U.S. Army song)
http://www.dtic.mil/soldiers/july94/p45.html

575. Wilson, John B. *Maneuver and Firepower: The Evolution of Divisions and Separate Brigades* (1998; in the "Army Lineage Series"—traces the subject from the Revolutionary War to late twentieth century)
http://www.army.mil/cmh-pg/books/Lineage/M-F/index.htm

576. Wright, Jr., Robert R. "Clio in Combat: The Evolution of the Military History Detachment" (from *Army Historian*, No. 6 [Winter 1985], pages 3-6)
http://www.army.mil/cmh-pg/reference/History/clio.htm

NAVAL FORCES

577. Aircraft Carrier Study Group. *Home Page* (issues studies on carriers from the first built to the most recent; issues 1-100 downloadable; 101-203 readable on line; click on "Back Issues" button)
http://www.carriersg.org/

578. Bauer, Jim. *Naval Construction Authorizations* (U.S., 1931-1945)
http://www.ww2pacific.com/authoriz.html

579. Baugher, Joe. *U.S. Navy and U.S. Marine Corps Aircraft Serial Numbers and Bureau Numbers—1911 to Present*
http://home.att.net/~jbaugher/navyserials.html

580. Clancey, Patrick. *Ships of the U.S. Navy, 1940-1945* (with links to ships that fall under each letter of the alphabet)
http://www.ibiblio.org/hyperwar/USN/USN-ships.html
http://www.ibiblio.org/hyperwar/USN/ships/ships-ss.html (submarines, by type)

581. Cressman, Robert J. *Official Chronology of the U.S. Navy in World War II*
http://www.ibiblio.org/hyperwar/USN/USN-Chron.html

582. DANF's Online. *Torpedo Boats*
http://www.hazegray.org/danfs/destroy/tb.htm

583. [Department of Defense.] *NV: Naval Vessel Register: Official Inventory of U.S. Naval Ships and Service Craft* (with search capacity)
http://www.nvr.navy.mil/

584. Department of Navy. *Dictionary of American Naval Aviation Squadrons; Volume 1: VA, VAH, VAK, VAL, VAP, and VFA Squadrons*
http://www.history.navy.mil/branches/dictvol1.htm

585. Department of Navy. *Dictionary of American Naval Aviation Squadrons; Volume 2: VP, VPB, VP(H), and VP(AM) Squadrons*
http://www.history.navy.mil/branches/dictvol2.htm

586. Department of Navy. *Nomenclature of Naval Vessels* (Revised, February 1942; includes a glossary of terms)
http://www.ibiblio.org/hyperwar/USN/ref/NNV/

587. Design, John L. *Aircraft Carriers of World War 2* (covers all combatants)
http://www.voodoo.cz/ww2car/

588. Duncan, George. *Maritime Disasters of World War II* (concise summaries of each)
http://members.iinet.net.au/~gduncan/maritime.html

589. Faville, Doc. *Navy Corpsman* ("home of the military medicine webring")
http://www.corpsman.com/

590. Frankel, Nevins A. *VPNAVY* (internet accessible information on over 200 past and present U.S. Navy patrol squadrons)
http://www.vpnavy.org/

591. Guttery, Randy. *Submarine Tenders of the U.S. Navy*
http://tendertale.com/

592. Harris, K. *USS LST 173* (pictures, action reports, film footage; links page has links to many other specific LST histories/groups)
http://users.erols.com/reds1/LST173.htm

593. Historic Naval Ship Association. *Historic Naval Ship Visitors' Guide* (historic vessels listed by name and location)
http://www.maritime.org/hnsa-guide.htm

594. Hayes, John D. *Developments in Naval Warfare*
http://gi.grolier.com/wwii/wwii_12.html

595. Hoyt, Michael J. *PT Boat Page*
http://ourworld.compuserve.com/homepages/mandm/ptboatp1.htm

596. Jackson, Ramon. *Army Ships—The Ghost Fleet* (discusses that large number of ships that were actually under Army rather than Navy control)
http://www.dc.net/jacksonr/Army.htm

597. Johnson, Robert E. *Coast Guard-Manned Naval Vessels in World War II*
http://www.uscg.mil/hq/g-cp/history/h_cgnvy.html

598. Karoly, Charles. *War Memoirs* (a Navy aviator; did not see combat during the war, but provides a detailed description of flight training in the last year or two of the conflict)
http://home.nc.rr.com/ww2memories/memoirs_karoly.txt

599. Kennedy, David M. *Victory at Sea* (articles from the *Atlantic Monthly*)
(part 1:) http://www.theatlantic.com/issues/99mar/victory.htm
(part 2:) http://www.theatlantic.com/issues/99mar/victory2.htm
(part 3:) http://www.theatlantic.com/issues/99mar/victory3.htm
(part 4:) http://www.theatlantic.com/issues/99mar/victory4.htm
(part 5:) http://www.theatlantic.com/issues/99mar/victory5.htm

600. King, Ernest J. (Fleet Admiral). *First Report to the Secretary of the Navy Covering Our Peacetime Navy and our Wartime Navy and including Combat Operations up to 1 March 1944* (issued 23 April 1944)
http://www.ibiblio.org/pha/cno/cnorpt_1.html

601. King, Ernest J. (Fleet Admiral). *Third and Final Report to the Secretary of the Navy, Covering the Period 1 March 1945 to 1 October 1945* (issued 8 December 1945)
http://www.unclesam.net/cny/honors/hon-07a.htm

602. King, Ernest J. (Fleet Admiral). *U. S. Navy at War, 1941-1945: Official Reports to the Secretary of the Navy* (Washington: U.S. Navy Department, 1946)
http://www.ibiblio.org/pha/cno/cnointro.html

603. Marlatt, Gregta E., and Michaele L. Huygen. *Sea Mines & Countermeasures in the Twentieth Century: A Bibliography*
http://web.nps.navy.mil/~library/bibs/sea20thtoc.htm

604. Mosher, Bill. *The Lucky Ship Online: The story of the U.S.S. Wilkes (DD-441)* (served in both the Atlantic and the Pacific; multiple chapters in detailed narrative)
http://www.geocities.com/wilkesdd441/441action.html

605. Naval Historical Center. *Casualties: U.S. Navy and Coast Guard Vessels, Sunk or Damaged beyond Repair during World War II—7 December 1941-1 October 1945*
http://www.history.navy.mil/faqs/faq82-1.htm

606. Naval Historical Center. *Casualties: U.S. Navy and Marine Corps Personnel Killed and Wounded in Wars, Conflicts and Incidents with Hostile Forces, 1775-Present*
http://www.history.navy.mil/faqs/faq56-1.htm

607. Naval Historical Center. *Dates in American Naval History* (arranged by month)
http://www.history.navy.mil/wars/dates.htm

608. Naval Historical Center. *Sources of Ship Plans* (microfilm and other sources)
http://www.history.navy.mil/faqs/faq26-1.htm

609. Naval Historical Center. *Typhoons and Hurricanes: The Effects of Cyclonic Winds on U.S. Naval Operations*
http://www.history.navy.mil/faqs/faq102-1.htm

610. Naval Historical Center. *U.S. Navy Abbreviations of World War II*
http://www.history.navy.mil/books/OPNAV20-P1000/index.html

611. Naval Historical Center. *U.S. Navy and Marine Corps Personnel Casualties in World War II*
http://www.history.navy.mil/faqs/faq11-1.htm

612. Naval Historical Center. *"USS Yorktown" (CV-5), 1937-1942: Overview and Special Image Selection*
http://www.history.navy.mil/photos/sh-usn/usnsh-xz/cv5.htm

613. Naval History Division, Office of Naval Operations. *U.S. Naval Chronology of World War II* (1955)
http://www.ibiblio.org/pha/chr/chrface.html
http://www.metalab.unc.edu/pha/chr/chrface.html (entire document downloadable; also has link to 1996 edition)

614. Navy Department. *Communiques and Pertinent Press Releases, December 10, 1941-May 24, 1945*
http://www.ibiblio.org/pha/comms/index.html

615. Office of Naval History. *Glossary of U.S. Naval Code Words* (NAVEXOS P474; revised March 1948)
http://www.ibiblio.org/hyperwar/USN/ref/USN-NAVEXOS_P-474.html

616. Office of Naval Records and History. *Glossary of U.S. Naval Abbreviations* (OPNAV 29-P1000; revised April 1949)
http://www.ibiblio.org/hyperwar/USN/ref/OPNAV_29-P1000.html

617. Office of Public Relations, Navy Department. *Report on the Navy and the War* (October 12, 1943; prepared for the U.S. Senate)
http://www.ibiblio.org/pha/USN/77-1s107.html

618. Patrick, Bethanne. *Adm. Russell R. Waesche* (oversaw wartime expansion of Coast Guard)
http://www.military.com/Content/MoreContent?file=ML_waesche_bkp

619. Patrol Craft Sailors Association. *Too Good to be Forgotten* (information and statistics on different types of WWII patrol craft of U.S. Navy)
http://www.ww2pcsa.org/

620. Scheina, Robert. *The Coast Guard At War*
http://www.uscg.mil/hq/g-cp/history/h_CGatwar.html

621. Senate Committee on Naval Affairs. *The Decline and Renaissance of the Navy, 1922-1944* (Senate document 202; June 7, 1944; brief survey of government policy and Naval legislation)
http://www.ibiblio.org/pha/USN/77-2s202.html

622. Short, Randy, and Cindy Ferguson. *U.S. Navy [Warship] Camouflage, 1941-1945*
http://www.shipcamouflage.com/warship_camouflage.htm

623. Toppan, Andrew, Project Manager. *DANFS Online: Dictionary of American Naval Fighting Ships* (nine large hard print volumes covering 7,000 ship histories, partially available online)
http://www.hazegray.org/danfs/
search engine: http://www.hazegray.org/search.htm

624. [Unidentified.] *American Merchant Marine Heroes and their Gallant Ships in World War II* (concise summary with links)
http://www.usmm.org/men_ships.html

625. [Unidentified.] *An Unofficial History of H.M.S. Attacker* (British carrier)
http://www.gavinbull.pwp.blueyonder.co.uk/attacker.html

626. [Unidentified.] *British Submarines of World War II*
http://web.ukonline.co.uk/chalcraft/sm/ww2sm2.html

627. [Unidentified.] *Convoy Routing Codes: World War II* (letter abbreviations utilized)
http://www.ibiblio.org/hyperwar/USN/ref/ConvoyCodes.html

628. [Unidentified.] *Destroyers Online Home Page* (with links to various types of data)
http://www.plateau.net/usndd/

629. [Unidentified.] *52 Still on Patrol* (discussion of American submarines that "vanished" during the war, presumably sunk)
http://users2.ev1.net/~crashevansss343/52onpatrol/

630. [Unidentified.] *H.M.S. Ramilles* (battleship; torpedoed but not sunk in Far East)
http://www.hmsramillies.org.uk/index.htm

631. [Unidentified.] *International Registry of Sunken Ships* (includes pre-
and post-war sinkings as well)
http://www.cableregina.com/users/shipwreck/

632. [Unidentified.] *Lost Boats* (from 1915 to most recent, with brief discussion of number of personnel lost and the circumstances)
http://www.subnet.com/MEMORIAL/lostboat.htm

633. [Unidentified.] *Naval Actions and Losses, 1939-1945* (choose year desired)
http://www.wolftree.freeserve.co.uk/Naval/Naval_Actions_WW2.html

634. [Unidentified.] *102 Ocean Minesweepers (MSO)* (complete account of
all every built by U.S.)
http://www.geocities.com/Pentagon/Bunker/2170/minesweeperlist.html

635. [Unidentified.] *Ships of the U.S. Coast Guard in World War II* (divided
by type and class and includes selected histories and photographs)
http://www.ibiblio.org/hyperwar/USN/ships/ships-cg.html

636. [Unidentified.] *Sources of Official Information for U.S. Naval Vessels*
(this section follows the one on veterans' information and includes locations and approximate prices for deck logs, muster rolls, etc.)
http://www.ibiblio.org/hyperwar/USN/USN-ref.html

637. [Unidentified.] *S.S. Jeremiah O'Brien* (one of only two surviving Liberty ships that remain fully operational)
http://www.geocities.com/jeremiahobrien/obrien.html

638. [Unidentified.] *Submarines of the Royal Navy* (aspires to be a complete listing, past and present)
http://www.argonet.co.uk/users/jdholt/index.html

639. [Unidentified.] *The Floating Drydock* (source for photographs, plans,
model kits, etc. related to U.S. war vessels)
http://www.floatingdrydock.com/

640. [Unidentified.] *The U.S. Navy 1900-1945: Looking at the Peacetime
Aspects of the U.S. Navy in the First Half of the Twentieth Century*
http://www.geocities.com/scs028a/index.html

641. [Unidentified.] *U.S. Army Hospital Ship "Thistle"*
http://members.aol.com/rseiple766/PAGE1.htm

642. [Unidentified.] *World War II Cruiser Operations* (of all combatants)
http://www.world-war.co.uk/index2.php3

643. [Unidentified.] *World War II Troopship Crossings*
http://members.aol.com/troopship/index.htm

644. [Unidentified,] Pollard. *Pollard's Page* (served in merchant marine in both Atlantic and Pacific)
http://www.geocities.com/sam_pollard_2000/index.html

645. United States Coast Guard. *Russell Randolph Waesche, Admiral, U.S. Coast Guard* (biography of Admiral who oversaw its war expansion)
http://www.arlingtoncemetery.com/waesche.htm

646. United States Government Printing Office. *Naval History Bibliography* (books on WWII and other wars currently available, with their prices)
http://bookstore.gpo.gov/sb/sb-236.html

647. U.S. Maritime Service Veterans *U.S. Merchant Marine in World War II* (concise summary with links)
http://www.usmm.org/ww2.html

648. U.S. Maritime Service Veterans. *U.S. Merchant Ships Sunk or Damaged in World War II* (over 1,200 listed)
http://www.usmm.org/shipsunkdamaged.html

649. Venzi, Maureen. *The Allied Merchant Navy of World War Two Website: Index Page*
http://members.tripod.com/~merchantships/

650. Washichek, Richard J. *Knights of the Sea* (PT boat drawings, stories, etc.)
http://www.geocities.com/Pentagon/4017/page-001.html

651. Wilson, Randy. *U.S. Naval Aircraft Designations 1939-1945—or Why a Navy AT-6 Is Really an SNJ*
http://rwebs.net/avhistory/acdesig/usnavy.htm

TANK AND ARMORED FORCES

652. Haugh, David. *Armored Car: The Wheeled Fighting Vehicle Website*
http://www.geocities.com/Pentagon/6138/

653. [Newspaper.] *Armored Force News—World War II* (first issue; 10 May 1943)
http://carlisle-www.army.mil/usamhi/Sampler/10051943/index.htm

654. Paesani, Mario. *World War II Tanks*
http://www.geocities.com/Pentagon/Quarters/1975/ww2tank.htm

655. Pitonak, Jaroslav. *Tanks in World War II*
http://www.military.cz/panzer/index.htm

656. Spoelstra, Hanno. *Sherman Register* (details on the Sherman M4 medium tank)
http://web.inter.nl.net/users/spoelstra/g104/index.htm

657. [Unidentified.] *Armored Division TO&E—1945* (Table of Organization; no. 17—16 June 1945)
http://carlisle-www.army.mil/usamhi/Sampler/16061945/index.htm

658. [Unidentified.] *Armoured! British Armoured Groups in World War II*
http://www.warlinks.com/armour/enter.html

659. [Unidentified.] *Tanks! Armored Warfare Prior to 1946* (studies of all combatants—and a number of nations not usually considered such)
http://mailer.fsu.edu/~akirk/tanks

CANADIAN FORCES

660. Policy Publishers. *"Seasoned Sailors:" Canadian Naval Heritage in Video* (description of videotapes, available for free loan inside Canada)
http://www.oldsalts.com/

661. Sollers, Gordon. *Stories of a Merchant Sailor* (Canadian who entered merchant marine at age fourteen in 1942)
(part 1:) http://members.tripod.com/~merchantships/storiesofamerchantsailor1.html
(part 2:) http://members.tripod.com/~merchantships/storiesofamerchantsailor2.html
(part 3:) http://members.tripod.com/~merchantships/storiesofamerchantsailor3.html

662. [Unidentified.] *Canadian Navy of Yesterday and Today* (1910-today; includes ship listings and photographs)
http://www.hazegray.org/navhist/canada/

MAPS AND PHOTOGRAPH

663. Augustus, Jim. *Naval Liberator and Privateers: Image Archive and Reference* (over 500 photographs)
http://www.navylib.com/

664. British Army. *The British Army Picture Library*
http://www.army.picture-library.com/

665. Campbell, W. A. *The Edge of War* (photographs from late in the war in both Europe and the Far East)
http://www.wtj.com/archives/gallery-edge/

666. Indiana State University. *World War II Theaters* (maps)
http://baby.indstate.edu/gga/gga_cart/gecar127.htm

667. McDonald, Jason. *World War II Multimedia Database* (includes over 1800 photos, 93 film clips, and other data)
http://www.worldwar2database.com/

668. Muche, Lani. *Muche's Warbirds: Warbird Photograph at Its Best* (covers gauntlet from World War I to Vietnam)
http://www.mucheswarbirds.com/

669. Naval Historical Center. *Merchant Ship Photograph Sources* (libraries and similar facilities)
http://www.history.navy.mil/faqs/faq16-1.htm

670. Perry-Castaneda Library Map Collection (University of Texas at Austin). *World War II Maps* (dozens on different aspects of the two theaters of conflict)
http://www.lib.utexas.edu/maps/historical/history_ww2.html

671. Time-Life. *World War II Gallery*
http://www.pathfinder.com/photo/gallery/war/ww2/gallery_ww2.html

672. [Unidentified.] *B-24* (claims over 1,600 pictures)
http://www.b24bestweb.com/

673. [Unidentified.] *Naval Liberators and Privateers* (with over 500 photos)
http://www.navylib.com/index.html

674. [Unidentified.] *The GI Legacy: A Collection of Graphics and Thoughts Concerning America's Sons and Daughters during World War II*
http://www.geocities.com/SoHo/Bistro/8879/G.html

675. [Unidentified.] *Warships of World War II* (photographs of representative British, French, Italian, German, Japanese, and U.S. craft)
http://www.geocities.com/Pentagon/2776/2war_i.htm

676. [Unidentified.] *World War II Battles* (over 900 photos plus textual descriptions of battles)
http://www.merkki.com/

677. [Unidentified.] *World War II Color Photographs*
http://go.to/acoloredww2

678. [Unidentified.] *World War II Maps* (twelve maps; primarily pre-1941 maps of Europe and China)
http://history.acusd.edu/gen/WW2Timeline/maps2.html

679. [Unidentified.] *World War II Maps by Date*
http://history.acusd.edu/gen/WW2Index/picindexmapsi.html

680. [Unidentified.] *World War II Theaters, Maps and Information*
http://baby.indstate.edu/gga/gga_cart/gecar127.htm

681. [Unidentified.] *World War II Warship Photos* (of major combatant nations)
http://www.warlinks.com/cgi-bin/links/jump.cgi?ID=302

682. [Various Sources.] *World War II Maps* (maps of varied types published during the war)
http://www.usd230.k12.ks.us/PICTT/publications/maps/maps.html

683. Yarnall, Paul. *New Source Naval History* (self-described as "the largest U.S. Navy warship photo collection on the internet")
http://navsource.org/Archives/home.html

OTHER MATERIALS

684. American War Library. *American Friendly Fire Notebook[: Comparative Losses from Various Wars]*
http://members.aol.com/amerwar/ff/ff.htm

685. American War Library. *U.S. Civil and Military Populations* (1940-1946)
http://members.aol.com/forcountry/ww2/pop.htm

686. American War Library. *U.S. Servicemen Profile (1941-1945): Volunteerism* (number, length of service, mortality)
http://members.aol.com/forcountry/ww2/vol.htm

687. American War Library. *World War II Friendly Fire Notebook[: Examples]*
http://members.aol.com/amerwar/ff/ff2.htm

688. Bacon, Katie. *The Other Side of War* (an interview with Paul Fussell, a historian and veteran of the conflict; from the February 1997 *Atlantic Monthly*)
http://www.theatlantic.com/unbound/bookauth/battle/pfint.htm

689. Bartam, Graham. *Historical Flags of World War II* (flags of the various nations as they appeared in the war years)
http://www.flags.net/WWII.htm

690. Bauer, Jim. *First Occurrence: When Were Features Introduced* (innovations in technology during the war with an impact on combat)
http://www.ww2pacific.com/notuntil.html

691. Bauer, Jim. *Ideas Introduced that Did—and Didn't—Work* (technological innovations and their degree of success—some of which were only made fully workable decades later)
http://www.ww2pacific.com/ideas.html

692. Bauer, Jim. *Little Known Facts: Attacks and [Potential] Threats on U.S., 1939-1945*
http://www.ww2pacific.com/attacks.html

693. Blakebrough, Ken. *The Nissen Hut and the Unknown Pilot* (war-time life in a Nissen hut)
http://457thbombgroup.org/New/Recollections/The_Cave/Nissen.html

694. Bodife, Paul. *Signals Collection: '40 to '45—Home of Allied Army, Navy & Airforce Radio and Radar Equipment of World War II*
http://www.qsl.net/pe1ngz/

695. Braakhuis, Wilfried. *The World at War: History of World War II, 1939-1945* (actually background information as far back as late 1800s is also included)
http://www.wwiitech.net/main/index.html

696. Braun, Ed. *Post Exchanges* (operation and characteristics of)
http://members.aol.com/famjustin/braun20.html

697. Braun, Ed. *The Night He Got Lucky* (treatment of sexually transmitted diseases in the military)
http://members.aol.com/famjustin/braun10.html

698. Brooke, Ken. *Sounds Like the Enemy* (served with a sound ranging battery in North Africa, Sicily, and the Normandy invasion)
http://freepages.family.rootsweb.com/~sarker/Sound/contents.html

699. Clancey, Patrick. *Glossary of Abbreviations, Acronyms, Codewords, and Other Terms*
http://www.ibiblio.org/hyperwar/Glossary.html

700. Coleman, Garth. *Great Battles of World War II* (only a few battles covered)
http://members.tripod.com/~colemangr/contents.html

701. Conn, Stetson. *Highlights of Mobilization, World War II, 1938-1942* (1959; manuscript prepared for use of U.S. Army Center of Military History)
http://www.army.mil/cmh-pg/documents/wwii/ww2mob.htm

702. Copp, Terry. *Selective Reasoning in World War II* (determining standards for eligibility for military service)
http://www.legionmagazine.com/features/canadianmilitaryhistory/96-05.asp

703. Department of History, Florida State University. *The Institute on World War II and the Human Experience*
http://www.fsu.edu/~ww2/

704. Depickere, Dave, and Michael Meister. *World War II Analyzed*
http://www.worldwar2.be/

705. Duncan, George. *Lesser Known Facts of World War II*
http://members.iinet.net.au/~gduncan/facts.html

706. Duncan, George. *Massacres and Atrocities of World War II* (short summaries of events surrounding each)
http://members.iinet.net.au/~gduncan/massacres.html

707. EarthStation1.com. *The World War II Sound and Image Archive* (thousands of audio and visual clips; site available in six languages)
http://www.earthstation1.com/wwii.html

708. Elson, Aaron. *Interview* (Elson interviews Dr. Gerald Levine and Jerry Rutigliano [a World War II vet] on post traumatic stress syndrome as manifested in that conflict)
http://www.tankbooks.com/ptsd.htm

709. Enfield Research Associates. *Enfield Rifle Research*
http://www.uidaho.edu/~stratton/en-page.html

710. Feldmeth, Greg D. *American Involvement in World War II* (with dates and what happened)
http://home.earthlink.net/~gfeldmeth/chart.ww2.html

711. Fisher, Robert. *The Vickers .303 Machine Guns*
http://www.vickersmachinegun.org.uk/

712. Flores, Ruben. *K-Rations Kept Troops Kicking*
http://www.utexas.edu/projects/latinoarchives/narratives/vol1no2/K_RATIONS/K_RATIONS.HTML

713. Friedlander, Gardner L. *Early Days of Radar: Secrets and My Recollections of World War II*
http://freepages.military.rootsweb.com/~memoirs/

714. Fussell, Paul. *The Real War, 1939-1945* (from the *Atlantic Monthly*, August 1989)
http://www3.theatlantic.com/unbound/bookauth/battle/fussell.htm

715. Gerlach, Charles. *World War II Homepage* (actually a site on tempo-

rary graveyards utilized by the military in Europe; links to other geographic locations and the history of the practice)
http://www.geocities.com/pentagon/barracks/1267/ww2/index.html

716. Greenfield, Kent R., editor. *Command Decisions* (2000; various scholars analyze key military decisions made by the nations involved in the war)
http://www.army.mil/cmh-pg/books/70-7_0.htm

717. Grolier. *World War II Commemoration Quiz*
http://gi.grolier.com/wwii/wwiiquiz.htm

718. Hadley, Arthur T. *"In This Like Your War, Sir?" The Line of Battle, 1944-1945* (comparison of this war with Vietnam)
http://www3.theatlantic.com/unbound/bookauth/battle/hadley.htm

719. Herr, Ernest. *Combat Stories of World War II*
http://www.netunlimited.net/~ernieh

720. History Department. *Rutgers Oral History Archives of World War II Web Archives* (interview with graduates of war and civilian activities during the conflict)
http://fas-history.rutgers.edu/oralhistory/index.html

721. History Place. *Statistics of World War II* (deaths in numbers and percentages)
http://www.historyplace.com/worldwar2/timeline/statistics.htm

722. Jones, Edgar J. *One War Is Enough* (a combat veteran's evaluation of popular GI attitudes toward the homefront and a plea against non-war conscription; from the February 1946 *Atlantic Monthly*)
http://www.theatlantic.com/unbound/bookauth/battle/jones.htm

723. Jones, Samuel. *WWII Tech.net* (studying the technologies of war utilized in the various conflicting powers)
http://www.wwiitech.net/main/index.html

724. Kelly, Mike. *Morris Commercial Military Vehicles* (made in Britain for the Army)
http://geocities.com/motorcity/street/1759/

725. Lanham, Howard G. *American Military Patches, Other Insignia and Decorations of World War Two*
http://www.angelfire.com/md2/patches/

726. Lippman, David H. *World War II Plus 55: Daily Events from Around the Globe as They Happened 55 Years Ago* (covers 1941-1943)
http://www.usswashington.com/dl_index.htm

727. Matloff, Maurice. *Grand Strategy and Washington High Command* (extract from *American Military History)*
http://www.army.mil/cmh-pg/books/amh/amh-21.htm

728. Mills, T. R. *Land Forces of Britain, the Empire, and Commonwealth*
http://www.regiments.org/milhist/

729. National Gallery of Art. *A Guide to Resources Relating to World War II* (uses Adobe Acrobat)
http://www.nga.gov/pdf/ww2.pdf

730. Naval Historical Center. *A Guide to U.S. Navy Museums in the United States*
http://www.history.navy.mil/branches/org8-9.htm

731. Naval Historical Center. *Quonset Huts*
http://www.history.navy.mil/faqs/faq75-1.htm

732. Naval Historical Center. *Radio Proximity (VT) Fuzes*
http://www.history.navy.mil/faqs/faq96-1.htm

733. Niehorster, Leo. *World War II Armed Forces Orders of Battle*
http://www.freeport-tech.com/WWII/index.htm

734. Ordnance Office, War Department. *Carbine, Cal. 30, M1* (1942 technical bulletin on operation of M1 carbine)
http://www.geocities.com/buckrodgrs/M1/TB_23-7-1/Page1.html

735. Paisley, Todd. *Holabird Vehicle Testing Track* (from 1920 to early postwar, it carried out testing and development of general purpose military vehicles)
http://users.erols.com/paisley/warehouse/holabird.htm

736. Rothwell, Steve. *Commonwealth Orders of Battle* (by nationality)
http://homepages.force9.net/rothwell/

737. Ryan, David A. *Commonwealth Orders of Battle, 1939-1945*
http://home.adelphia.net/~dryan67/orders/army.html

738. Schoenherr, [?]. *Myths of World War II*
http://history.sandiego.edu/gen/classes/media/myths.html

739. Scottish Military History Web Project. *Scots at War* (covers entire twentieth century)
http://www-saw.arts.ed.ac.uk/saw.html

740. Sentimental Journey. *Sentimental Journey to the Southwestern Proving*

Grounds (located at Hope, Arkansas, and used to test ordinance and new weapons)
http://www.sentimentaljourney.org/

741. Steinberg, Glenn A. *European Royalty during World War II*
http://gsteinbe.intrasun.tcnj.edu/royalty/royalty.html

742. Stephenson, Frank. *War Stories* (articles on wartime experiences of 8 faculty members at Florida State University)
http://mailer.fsu.edu/~research/RinR/War_Stories.html

743. Stoftt, William A., editor. *American Military History* (1989; tracing the U.S. military from the Revolutionary War to post Vietnam)
http://www.army.mil/cmh-pg/books/amh/amh-toc.htm

744. Stokes, Phil. *The Second World War: 1939-1945* (includes biography of Hitler, consideration of the high command of the various combatants, statistics, etc.)
http://www.stokesey.demon.co.uk/wwii/index.html
(glossary of terms:) http://www.stokesey.demon.co.uk/wwii/glossa.html
(trivia:) http://www.stokesey.demon.co.uk/wwii/trivia1.html

745. Suen, Gary. *World War II Quotes* (from a variety of different countries)
http://www.angelfire.com/la/raeder/worldwarIIquotes.html

746. Sworn to Secrecy [program web site]. *World War II Trivia*
http://www.secretsofwar.com/html/trivia.html

747. Tutt, Bob. *World War II Remembered* (a series of articles by a *Houston Chronicle* journalist)
http://www.chron.com/content/interactive/special/wwII/

748. [Unidentified.] *Balance of Power during World War 2* (in population, army size, aircraft, etc.)
http://members.aol.com/forcountry/ww2/bal.htm

749. [Unidentified.] *Battle Units Composition during World War II*
http://members.aol.com/forcountry/ww2/unt.htm

750. [Unidentified.] *British and Dominion Armed Forces* (by "administrative orders of battle," "theatre orders of battle," and "military organizations")
http://www.freeport-tech.com/WWII/017_britain/__uk.htm

751. [Unidentified.] *British and U.S. Military Ranks Compared*
http://www.helsinki.fi/~degroot/anglomil.html

752. [Unidentified.] *[British] Squadron Codes of World War Two* (letter codes, years used, and by what units—use "squadron codes" link)
http://www.pboro-memorial.com/

753. [Unidentified.] *Cost of the War* (financial, to the various combatant nations)
http://members.aol.com/forcountry/ww2/wc1.htm

754. [Unidentified.] *Counterintelligence in World War II* (includes chapters on counterintelligence, OSS, and Magic)
http://www.fas.org/irp/ops/ci/docs/ci2/index.htm

755. [Unidentified.] *Famous Fighters* (men who served in the war who were already famous or who became so after the war, along with the decorations they received)
http://www.geocities.com/ResearchTriangle/Facility/3991/ww2stars.htm

756. [Unidentified.] *Forgotten Battles of the Second World War*
http://www.geocities.com/Pentagon/Bunker/3351/index.html

757. [Unidentified.] *Glossary of Military Units, Phrases, Abbreviations, Slang* (click on first letter of term being researched)
http://members.aol.com/usmilbrats/glossary

758. [Unidentified.] *Kremm's World: Military Interest Sites* (including unusual war related photos)
http://web.ukonline.co.uk/gaz/

759. [Unidentified.] *Mac & Doug's World War History* (emphasizes service of their relatives in both world wars)
http://members.tripod.com/macsairforce66/

760. [Unidentified.] *Medal of Honor Statistics as of 13 May 1997* (by wars and specific branch of service)
http://www.army.mil/cmh-pg/mohstats.htm

761. [Unidentified.] *MilitarEbooks.com* (commercial publisher of e-books, but includes considerable information on line on history of Colt firearms)
http://users.skynet.be/HL-Editions/militarebook/militarebook.htm

762. [Unidentified.] *Military Order of the Purple Heart* (requirements to obtain, etc.)
http://www.purpleheart.org/

763. [Unidentified.] *Military Records of World War II Veterans* (how to obtain information)
http://www.ibiblio.org/hyperwar/USN/USN-ref.html

764. [Unidentified.] *National Museum of Naval Aviation*
http://www.naval-air.org/

765. [Unidentified.] *Number People Who Died during World War Two* (by
nation, military, POW, civilian status etc.)
http://members.aol.com/forcountry/ww2/peo.htm

766. [Unidentified.] *Radio News* (audio of key events such as Munich Crisis and reports of most respected reporters of the time)
http://www.otr.com/news.html

767. [Unidentified.] *Signal Collections '40-'45* (all types including portable
radios and radar)
http://www.qsl.net/pe1ngz/signalscollection.html

768. [Unidentified.] *The Language of World War 2* (emphasizing British
awards, ranks, abbreviations, and slang)
http://cap.estevan.sk.ca/ssr/language.html

769. [Unidentified.] *The Second World War Experience Centre* (dedicated
to preserving contemporary records of that conflict)
http://www.war-experience.org/

770. [Unidentified.] *Victoria Cross Reference* (Great Britain's highest military award; contains names of all recipients and why they received it)
http://www.chapter-one.com/vc/

771. [Unidentified.] *War Sports, 1905-1945* (photographs of military personnel involved in athletics)
http://www.wtj.com/archives/gallery-edge/

772. [Unidentified.] *Wartime Memories Project* (many short essays concerning specific events of the war around the world by those who went
through them)
http://uk2.net/ukpop.htm

773. [Unidentified.] *White Star* (World War II military vehicles)
http://home.planet.nl/~whitestar/

774. [Unidentified.] *Wireless Set No. 19* (a radio communication device
designed for tanks; extensive details)
http://www.qsl.net/ve3bdb/picsindex.html

775. [Unidentified.] *World War II* (concise summary)
http://www.army.mil/cmh-pg/reference/apcmp.htm

776. [Unidentified.] *World War II* (concise year-by-year summary, with in-site links to more details on specific battles and events)
http://www.unverse.com/WW2.html

777. [Unidentified.] *World War II Analyzed*
http://www.geocities.com/Pentagon/Quarters/1695/

778. [Unidentified.] *World War II Medal of Honor Recipients: A-F* (with concise description of reasons for award)
http://www.army.mil/cmh-pg/mohiia1.htm

779. [Unidentified.] *World War II Medal of Honor Recipients: G-L* (with concise description of reasons for award)
http://www.army.mil/cmh-pg/mohiia2.htm

780. [Unidentified.] *World War II Medal of Honor Recipients: M-S* (with concise description of reasons for award)
http://www.army.mil/cmh-pg/mohiib1.htm

781. [Unidentified.] *World War II Medal of Honor Recipients: T-Z* (with concise description of reasons for award)
http://www.army.mil/cmh-pg/mohiib2.htm

782. [Unidentified.] *World War II Tanks*
http://www.geocities.com/Pentagon/Quarters/1975/ww2tank.htm

783. [Unidentified.] *World War II Terms and Facts*
http://frontiernet.net/~pendino/World-War-Two-Facts.htm

784. [Unidentified.] *World War II: The Defensive Phase* (extract from *American Military History*)
http://www.army.mil/cmh-pg/books/amh/amh-20.htm

785. [Unidentified.] *World War II Timeline* (covers 1939-1945 on a day by day basis; divided into ten regional treatments)
http://www.worldwar-2.net/

786. [Unidentified,] William. *Williams' World War II Page: Essays and Reviews*
http://www.geocities.com/wmaxwell/index1.html

787. United States Government Printing Office. *Military History Bibliography* (books on WWII and other wars current available and their prices)
http://bookstore.gpo.gov/sb/sb-098.html

788. U.S. Army Center of Military History. *Index of Operational and Code Names*
http://www.army.mil/cmh-pg/reference/code.htm

789. U.S. Army Center of Military History. *World War II* (annotated bibliography of materials published by American government)
http://www.army.mil/cmh-pg/catalog/WWII-Pubs.htm

790. U.S. Armed Forces. *Combat Chronology, 1942-1945* (as published monthly by the services at the time)
http://www.ibiblio.org/pub/academic/history/marshall/
military/airforce/wwii_chronology/

791. Valero, Larry A. *An Impressive Record: The American Joint Intelligence Committee and Estimates of the Soviet Union, 1945-1947* (also includes material on intra-war intelligence estimate making)
http://www.cia.gov/csi/studies/summer00/art06.html

792. Weinberg, Gerhard. *Archives Surviving from World War II*
http://www.nara.gov/alic/milrsrcs/ww2.html

793. Wendell, Marcus. *World War II Factbook*
http://www.skalman.nu/worldwar2/

Prisoners of War and Evadees

794. Allard, Mike. *Clinton Prisoner of War Camp (Clinton, Mississippi)*
http://www2.netdoor.com/~allardma/powcamp2.html

795. Anderson, P. *A Raid on Munich* (his father's account of an RAF raid on Munich and his imprisonment as a POW after his plane was shot down)
http://www.camomilesworld.com/raid/

796. Angell Productions. *The Forgotten Prisoners of Rabaul* (internal links to other abused POWs/internees stories)
http://www.angellpro.com.au/rabaul.htm

797. Barker, Tom. *Memories of Pvt Tom Barker 2982252, 1st Bn Argyll & Sutherland Highlanders* (served in Palestine and Desert Long Range Group before capture)
http://www.warlinks.com/cgi-bin/links/jump.cgi?ID=76

798. Beaver, Johnnie R. *[Letters Home]* (after being captured during the Battle of the Bulge)
http://www.military.com/Content/MoreContent?file=beaver_02

799. Beckett, Anthea. *The Java Index: British & Commonwealth Prisoners of War held in Java, 1942-1945* (the list approaches 5,000 names)
http://myweb.tiscali.co.uk/abeckett/pow/index.html

800. Bernard, Yves, and Caroline Bergeron. *Trop loin de Berlin* (summary of book on German POWs in Canada that were temporarily retained at detainees after the war ended)
http://www.cam.org/~ybern/septentrionE.html

801. Bowers, Everett. *Expert POW Liberator* (soldier interviewed participated in successful POW liberation raids in both World War II and Vietnam)
http://www.military.com/Content/MoreContent?file=PRpowlib

802. Brett, Exton. *Island Farm Prisoner of War Camp 198/Special Camp XI (Bridgend, South Wales)* (with stress on the unprecedently large March 1945 escape of 67 German POWs)
http://www.islandfarm.fsnet.co.uk/

803. Brown, Charles M. *The Oroyuku Maru* (about 3/4 of the POWs died on board while being shipped from Philippines to Japan)
http://www.geocities.com/oryokumaru/oryoku_maru_story.html

804. Cave, A. H. *Escape Narrative* (member of the Desert Long Range Reconnaissance Group; account of his capture and escape in Spring of 1941)
http://www.lrdg.org/Titch_Story.htm

805. Christie, [?]. *Muken 1940-1945: In Search of a Captive* (a British POW of the Japanese)
http://www.btinternet.com/~m.a.christie/insearch.htm

806. Coleman, Rusty. *Lloyd A. Dodd: An American Soldier's Experience* (captured during the Battle of the Bulge)
http://www.memoriesofwar.com/veterans/dodd.asp

807. Costales, Elmer. *Memoirs* (nearly perished of injuries received when shot down)
http://www.geocities.com/Athens/Parthenon/9800/

808. Danner, Dorothy S. *U.S. Navy Nurse Prisoner of War in the Philippines, 1942-1945* (captured in Manila, Philippines)
http://www.history.navy.mil/faqs/faq87-3f.htm

809. Daws, Gavan. *Outram Road Prison, Singapore*
http://www.danford.net/death.htm

810. Dean, Paul. *Colditz Castle Oflag IVC*
http://www.geocities.com/Pentagon/Bunker/8963/

811. Deuitch, Jack. *[Auto]Biography of Jack Deuitch* (410th Bomber Group, 9th Air Force)
http://members.aol.com/famjustin/Deuitchbio.html

812. Deuitch, Jack. *Stalag Luft IV*
http://members.aol.com/famjustin/Luft4.html

813. Dorsey, Mason H. *"Button Up" Phillips* (on the sometimes difficulty of surrendering)
http://members.aol.com/famjustin/Dorsey5.html

814. Dougherty, Kevin. *Rescue in the Philippines*
http://www.dtic.mil/soldiers/feb95/p52.html

815. Duffy, George. *Captain George Duffy's POW Home Page* (Duffy was held as a prisoner by both the Germans and the Japanese during the War)
http://www.usmm.org/duffy.html

816. Dungey, Peter. *British POW Diary* (Dungey served in the 44th Battalion Royal Tank Regiment and was captured in North Africa in 1942)
http://members.tripod.co.uk/billdungey/petersdiary.html

817. Dunne, Dermot. *The Old Man's War* (held prisoner in Singapore and Japan)
http://www.labmed.umn.edu/students/hinf5430/dunne/oldman.htm

818. Durey, Jack. *[Experiences]* (captured in France; section listings on left hand side of screen)
http://www.warlinks.com/memories/durey/index.html

819. DuVall, Gene. *A Most Memorable Christmas*
http://tec.uno.edu/George/myBestWork/christmas44.html

820. Dyas, Tim. *Interview* (82nd Airborne paratrooper taken prisoner in Sicily)
http://www.tankbooks.com/intviews/dyas/dyas1.htm

821. Fisher, O. E. (Dr.) *War Diaries* (describes fall of Singapore and his imprisonment 1942-1945)
http://freespace.virgin.net/sam.campbell/diary.htm

822. Flynn, Sam. *History of Camp King* (major interrogation center for downed Allied flymen; traces use of center into post-war years)
http://home.earthlink.net/~sflynn33/History.html

823. Ford, Dan. *The Prisoners of Rabaul* (POWs known to have been held, at least temporarily, on Rabaul)
http://www.danford.net/prisoner.htm

824. Geiger, Bill. *Bill Geiger, RAF, Eagle Squadron* (American fighting in the RAF, spent bulk of war as a POW; interview)
http://www.military.com/Content/MoreContent?file=geiger01

825. Graham, Charles. *Interview* (shot down September 27, 1944)
http://www.tankbooks.com/intviews/graham/graham1.htm

826. Grokett, Sr., Russell. *Twelve Hundred Days* (survived Bataan Death March)
http://www.jacksonville.net/~rgrokett/POW/index.htm

827. Haeuser, Karl. *A Surprised Landing* (410th Bomber Group, 9th Air Force)
http://members.aol.com/famjustin/0410land.html

828. Hale, Edward E. *First Captured, Last Freed: Memoirs of a P.O.W. in World War II Guam and Japan* (captured December 8, 1941)
http://home.nc.rr.com/ww2memories/memoirs_hale.html

829. Hamlett, Eugene J. *World War II Memoirs of a German POW* (captured at Anzio)
http://www.geocities.com/eugenejhamlett/index.html

830. Hays, Ed. *Interview* (tail-gunner; shot down over Denmark)
http://www.tankbooks.com/intviews/hays/hays1.htm

831. Herder, Ludeke. [*Life as a POW in Florida*] (at top of screen click on "H-L;" pick "Mrs. Eva Knapp" from list on left screen [Hereder's remarks are a letter to her and her class]; text appears to right)
http://www.warlinks.com/memories/index.html

832. Hewitt, A. R. *Masonic Activities of Prisoners-of-War* (treats World War I and both theaters in the Second World War)
http://www.geocities.com/Athens/Acropolis/8291/prisoner.html

833. House, Pete. *Memories of Peter House* (at top of screen click on "H-L;" pick this person's name from list on left screen; text appears to right)
http://www.warlinks.com/memories/index.html

834. Injerd, Wes. *Prisoner of War Camp #1, Fukuoka, Japan: An Insight into Life and Death at a POW Camp in War-time Japan* (over a thousand Allied POWs passed through the camp)
http://www2.gol.com/users/winjerd/Pwcmp1_a.htm

835. Koerner, Jim. *Interview* (captured at the Battle of the Bulge)
http://www.tankbooks.com/intviews/koerner/koerner1.htm

836. Levine, Bernie. *Interview* (100th Bombardment Group; a Jewish American POW in a German camp)
http://www.tankbooks.com/intviews/bernie/bernie1.htm

837. Levine, Bernie. *The Espionage System* (detailed description of his crash and capture)
http://www.tankbooks.com/stories/story92.htm

838. Levine, Bob. *Interview* (90th Infantry Division; captured after being wounded and soon thereafter the Americans over-ran the German line and he was among the liberated)
http://www.tankbooks.com/intviews/boblevine/boblevine1.htm

839. Levine, Murray. *Interview* (45th Infantry Division; captured at Anzio)
http://www.tankbooks.com/intviews/murray/murray1.htm

840. Naval Historical Center. *U.S. Navy Prisoners of War during World War II: A Bibliography*
http://www.history.navy.mil/faqs/faq41-1.htm

841. Newell, Emmett L. *Diary of Emmett L. Newell* (a construction worker at Wake Island; held prisoner in China until 1945)
http://www.excelwithus.com/Emmett%20POW.htm

842. Notte, Giovanni. *Prigionia di guerra; Diario dei primi quattro mesi* (covering September 1943 to January 1944; Italian/English versions of this POW diary)
http://www.geocities.com/Heartland/Plains/4142/prigioni.htm

843. Osborne, J. D. *Affidavit* (*U.S.S. Napa* crewman taken prisoner in Philippines and held as POW in Manchuria for duration of war)
http://www.military.com/Content/MoreContent?file=osborne01

844. Parker, Dennis M. *World War II Diary of Dennis M. Parker* (part of 325th Fighter Group; imprisoned at Stalag Luft III)
http://www.checkertail.com/

845. Patrick, Bethanne K. *Col. Vernon P. Ligon, Jr.* (POW in three wars: WWII [Stalagluft III], Korea, and Vietnam)
http://www.military.com/Content/MoreContent?file=ML_ligon_bkp

846. Patrick, Bethanne K. *Lt. Michael Mauritz* (captured and escaped from Italian German confinement)
http://www.military.com/Content/MoreContent?file=ML_mauritz_bkp

847. Patrick, Bethanne K. *Rear Admiral Richard Nott Antrim*
http://www.military.com/Content/MoreContent?file=ML_antrim_bkp

848. Patrick, Bethanne K. *2nd Lt. Reba Whittle* (flight nurse; only U.S. military woman to become a German POW during the war)
http://www.military.com/Content/MoreContent?file=ML_whittle_bkp

849. Pugh, William A. *RAF Memoirs of SE Asia, 358 Squadron* (follow links through entire story)
http://www.magweb.com/sample/ww2/wl027bp1.htm

850. Reeves, Robert D. *Peoria to Munich: A Prisoner of War* (part of 101st airborne; held in Stalag VII-a)
http://www.lp-net.com/pow/

851. Sanchez, Joanne R. *Faith Sustains Abel Ortega during Bataan Death March, Japanese Prisoners of War Camps, and Korean War Wounds*
http://www.utexas.edu/projects/latinoarchives/narratives/vol2no2/4orte-gaabel.html

852. Schmidt, Glenn E. *The POW diary of Glenn E. Schmidt* (captured in Alsace, France)
http://www.tankbooks.com/stories/hatten/hatten1.htm

853. Seefluth, Gus. *How Did the Germans Feel? A Veteran's Observations* (with emphasis on movements to keep from POWs from being overtaken by advancing Allies)
http://www.ww2heroes.com/article1008.html

854. Siddall, Harold J. *And So ... An Autobiography* (sailor captured at Crete)
http://www.naval-history.net/WW2MemoirAndSo00.htm

855. Siker, Fred. *Lest We Forget—the Railway of Death*
http://www.beverevivis.com/books/lestweforget/index.htm

856. Smith, Mary, and Barbara Williams. *Stalag Luft One Online* (photos, copies of secret stalag newspaper, and other data)
http://home.att.net/~merkki/

857. Taylor, Ron. *Colditz Castle* (intended for the most escape prone Allied prisoners)
http://www.britain-at-war.org.uk/Colditz/index.htm

858. Tenney, Harry. *The Great Escape* (at top of screen click on "R-Z;" pick this person's name from list on left screen; begins with newspaper article, with additional autobiographical material listed below on left; text appears to right)
http://www.warlinks.com/memories/tenny/index.html

859. Thomasian, Karnig. *Interview* (POW in Burma)
http://www.tankbooks.com/intviews/thomasian/thomasian1.htm

860. [Unidentified.] *Capture* (Stalag Luft Three)
http://www.usafa.af.mil/dfsel/sl3/capture/

861. [Unidentified.] *Document of an Atrocity* (article on Don Schloat, a POW and army medic at Bataan and the paintings he did to depict Japanese excesses)
http://www.geocities.com/Heartland/Plains/5850/prisoners.html

862. [Unidentified.] *German Prisoner of War Camps in 1942* (gives official designations and location; includes Italian facilities and internment camps as well—use "prison camp" link)
http://www.pboro-memorial.com/

863. [Unidentified.] *German Prisoners of War of World War 2* (available in English or German)
http://www.kriegsgefangen.de/

864. [Unidentified.] *Merchant Mariners at Milag Nord Prisoner of War Camp in Germany during World War II* (includes other materials, such as standing instructions to mariners as to how to act if facing capture)
http://www.usmm.org/milag.html

865. [Unidentified.] *"Paradise Road:" The Real Women* (female detainees)
http://www.foxsearchlight.com/paradise/story/women.html

866. [Unidentified.] *Prisoner of War* (centers on British empire personnel captured in Greece and imprisoned in Stalag 18A)
http://www.btinternet.com/~stalag18a/

867. [Unidentified.] *Prisoner of War Camp: Aliceville, Alabama*
http://www.pickens.net/~museum/page17.html

868. [Unidentified.] *Prisoner of War Camp Stalag VIIA (Moosburg)* (available in four languages; includes accounts by prisoners held there)
http://www.moosburg.org/info/stalag/indeng.html

869. [Unidentified.] *Stalag Luft One: The Men, Their Machines, and Their Missions*
http://www.stalag.net/

870. [Unidentified.] *Task Force Baum and the Hammelburg Raid* (to liberate POWs; German language site)
http://www.crosswinds.net/~pdomes/tfb/index.html

871. [Unidentified.] *Tatura Museum* (pictures and surviving paraphernalia from POW and internment camps in Australia)
http://www.maskell.com.au/museum.html

872. [Unidentified.] *The Interrogators: World War II Prisoners of War, Stalag Luft I*
http://home.att.net/~merkki/new_page_2.htm

873. U.S. Maritime Service Veterans. *American Merchant Marine Prisoners of War during World War II* (several concise biographies)
http://www.usmm.org/pow.html

874. U.S. Maritime Service Veterans. *American Merchant Marine Prisoners of War or Civilian Internees during World War II* (totals and specific names)
http://www.usmm.net/pownames.html

875. Walker, John Stanley. *John Stanley Walker: 1912-1960* (a Japanese prisoner confined to Changi Goal; includes text of a letter home and paintings by himself and fellow inmates)
http://homepage.ntlworld.com/the.carpenters/jsw1.htm

876. Walton, Pamela. *Hard Way Back* (biography of her father, Frank Hoeffer, who pulled Far East service prior to the war and was part of the infamous Bataan Death March)
http://wtv-zone.com/califPamela/A-Memorial-For-Dad.html

877. Weinstein, Ira. *Interview* (shot down during the 1944 bombing raid on Kassel, Germany)
http://www.tankbooks.com/intviews/weinstein/weinstein1.htm

878. Weiss, Edward W. *Under the Rising Sun: War, Captivity and Survival, 1941-1945* (hid from Japanese in Philippines six months; captured while trying to sail to Australia)
http://www.geocities.com/Pentagon/8660/

879. Wensyel, James W. *Odyssey of the Wake Island Prisoners*
http://www.military.com/Content/MoreContent?file=PRwakef

880. Williams, [?]. *World War II Prisoners of War: Stalag Luft I (Barth, Germany)* (official records, photographs, narratives of individual Air Force prisoners)
http://www.merkki.com/

881. Wrynn, V. Dennis. *Massacre at Palawan* (western POWs murdered in the Philippines)
http://www.military.com/Content/MoreContent?file=PRpalawan

882. Zywiczynski, Anthony J. *Behind Barbed Wire: A Look at Stalag Luft I*
http://www.behindbarbedwire.com/links.htm

Racial or National Minorities

BLACK AMERICANS

883. Anders, Steven E. *Private George Watson* (first black soldier of the war to earn the Distinguished Service Cross; posthumously increased to the Medal of Honor)
http://www.quartermaster.army.mil/oqmg/Professional_Bulletin/2001/Spring01/Private_George_Watson.html

884. Anders, Steven E. *WWII Quartermaster Hero Awarded Medal of Honor* (emphasis on private George Watson receiving the Congressional medal of honor)
http://www.quartermaster.army.mil/oqmg/Professional_Bulletin/1997/Spring/watson.html

885. Brandon, Linda E. *Black Pilots Shatter Myths*
http://www.af.mil/news/features/features95/f_950216-112_95feb16.html

886. Brown, Avonie. *The Tuskegee Airmen—The Sky Was the Limit*
http://www.afroam.org/history/tusk/tuskmain.html

887. Burger, Barbara L. *The Lions' History: Researching World War II Images of African Americans*
http://www.nara.gov/publications/prologue/burger.html

888. Detroit Free Press. *The Belle-Isle, Detroit, Race Riot (June 1943)*
http://www.freep.com/century/cent1_19991201.htm

889. Director of Selective Service. *Minority Groups in World War II* (extract from *Selective Service and Victory: The Fourth Report of the Director of Selective Service*)
http://www.army.mil/cmh-pg/documents/wwii/minst.htm

890. Douglass, Phyllis G. *Tuskegee Airmen: A Tribute to My Father*
http://www.geocities.com/Pentagon/Quarters/1350/

891. Emerick, Joanne. *[Black] U.S. Army Units Station in the Pacific Theater*
http://www.coax.net/people/lwf/ww2_aap.htm

892. Grinton, Phil. *Black Army/Air Corps Units Stationed in the United Kingdom*
http://www.coax.net/people/lwf/bu_uk.htm

893. Guttman, Jon. *Charles McGee: Tuskegee and Beyond* (interview)
http://www.military.com/Content/MoreContent?file=PRmcgee

894. History Place. *African-Americans in World War II*
http://www.historyplace.com/unitedstates/aframerwar/

895. Hodges, Jr., Robert *Buffalo Soldiers on the Gothic Line* (Italy)
http://www.military.com/Content/MoreContent?file=PRbuffalo

896. Hoyt, Davina. *Tuskegee Airmen of World War II*
http://ac.acusd.edu/History/WW2Timeline/Tuskegee.html

897. Indiana Historical Society. *"Nobody Wanted Us:" Black Aviators at
Freeman Field, Indiana*
http://www.indianahistory.org/heritage/freeman.html

898. Johnson, Gerald K. *Black Soldiers of the Ardennes*
http://www.bjmjr.com/ww2/ardennes.htm

899. Jones, Kevin K. *African-American Warriors* (from the Revolutionary
War onwards)
http://www.abest.com/~cklose/aawar.htm

900. Kitson, J. D. *Cook 3rd Class William Pinckney* (won the Navy Cross
at Guadalcanal)
http://www.military.com/Content/MoreContent?file=ML_pinckney_bkp

901. Lee, Ulysses. *Road Builders: Black Engineers in World War II* (extract
from Lee's larger work *The Employment of Negro Troops*)
http://www.army.mil/cmh-pg/topics/afam/rb.htm

902. MacGregor, Jr., Morris J. *Integration of the Armed Forces, 1940-1965*
(1985; in the "Defense Studies Series")
http://www.army.mil/cmh-pg/books/integration/IAF-FM.htm

903. Masko, David P. *CBI: No Place to be in 1945*
http://www.af.mil/news/May1995/n19950525_535.html

904. National Archives. *New Roles* (in the military)
http://www.nara.gov/exhall/people/newroles.html

905. Patrick, Bethanne K. *Gen. Daniel "Chappie" James* (from Tuskegee
airman to, decades later, four star Air Force general)
http://www.military.com/Content/MoreContent?file=ML_cjames_bkp

906. Patrick, Bethanne K. *Private George Watson* (honored for saving lives
of fellow crewmembers off the New Guinea coast)
http://www.military.com/Content/MoreContent?file=ML_watson_bkp

907. Patrick, Bethanne K. *2nd Lt. Vernon Baker* (Medal of Honor winner for bravery in Italy)
http://www.military.com/Content/MoreContent?file=ML_vbaker_bkp

908. Patrick, Bethanne K. *The Montford Point Marines*
http://www.military.com/Content/MoreContent?file=ML_montford_bkp

909. President's Committee on Fair Employment Practice. *Minorities in Defense* (1942)
http://worldwar2.smu.edu/cgi-bin/Pwebrecon.cgi?v1=91&ti=
51,91&CNT=50&Search_Arg=world+war&Search_Code=GKEY&x=
30&y=5&y=5&PID=3725&SEQ=20020105194602&SID=1

910. Public Broadcasting System. *Detroit Race Riots, 1943*
http://www.pbs.org/wgbh/amex/eleanor/peopleevents/pande10.html

911. Simpson, Diana. *African-Americans in Military History* (a bibliography)
http://www.au.af.mil/au/aul/bibs/afhist/aftoc.htm

912. Stewart, Ollie. *Invasion of France* (a black quartermaster unit)
http://www.afroam.org/history/OurWar/stewart1.html

913. Tubbs, Vincent. *The Southwest Pacific*
http://www.afroam.org/history/OurWar/tubbs.html

914. [Unidentified.] *African American Volunteers as Infantry Replacements* (study of late war program)
http://www.army.mil/cmh-pg/topics/afam/VolInfRpl.htm

915. [Unidentified.] *[Black] Combat Troops in the European Theater*
http://www.coax.net/people/lwf/combat.htm

916. [Unidentified.] *Examples Mentioned in The Negro Soldier* (details on the individuals cited in Capra's film)
http://history.sandiego.edu/gen/filmnotes/negrosoldier2.html

917. [Unidentified.] *Information Paper: 555th Parachute Infantry Battalion* (an experimental all black unit)
http://www.army.mil/cmh-pg/topics/afam/555pib.htm

918. [Unidentified.] *Integration of the Air Force*
http://www.afroam.org/history/tusk/integrate.html

919. [Unidentified.] *Smoke Jumpers: The 555th Parachute Infantry Battalion (PIB)* (originally trained for foreign combat, the potential of Japanese balloon attacks on the west coast had them shifted into a forest fire fighting unit)
http://www.triplenickle.com/smjprs.html

920. [Unidentified.] *The Negro Soldier* (background to of Frank Capra's public relations film)
http://history.sandiego.edu/gen/filmnotes/negrosoldier.html

921. [Unidentified.] *The Tuskegee Airmen: Facts and History*
http://www.dayton.net/~dieeoc/pages/tuske.htm

922. [Unidentified.] *World War II Black Medical of Honor Recipients* (with description of actions that brought about the awards)
http://www.army.mil/cmh-pg/mohb.htm

923. U.S. Air Force Museum. *African-American Aviation Engineer Battalions*
http://www.wpafb.af.mil/museum/history/wwii/aeb.htm

924. U.S. Maritime Service Veterans. *Afro-Americans in the U.S. Merchant Marine and U.S. Maritime Service*
http://www.usmm.org/african-americans.html

925. [Various Writers.] *This Is Our War* (book version of dispatches filed with the Baltimore *African American* newspaper)
http://www.afroam.org/history/OurWar/intro.html

German Americans

926. Earle, Sarah M. *Germans, too, Were Imprisoned in WWII* (January 23, 2000 article in the *Concord Monitor* [New Hampshire])
http://www.foitimes.com/internment/ebelcm.htm

927. Fallon, [?], and [?] Jacobs. *Chronology—Suspicion, Arrest, and Internment* (extensive quotations from source documents)
http://www.foitimes.com/internment/chrono.htm

928. Greis, Guenther. *The Greis Story—Interned with Sons in the Military*
http://www.foitimes.com/internment/Greis.htm

929. Jacobs, Arthur D. *The Imprisoned American Schoolboy* (his account of his own treatment)
http://atschool.eduweb.co.uk/chatback/english/memories/~artj.html

930. Jacobs, Arthur D. *World War II—The Internment of German American Civilians* (includes texts of president proclamations authorizing internment of various nationalities)
http://www.foitimes.com/internment/

931. Smith, Deborah M. *Years of Silence: The Untold Story of German-American Internment*
http://www.foitimes.com/internment/udq.htm

932. [Unidentified.] *Internees by Nationality and Country*
http://www.foitimes.com/internment/numbers.htm

933. [Unidentified.] *Legislation, Testimony, Remarks on the Internment Issue*
http://foitimes.com/internment/legislation.htm

LATIN AMERICANS

934. Acosta, Ann. *A Generation of Change* (war-time anti-Hispanic sentiment)
http://www.utexas.edu/projects/latinoarchives/narratives/vol1no1/
Murillo.html

935. Davis, Alan. *Behind Enemy Lines* (about a 8th Air Force gunner; shot down over France and evaded the Germans till the Allied invasion)
http://www.utexas.edu/projects/latinoarchives/narratives/
vol2no2/4castroladislao.html

936. Dovalina, Fernando. *Ed Piniche* (Pinche parachuted with the airborne into both D-Day and Market Garden)
http://www.utexas.edu/projects/latinoarchives/narratives/
vol2no1/3penicheed.html

937. Emmott, Christine. *Hospital Corpsman Dedicates Life to Service* (emphasis on Guadalcanal service)
http://www.utexas.edu/projects/latinoarchives/narratives/
vol2no2/4castorenagilbert.html

938. Gonzalez, Mayella. *Tony Oliver* (description of Battle of Bulge)
http://www.utexas.edu/projects/latinoarchives/narratives/
vol2no2/4olivastony.html

939. Harris, Dartinya. *World War II Vet Makes Difference in Community and World* (about war experiences in Italy)
http://www.utexas.edu/projects/latinoarchives/narratives/
vol2no2/4aguilarvalentin.html

940. Luis, Bettina. *Lived to Tell* (about service in the CBI Theater)
http://www.utexas.edu/projects/latinoarchives/narratives/
vol2no2/4cantuthomas.html

NATIVE AMERICANS (INDIANS)

941. Bingaman, Jeff (Senator). *Navajo Code Talkers*
http://bingaman.senate.gov/code_talkers/

942. Lambert, Allen J. *Navajo Code Talkers, USMC*
http://www.angelfire.com/biz/550cafe/navajo.html

943. Molnar, Jr., Alexander. *Navajo Code Talkers* (in the "World War II
Fact Sheet, USMC" series)
http://www.usmc.mil/history.nsf/Table+of+Contents/
77f992b2acb682eb852564d70059c642?OpenDocument&Expand
Section=8

944. Naval Historical Center. *Navajo Code Talkers: A Select Bibliography*
http://www.history.navy.mil/faqs/faq12-1.htm

945. Naval Historical Center. *Navajo Code Talker's Dictionary* (revised as
of 15 June 1945)
http://www.history.navy.mil/faqs/faq61-4.htm

946. Patrick, Bethanne K. *Dr. Samuel Billison*
http://www.military.com/Content/MoreContent?file=ML_billison_bkp

947. [Unidentified.] *Choctaw Indians: The First Code Talkers in the U.S.
Armed Forces* (from *Bishinik,* official publication of Choctaw Nation,
August 1986)
http://members.aol.com/famjustin/Chocktaw1.html

948. United States Interior Departments. *Indians in the War* (1945; requires
Adobe Acrobat)
http://worldwar2.smu.edu/cgi-bin/Pwebrecon.cgi?v1
=78&ti=51,78&CNT=50&Search_Arg=world+war&Search_Code
=GKEY&x=30&y=5&y=5&PID=3725&SEQ=20020105194602&SID=1

JAPANESE AMERICANS

949. Brown, Jay M. *When Military Necessity Overrides Constitutional Guar-
antees: The Treatment of Japanese Americans during World War II* (emphasis on court decisions and questions/precedents raised by them)
http://www.cis.yale.edu/ynhti/curriculum/units/1982/3/82.03.01.x.html

950. Ito, Robert. *Concentration Camp or Summer Camp? A New Generation of Revisionists Tries to Put a Happy Face on the Japanese American
Relocation Camps*
http://www.mojones.com/news_wire/ito.html

951. McNaughton, James C. *Nisei Linguists and New Perspectives on the
Pacific War: Intelligence, Race, and Continuity* (a paper presented at the
1994 Conference of Army Historians)
http://www.army.mil/cmh-pg/topics/apam/Nisei.htm

952. Museum of the City of San Francisco. *Internment of San Francisco Japanese* (includes text of on-going 1942 series of articles in the *San Francisco News* encouraging concern over domestic presence of Japanese descendants)
http://www.sfmuseum.org/war/evactxt.html

953. Ninomuya, Calvin. *A Japanese American Man Visits the Place Where His Brother Died a Hero in World War II* (from *Seattle Times*, May 30, 1999)
http://seattletimes.nwsource.com/news/travel/html98/altbruz_
19990530.html

954. War Relocation Authority. *War Relocation Authority Photographs of Japanese-American Evacuation and Resettlement* (over 7,000)
http://www.oac.cdlib.org/dynaweb/ead/calher/jvac/@Generic__Book View

955. [Unidentified.] *America's Concentration Camps* (map of location of internment camps and links to additional materials)
http://www.janm.org/clasc/map.htm

956. [Unidentified.] *The Japanese American Internment* (with large selection of links to other sites dealing with aspects of the subject)
http://www.geocities.com/Athens/8420/main.html

957. [Unidentified.] *War Relocation Camps in Arizona, 1942-1946*
http://www.library.arizona.edu/images/jpamer/wraintro.html

958. U.S. Supreme Court. *Korematsu v. United States* (1944; right of government to intern is upheld; text of decision and commentary)
http://usinfo.state.gov/usa/infousa/facts/democrac/65.htm

959. Yamamoto, Saori (pseudonymn). *Oral History* (description of internment years and conditions)
http://www-personal.umich.edu/~amnornes/Young.html

Women as a War Resource

960. Bellafaire, Judith A. *The Army Nurses' Corps: A Commemoration of World War II Service* (in the "Fiftieth Anniversary Commemorative Histories" series)
http://www.army.mil/cmh-pg/books/wwii/72-14/72-14.htm

961. Bellafaire, Judith A. *The Women's Army Corps: A Commemoration of*

World War II Service (in the "Fiftieth Anniversary Commemorative Histories" series)
http://www.army.mil/cmh-pg/brochures/wac/WAC.HTM

962. Bernatitus, Ann. *Oral Histories: U.S. Navy Nurse in the Pacific Theater during World War II* (describes her service in the Philippines, escape by sub from Corregidor, and duty off shore at Okinawa)
http://www.history.navy.mil/faqs/faq87-3b.htm

963. Brown, Dorothy M. *Edith Nourse Rogers* (World War II Congresswoman; lobbied for a women's auxiliary military service)
http://www.rice.edu/fondren/woodson/exhibits/wac/rogers.html

964. Burgess, Jerry G. *Partners in Progress* (women in the military and the museum devoted to their role)
http://www.quartermaster.army.mil/oqmg/Professional_Bulletin/1999/winter1999/Partners%20in%20History.htm

965. Copp, Terry. *[Canadian] Servicewomen of World War II*
http://www.legionmagazine.com/features/canadianmilitaryhistory/96-11.asp

966. Copp, Terry. *The Role of Jill Canuck* (women in Canadian military service)
http://www.legionmagazine.com/features/canadianmilitaryhistory/96-10.asp

967. Douglas, Deborah G. *WASPS of War* (Nancy H. Love, pioneer military pilot)
http://www.military.com/Content/MoreContent?file=PRqueenwasps

968. Hailey, C. Andy. *Women Airforce Service Pilots Killed in Action* (details on the death of the 38 women pilots who lose their lives during the war)
http://www.icct.net/~cahailey/WASP_KIA/38KIA.html

969. Harcourt School Publishers. *A Real-Life "Rosie the Riveter"*
http://www.harcourtschool.com/newsbreak/rosie.html

970. Hinman, Krista. *Women on the Homefront: World War II* (includes many posters of the period)
http://www.cs.olemiss.edu/~kmhinman/

971. Historical Section, Headquarters, European Theater of Operations. *WAAC-WAC, 1941-1944* (manuscript prepared near end of the war)
http://www.army.mil/cmh-pg/topics/women/waac.htm

972. Hobby, Bill. *Oveta Culp Hobby* (first commanding officer of the WACs)
http://www.rice.edu/fondren/woodson/exhibits/wac/hobby.html

973. Library of Congress. *Women Come to the Front: Journalists, Photographers, and Broadcasters during World War II*
http://lcweb.loc.gov/exhibits/wcf/wcf0001.html

974. McIntyre, Hannah. *Women Fill the Gap in the Workforce*
http://www.utexas.edu/projects/latinoarchives/narratives/
vol1no2/WOMEN_WORKERS/WOMEN_WORKERS.HTML

975. Minnich, Mike. *WAVES Air Navigators*
http://www.military.com/Content/MoreContent?file=PRwaves

976. Morden, Bettie J. *Women's Army Corps, 1945-1978* (Center of Military History, 2000)
http://www.army.mil/cmh-pg/books/wac/index.htm#contents

977. National Archives. *Women Who Served*
http://www.nara.gov/exhall/people/women.html

978. Patrick, Bethanne K. *Capt. Mildred McAfee Horton* (first director of the WAVES)
http://www.military.com/Content/MoreContent?file=ML_horton_bkp

979. Patrick, Bethanne K. *Lt. Cmdr. Nida Glick* (Coast Guard)
http://www.military.com/Content/MoreContent?file=ML_glick_bkp

980. Patrick, Bethanne K. *Lt. Col. Florence Aby Blanchfield*
http://www.military.com/Content/MoreContent?file=ML_blanchfield_bkp

981. Patrick, Bethanne K. *Lt. Col. Harriet W. Waddy* (one of two blacks to reach the rank of Major in the wartime WACs)
http://www.military.com/Content/MoreContent?file=ML_waddy_bkp

982. Patrick, Bethane K. *Maj. Gen. Jeanne Holm*
http://www.military.com/Content/MoreContent?file=ML_holm_bkp

983. Reading, Shirley N. *From Shell Inspector to Riveter to Typist for Military Intelligence*
http://www.memoriesofwar.com/veterans/reading/shirleyreading.asp

984. Roosevelt, Eleanor. *"Women at War"* (1944 *Reader's Digest* article)
http://newdeal.feri.org/texts/523.htm

985. Thomson, Robin J. *The Coast Guard & The Women's Reserve in World War II*
http://www.uscg.mil/hq/g-cp/history/h_wmnres.html

986. [Unidentified.] *American Women and the Military* (historical survey; extensive material on types of service of women in the Second World War)
http://www.gendergap.com/military/USmil.htm

987. [Unidentified.] *Oveta Culp Hobby: The Little Colonel*
http://www.rice.edu/fondren/woodson/exhibits/wac/wac.html

988. [Unidentified.] *Redstone [Arsenal at Huntsville, Alabama] World War
II Female "Production Soldiers"* (includes short film about the work of the
Arsenal at that time)
http://www.redstone.army.mil/history/women/welcome.html

989. [Unidentified.] *War Manpower Commission and Women*
http://history.acusd.edu/gen/WW2Timeline/WMC.html

990. [Unidentified.] *WASPs in World War II* (women pilots)
http://www.wasp-wwii.org/

991. [Unidentified.] *Women in the Marine Corps* (in the "World War II
Fact Sheet, USMC" series)
http://www.usmc.mil/history.nsf/Table+of+Contents/
77f992b2acb682eb852564d70059c642?OpenDocument&Expand
Section=13

992. U.S. Airforce Museum. *Women in the Army Air Force*
http://www.wpafb.af.mil/museum/history/wwii/waf.htm

993. U.S. Maritime Service Veterans. *Woman Mariners in World War
II*
http://www.usmm.org/women.html

994. [Various authors.] *What Did You Do in the War Grandma?* (oral history interviews focusing on the homefront)
http://www.stg.brown.edu/projects/WWII_Women/tocCS.html

995. Women's Bureau. *Choosing Women for War-Industry Jobs* (1943;
requires Adobe Acrobat)
http://worldwar2.smu.edu/cgi-bin/Pwebrecon.cgi?
v1=18&ti=1,18&CNT=50&Search_Arg=world+war&Search_Code
=GKEY&x=30&y=5&y=5&PID=3725&SEQ=20020105193815&SID=1

996. Women's Bureau. *Women Workers in Ten War Production Areas and
Their Postwar Employment Plans* (1946)
http://worldwar2.smu.edu/cgi-bin/Pwebrecon.cgi?v1=188&ti
=151,188&CNT=50&Search_Arg=world+war&Search_Code
=GKEY&x=29&y=8&y=8&PID=3767&SEQ=20020105201722&SID=1

Decryption and Code-Breaking

997. Dunn, Peter. *Central Bureau Intelligence: Interception and Cryptanalyzing of Japanese Intelligence*
http://home.st.net.au/~dunn/sigint/cbi.htm

998. Dunn, Peter. *Signal Intelligence Units and Other Secret Units in Australia during World War 2*
http://home.st.net.au/~dunn/sigint/sigint.htm

999. Erskine, Ralph. *Enigma* (in site links to detailed information)
http://uboat.net/technical/enigma.htm

1000. Friedman, William F. *Certain Aspects of MAGIC in the Cryptological Background of the Various Official Investigations into the Attack on Pearl Harbor* (SRH-125)
http://www.ibiblio.org/hyperwar/PTO/Magic/SRH-125/index.html

1001. Gange, David. *Codebreaking through the Battle of Midway*
http://raphael.math.uic.edu/~jeremy/crypt/contrib/gange.html

1002. Hamer, David. *Downloads* (Enigma related articles; link to Enigma computer simulations currently available)
http://www.eclipse.net/~dhamer/download.htm

1003. Hamer, David. *Enigma—and Some Other Cipher Machines*
http://www.eclipse.net/~dhamer/cipher_machines.htm

1004. Henson, Jennifer. *The Making of Magic*
http://history.acusd.edu/gen/WW2Timeline/magic.html

1005. Kurzeja, Karen. *Pearl Harbor & Ciphering Methods*
http://raphael.math.uic.edu/~jeremy/crypt/contrib/kurzeja.html

1006. Mariner's Museum. *The Battle of the Atlantic: Allied Naval Intelligence in World War II* (includes a film of the capture of U-505)
http://www.mariner.org/atlantic/

1007. Maziakowski, Lech. *The German Enigma Cipher Machine* (available in English or Polish)
http://home.us.net/~encore/Enigma/enigma.html

1008. O'Connor, Jerome M. *The Secret War*
http://www.military.com/Content/MoreContent?file=PRsecretf

1009. Parker, Frederic D. *A Priceless Advantage: U.S. Navy Communica-*

tions Intelligence and the Battle of Coral Sea, Midway, and the Aleutians (NSA Center for Cryptologic History, 1993)
http://www.ibiblio.org/hyperwar/PTO/Magic/COMINT-CoralSea/index.html

1010. Parker, Frederic D. *Pearl Harbor Revisited: U.S. Navy Communications Intelligence, 1924-1941* (NSA Center for Cryptologic History, 1994)
http://www.ibiblio.org/hyperwar/PTO/Magic/ComInt-1924-41/index.html
http://centurytel.net/midway/priceless/

1011. Safford, Laurence F. *A Brief History of Communications Intelligence in the U.S.* (SRH-149; declassified, 1982)
http://www.ibiblio.org/pha/ultra/SRH-149.html

1012. Safford, Laurence F. *Statement Regarding "Winds Message" Before the Joint Committee on the Investigation of the Pearl Harbor Attack* (SRH-210)
http://www.ibiblio.org/hyperwar/PTO/Magic/Safford-Winds.html

1013. Sale, Tony. *Codes and Ciphers in the Second World War: The Website for the History, Science and Engineering of Cryptanalysis in World War II* (focus on Bletchley Park and its work; includes contemporary documents and lectures on the work of BP)
http://www.codesandciphers.org.uk/

1014. Schorreck, Henry F. *The Role of COMINT in the Battle of Midway* (SRH-230)
http://www.ibiblio.org/hyperwar/PTO/Magic/COMINT-Midway.html

1015. Sharpe, Andrew R. W. *How Mathematics Saved the World: The Allies Decryption Efforts during World War II*
http://personal.nbnet.nb.ca/michaels/hist3300.htm

1016. [Unidentified.] *Brabant Farmstead Valkenhorst Housed 1943 German Spy Station* (site in Holland used for tapping and breaking security on transatlantic calls)
http://www.godutch.com/herald/ww2/981207.htm

1017. [Unidentified.] *Codebreaking and Secret Weapons in World War II* (10 part magazine series; downloadable)
http://home.earthlink.net/~nbrass1/enigma.htm

1018. [Unidentified.] *Enigma* (with in-site links to a Polish and French evaluation of the background)
http://webhome.idirect.com/~jproc/crypto/enigma.html

1019. [Unidentified.] *The Alan Turing Internet Scrapbook: Critical Crypt-analysis—the Second World War* (Turing played a pivotal role in breaking Enigma for the British)
http://www.turing.org.uk/turing/scrapbook/ww2.html

1020. [Unidentified.] *Ultra Timeline* (with links to other material)
http://history.acusd.edu/gen/WW2Timeline/CRAIGE/ultra.html

1021. Weadon, Patrick D. *Battle of Midway (June 3-6, 1942): "AF Is Short of Water"—How Cryptology Enabled the United States to Turn the Tide in the Pacific War* (NSA pamphlet)
http://www.nsa.gov/docs/history/AFWater.html

Homefront: U.S.A. and Canada

CANADA

1022. Base, Linda Di. *Japanese Canadian Internment: Information at the University of Washington Libraries and Beyond*
http://www.lib.washington.edu/subject/Canada/internment/intro.html

1023. Dowall, Duncan. *Due Diligence: A Report on the Bank of Canada's Handling of Foreign Gold during World War II*
http://www.bankofcanada.ca/en/gold/gold97-1.htm

1024. [Kent School District.] *The Canadian Nikkei Evacuation Experience*
http://www.kent.wednet.edu/KSD/SJ/Nikkei/Canadian_Nikkei.html

1025. Neary, Peter. *A Garrison Country: Newfoundland and Labrador during the Second World War*
http://www.warmuseum.ca/cwm/disp/dis004_e.html

1026. Public Relations, CBC Head Office, Ottawa. *A Brief History of the Canadian Broadcasting Corporation* (July 1976)
http://www.radio.cbc.ca/facilities/cbc-history.html

1027. [Unidentified.] *My Grandmother's Wartime Diary* (accounts by a number of women)
http://www.vac-acc.gc.ca/general/sub.cfm?source
=history/secondwar/diary/grandmother

1028. [Unidentified.] *They Serve that Men May Fly* (women in support roles)
http://collections.ic.gc.ca/high_flyers/wwii.htm

UNITED STATES

1029. American War Library. *U.S. Weapon Production (1942-1945)*
http://members.aol.com/forcountry/ww2/wea.htm

1030. Barnes, Shirley M. *War on Their Minds* (stateside service as a military nurse)
http://www.whshistoryproject.org/ww2/Interviews/mrs_barnes.html

1031. Bennett, Andrew C. *Coastal Defenses on the Gulf of Mexico*
http://andy_bennett.home.mindspring.com/coastal.html

1032. Bergreen, Laurence. *Irving Berlin: "This Is the Army"* (history of the stage show and movie)
http://www.nara.gov/publications/prologue/berlin1.html

1033. Berhow, Mark. *The Coastal Defense Study Group*
http://www.cdsg.org/

1034. Blitzer, Carol. *The 1940s: On the Home Front* (California)
http://server4.service.com/paw/Centennial/1994_Apr_15.1940SA.html

1035. Bonito, Joe. *Oral History* (age seven when war began; memories of every day life)
http://www-personal.umich.edu/~amnornes/Joseph.html

1036. Boy Scouts. *Historical Highlights—1940s*
http://www.bsa.scouting.org/factsheets/02-511/1940.html

1037. Braun, Ed. *The Greenbrier* (used by the government during the war as the Ashford General Army Hospital)
http://members.aol.com/famjustin/braun5.html

1038. Brightman, Norma L. *War on Their Minds* (interview about home-front conditions)
http://www.whshistoryproject.org/ww2/Interviews/mrs_brightman.html

1039. Browning, Jr., Robert M. *Coast Guard Captains of the Port* (war-time responsibility over ports)
http://www.uscg.mil/hq/g-cp/history/h_cptprt.html

1040. Camden County Historical Society. *New York Ship-Building in World War II*
http://members.aol.com/nyship/home.html

1041. Chin, Brian B. *Defense Guns at San Francisco*
http://www.angelfire.com/bc/sanfranartillery/index.html

1042. Combs, James E., and Sara T. Combs. *Film Propaganda and American Politics* (book review and summaries of each chapter)
http://www.youknow.com/chris/essays/filmproprev.html

1043. Crouch, Jacob, Ben Gould, and Scott Hays. *World War II: The Homefront* (also includes chronology of events)
http://library.thinkquest.org/15511/?tqskip=1

1044. De Angelo, Don. *Washington Goes to War* (examines the dramatic transition of the city in 1940 and 1941)
http://history.acusd.edu/gen/WW2Timeline/brinkley.html

1045. Dirks, Tim. *War and Anti-War Films*
http://www.filmsite.org/warfilms.html

1046. ["Dr. Suess."] *Dr. Suess Went to War: A Catalog of Political Cartoons by Dr. Suess* (over 400)
http://orpheus.ucsd.edu/speccoll/dspolitic/

1047. Federal Bureau of Investigation. *German Espionage and Sabotage against the U.S. in World War II: George John Dasch and the Nazi Saboteurs* (FBI handout; revised by the FBI in 1984)
http://www.history.navy.mil/faqs/faq114-2.htm

1048. Feldmeth, Greg G. *New Deal Programs*
http://home.earthlink.net/~gfeldmeth/chart.newdeal.html

1049. Field, Gregory. "*From Regional Development to National Defense: TVA, World War II, and the Making of the Military-Industrial Complex.*"
http://www.hts.gatech.edu/cssi/2ndwave/field.html

1050. Fort MacArthur Historic Association. *The Fort MacArthur [San Pedro, California] Museum: Battery Osgood—Farley Historic Site*
http://www.ftmac.org/

1051. Goodwin, Susan. *American Cultural History: The Twentieth Century, 1940-1949*
http://www.nhmccd.edu/contracts/lrc/kc/decade40.html

1052. Grottola, Helen. *Interview* (description of life during the war years)
http://www.tankbooks.com/intviews/grottola/grottola1.htm

1053. Infante, Andria. *Home Front Rations*
http://www.utexas.edu/projects/latinoarchives/narratives/vol1no2/HOME_RATIONS/HOME_RATIONS.HTML

1054. Jones, Eleanor, and Florian Ritzmann. *CocaCola Goes to War*
http://wsrv.clas.virginia.edu/~tsawyer/coca_cola/coke.html

1055. Justin, James. *The Shot Heard around the Meadowland* (member of New Jersey State Guard patrolling a railroad bridge in 1941)
http://members.aol.com/famjustin/halt.html

1056. Kingwood College Library. *American Cultural History: The Twentieth Century, 1940-1949*
http://www.nhmccd.edu/contracts/lrc/kc/decade40.html

1057. Library of Congress. *Air Raid on Pearl Harbor* (radio broadcast texts, "man in the street" interviews about the attack, and other data)
http://memory.loc.gov/ammem/today/dec07.html

1058. Library of Congress. *America from the Great Depression to World War II: Photos from the FSA-OWI, 1934-1945*
http://lcweb2.loc.gov/ammem/fsowhome.html

1059. *Life* [magazine]. *"Life:" V-J Day Kiss 50 Years Later* (the famous cover picture from *Life*, with links to other materials on the photographer who took the photo)
http://www.lifemag.com/Life/special/kiss01.html

1060. National Archives. *Power of Persuasion: Poster Art from World War II*
http://www.nara.gov/exhall/powers/powers.html

1061. Nelson, Stacy. *Shortages during World War II*
http://www.utexas.edu/projects/latinoarchives/narratives/vol1no2/SHORTAGES/SHORTAGES.HTML

1062. [Newspaper Article.] *Skilled Staff Operates Hospital Trains Carrying Wounded Veterans* (from the *Falmouth Enterprise*, June 1, 1945)
http://www.milhist.net/global/hosptrain.shtml

1063. Noble, Dennis L. *Beach Patrol and Cosair Fleet*
http://www.uscg.mil/hq/g-cp/history/h_beachpatrol.html

1064. Office of Naval Intelligence. *"German Espionage and Sabotage against the United States"* (1946; declassified)
http://www.history.navy.mil/faqs/faq114-1.htm

1065. Oregon State Archives. *Fighters on the Farm Front: Oregon's Emergency Farm Labor Service, 1943-1947*
http://arcweb.sos.state.or.us/osu/osuhomepage.html

1066. Roberts, Malia. *Life in California around the Time of the Pacific War*
http://cstl.semo.edu/us107/mainst/HoffmanClasses/roberts/index.htm

1067. Roosevelt, Franklin D. *Proclamation of Unlimited National Emergency (May 27, 1941)*
http://www.sunsite.unc.edu/pha/policy/1941/410527a.html

1068. Rose, Elizabeth. *"Essential Patriotic Service:" Mothers and Day Care in World War II Philadelphia*
http://www.indiana.edu/~oah/97program/rose.htm

1069. Rudomin, Yitschak. *The Second World War and Jewish Education in America: The Fall and Rise of Orthodoxy* (MA Thesis, 1983)
http://www.jpi.org/holocaust/

1070. Saleeby, Catherine. *Brief History of World War II Ad Campaigns*
http://scriptorium.lib.duke.edu/adaccess/wwad-history.html

1071. Schoenherr, Steve. *Military Bases in San Diego [California]—World War II, 1921-1945*
http://history.sandiego.edu/gen/local/kearny/page00e.html

1072. Schubert, Frank N. *Mobilization—Fiftieth Anniversary of World War II* (in the "Fiftieth Anniversary Commemorative Histories" series of the U. S. Army)
http://www.army.mil/cmh-pg/documents/mobpam.htm

1073. Schultz, Stanley K. *World War II: The Home Front*
http://us.history.wisc.edu/hist102/lectures/lecture21.html

1074. Short, Gloria. *Memories from the Homefront* (she was seven years old at the time the war began)
http://www.ww2heroes.com/article1011.html

1075. Siegel, George U. *Hollywood's Army: The First Motion Picture Unit, U.S. Army Air Forces (Culver City, California)* (composed exclusively of veteran Hollywood writers, producers, directors, etc., this unit ground out instructional and other films for the military)
http://www.militarymuseum.org/1stmpu.html

1076. ThinkQuest. *World War II: The Homefront*
http://library.thinkquest.org/15511/index.htm

1077. Thomas, Michele. *World War II: The War Bride Experience*
http://www.geocities.com/Heartland/Meadows/9710/WarBrides.html

1078. [Unidentified.] *Comic Book Covers from the 1940s*
http://www.ultranet.com/~adjm/comics/cover.shtml

1079. [Unidentified.] *Mobilization of the Home Front* (with links to individual aspects)
http://history.acusd.edu/gen/WW2Timeline/mobilization.html

1080. [Unidentified.] *My Dog Murphy's Historical Goods* (commercial site but includes posters and other items that can be "blown up" for better viewing)
http://www.mydogmurphy.com/wp/

1081. [Unidentified.] *North American Fortifications: Forts and Fortresses, Frontier Posts and Camps, Blockhouses and Seacoast Batteries in the United States and Canada*
http://www.geocities.com/naforts/forts.htm

1082. [Unidentified.] *OCD and Civilian Defense*
http://history.acusd.edu/gen/WW2Timeline/OCD.html

1083. [Unidentified.] *OPA and Rationing*
http://history.acusd.edu/gen/WW2Timeline/OPA.html

1084. [Unidentified.] *Port Chicago (Sacramento River, California) Disaster—17 July 1944* (various materials related to explosion of ammunition ships on that date)
http://www.ibiblio.org/hyperwar/USN/fac/PC/index.html

1085. [Unidentified.] *Poster Girls of World War II*
http://www.geocities.com/queenknuckles/postergirls.htm

1086. [Unidentified.] *Songs of World War II*
http://www.fortunecity.com/tinpan/parton/2/ww2.html#top

1087. [Unidentified.] *The Stars Go to War*
http://history.sandiego.edu/gen/st/~ksoroka/hollywood7.html

1088. [Unidentified.] *Various Documents Related to the Port Chicago Disaster*
http://www.ibiblio.org/hyperwar/USN/fac/PC/

1089. [Unidentified.] *WW2Homefront.com* (collector's site, but includes large collection of photographs of items of period and other information)
http://www.ww2homefront.com/

1090. [Unidentified.] *World War II: The Homefront Encyclopedia* (student created; actually is concerned with all aspects of the war rather than the homefront)
http://library.thinkquest.org/15511/data/encyclopedia/index2.htm

1091. [Unidentified.] *World War II Films*
http://www.intelligentsianetwork.com/wwfilms/wwfilms.htm

1092. United States Air Force Museum. *Air Defense of the United States*
http://www.wpafb.af.mil/museum/history/wwii/adus.htm

1093. United States Government. *Historic Government Publications from World War II* (over 200, mainly homefront orientated documents on line; click "browse titles" for list)
http://worldwar2.smu.edu/

1094. Victory Seed Company. *The Victory Garden* (small gardens families encouraged to plant to meet some of their own food needs)
http://www.victoryseeds.com/TheVictoryGarden/index.html

1095. Vintage Vixen Clothing. *The New Look: Women's Fashions of the 1940s*
http://www.vintagevixen.com/history/1940s.asp

1096. Wall, Bill. *World War II's Biggest Troop Movement* (Third Armored Division moved to the American Southwest)
http://www.cwrr.com/Lounge/Stories/troops/troops.html

1097. Warinner, Andrew. *The Philadelphia Experiment* (a critical look at the claim, with links)
http://home.xnet.com/~warinner/phexp.html

1098. Widner, Robert. *Aircraft Accidents in Florida from Pearl Harbor to the Atomic Bomb*
http://www.geocities.com/bwidner1/

1099. Wolfe, Richard. *Crimeboss: Crime Comic Books of the 1940's and 1950's*
http://www.crimeboss.com/

Homefront: European Nations

Austria

1100. Blaschke, Ernest. *Growing up with the Russian Occupation* (with comparisons to German attitudes preceding it)
http://atschool.eduweb.co.uk/chatback/english/memories/~ernest.html

France

1101. Delattre, Helen. *[Three Narratives of the Occupation of France]*
(We are Occupied by the German Army:) http://atschool.eduweb.co.uk/chatback/english/memories/~helene.html
(Life under the Occupation:) http://atschool.eduweb.co.uk/chatback/english/memories/~helene2.

(Coping with the Lack of Anything and Everything:) http://
atschool. eduweb.co.uk/chatback/english/memories/~helene3.html

1102. Lindsey, Dorice. *France, 1944: A View from the Ground* (she was a
teenager at the time)
http://www.memoriesofwar.com/veterans/lindsey.asp

1103. Renelle, V. *Letters from Jail: V. Renelle, 1940-1941* (Renelle was a
trade unionist arrested and eventually executed by the German occupiers)
http://a.webring.com/hub?ring=ww2&id=379&go

1104. Wassem, Violette. *[Three Narratives of the Occupation of Paris]*
(Paris Is Occupied:) http://atschool.eduweb.co.uk/
chatback/english/memories/~viole.html
(Paris: Life during the Occupation:) http://atschool.eduweb.co.uk/
chatback/english/memories/~viol2.html
(Paris Is Liberated:) http://atschool.eduweb.co.uk/
chatback/english/memories/~viol3.html

GERMANY

1105. Barthel, Heinz. *Potsdam Schoolboy's Story*
http://www.timewitnesses.org/english/~heinz1.html
http://atschool.eduweb.co.uk/chatback/english/memories/~heinz1.html

1106. Basham, Horace A. *Rationing in World War Two* (personal reminiscences)
http://youth.net/memories/hypermail/0189.html

1107. Blaich, Roland. *A Church in Crisis: Historical Reflections* (concerning how the German church reacted to the challenge of Nazism)
http://www.wwc.edu/about-us/lectures/blaich.html

1108. Dixon, Ursula G. *Living through the Gotterdammerung of the Third
Reich* (first hand account of the last days of the Reich)
http://www.ursulashistoryweb.f2s.com/gotter.html

1109. Duncan, George. *Women of the Third Reich* (short summaries of a
number of prominent individuals)
http://members.iinet.net.au/~gduncan/women.html

1110. Harm, Marie, and Hermann Wiehle. *Biology for the Middle School*
(extract from a fifth grade textbook published in 1942)
http://www.calvin.edu/academic/cas/gpa/textbk01.htm

1111. Kern, David H. *Die Bahnschutzpolizei: History and Traditions of Germany's Railway Police* (1835-1945)
http://home.earthlink.net/~davidbear/

1112. Long, Jason. *The Sinews of War: Economics, Production and Logistics during the Second World War*
http://members.tripod.com/~Sturmvogel/WarEcon.html

1113. Muller, Reinhard. *People without Space* (extract from a 1943 geography textbook for middle school use)
http://www.calvin.edu/academic/cas/gpa/textbk02.htm

1114. Sanders, Ian J. *World War Two Locations in Modern Berlin* (photographs)
http://www.geocities.com/isanders_2000/ww2index.htm

1115. [Unidentified.] *Places of World War II* (industries, monuments, etc. erected by the Germans during the War)
http://www.geocities.com/Pentagon/7087/

1116. [Unidentified.] *The Functioning of the Nazi Regime: State and Society*
http://www.colby.edu/personal/r/rmscheck/GermanyE5.html

1117. [Unidentified.] *The German Conspiracy to Destroy Hitler, 1938-1944*
http://www.joric.com/Conspiracy/Conspiracy.htm

1118. [Unidentified,] Dennis. *Unpublished Images of Nazi Germany, 1939-1941*
http://members.aol.com/dennisr48/german/nazpics.htm

1119. Wendel, Marcus. *Third Reich Fact Book* (political, military, and other organizations, awards, etc.)
http://www.skalman.nu/third-reich/

1120. Wittenstein, George J. *Memories of the White Rose* (anti-Nazi youth)
http://www.historyplace.com/pointsofview/white-rose1.htm

1121. Yoder, Brian. *Nazi & Soviet Art*
http://www.primenet.com/~byoder/artofnz.htm

Great Britain

1122. Ainsbury, Frank. *The Catastrophe of Coventry* (at top of screen click on "A-G;" pick this person's name from list on left screen; text appears to right)
http://www.warlinks.com/memories/index.html

1123. Baker, Dot. *Dot's Story*
http://www.timewitnesses.org/english/~dot.html
http://atschool.eduweb.co.uk/chatback/english/memories/~dot.html

1124. Benvenuto, Bob. *White Caps, Watch Caps and Dress Blues* (Americans on liberty in Britain immediately after Normandy invasion)
http://members.aol.com/famjustin/LST8.html

1125. Bergonzi, Bernard. *Buzz-Bombs and Doodle-Bugs* (V-1s and V-2 in the latter part of the war)
http://atschool.eduweb.co.uk/chatback/english/memories/doodbug.html

1126. Bradley, Daphne. *The Day War Broke Out* (at top of screen click on "A-G;" pick this person's name from list on left screen; text appears to right)
http://www.warlinks.com/memories/index.html

1127. Davis, Walter. *A GI's Trip to London, 1944* (Davis' letter to his wife describing a long trip by himself and three other soldiers)
http://www.ibiscom.com/gilondon.htm

1128. Fletcher, Tom. *Civvy Street in World War II* (life as a civilian in wartime; he was eleven when war was declared)
http://www.macksites.com/PART1.htm

1129. Henderson, Diana M. *The Alleged [Anti-]British "Fifth Column"—Scotland*
http://www-saw.arts.ed.ac.uk/secret/fifthcolumn.html

1130. Hoffman, Marion C. *An English Girl's Impression of the Invasion by the Yanks*
http://www.geocities.com/oralbio/englishgirl.html

1131. Holloway, Tom. *Teatime for Tomy: Home from School in 1942*
http://www.timewitnesses.org/english/~tommy.html
http://atschool.eduweb.co.uk/chatback/english/memories/~tommy.html

1132. Johnson, David A. *Americans in Britain*
http://www.military.com/Content/MoreContent?file=PRperspectivesf

1133. Johnson, Stephen. *Plymouth's World War Two Underground Air Raid Shelters*
http://ourworld.compuserve.com/homepages/StephenJohnson1/

1134. Joyce, Doreen. *Memories of Doreen Joyce* (she was eight when the war began; at top of screen click on "H-L;" pick this person's name from list on left screen; text appears to right)
http://www.warlinks.com/memories/index.html

1135. Knapp, Yvonne E. *One Woman's War* (her account of British Army service)
http://www.tankbooks.com/stories/onewoman/onewoman1.htm

1136. Leadbeater, Noel. *Any Volunteers* (being an "extra" in a war-time movie; at top of screen click on "H-L;" pick this person's name from list on left screen; text appears to right)
http://www.warlinks.com/memories/index.html

1137. Martin, Gerry. *Memories* (at top of screen click on "M-Q;" pick this person's name from list on left screen; text appears to right)
http://www.warlinks.com/memories/index.html

1138. National Archives Learning Curve. *Home Front, 1939-1945*
http://learningcurve.pro.gov.uk/homefront/default.htm

1139. Pay, Arthur. *A Conscientious Objection to War*
http://www.timewitnesses.org/english/~arthurp.html
http://atschool.eduweb.co.uk/chatback/english/memories/~arthurp.html

1140. Penn, Marjorie. *The Little Nurse* (her wartime experiences in London—during the blitz—and in other hospitals in the country)
http://positiveinteraction.com/littleNurse

1141. Public Record Office. *Release of MI5 Material Related to the Second World War* (selected samples)
http://www.pro.gov.uk/releases/nov2000/mi5_1.htm

1142. Reese, A. Willard. *Picadilly Commandoes* (prostitution)
http://members.aol.com/famjustin/Reese2.html

1143. Reid, Brian A. *The German Occupation of Jersey in the Channel Islands* (a youth's memories)
http://atschool.eduweb.co.uk/chatback/english/memories/~brian.html

1144. Risbey, Peter. *Midnight Watch* (civil defense activities)
http://www.fortunecity.co.uk/meltingpot/oxford/330/mwindex.html

1145. Stratford, Stephen. *Stephen's Study Room* (analysis of spying, courts-martials, and other phenomena in Britain during the twentieth century)
http://www.stephen-stratford.co.uk/

1146. [Unidentified.] *Brum Homefront* (Birmingham air raids and related information)
http://www.brumhomefront.co.uk/

1147. [Unidentified.] *Dover Past and Present* (section on World War II Dover)
http://www.doverpages.fsnet.co.uk/

1148. [Unidentified.] *Eastbourne during the Second World War*
http://freepages.pavilion.net/users/enigma/ebwar0.htm

1149. [Unidentified.] *German Occupation of the Channel Islands*
http://www.jersey-channel-isles.com/page10.html

1150. [Unidentified.] *Great Britain's Deception Campaign against the German Invader During World War II* (dummy warfields, disguising location of actual war resources, etc.)
http://history.acusd.edu/gen/WW2Timeline/britain.html

1151. [Unidentified.] *Memories from My Wartime Youth* (1939-1942, the year in which she married)
http://www.warlinks.com/cgi-bin/links/jump.cgi?ID=509

1152. [Unidentified.] *Register of Essex-Related Dead of World War II* (also includes information on airfields and the area itself during the war)
http://www.goring1941.freeserve.co.uk/reg01.html

1153. [Unidentified.] *Squaddie Songs* (British and Commonwealth barrack songs [audio]; unedited)
http://www.squaddiesongs.f2s.com/

1154. [Unidentified.] *The Home Guard*
http://www.users.dircon.co.uk/~tdschild/index.html

1155. [Unidentified.] *Wartime Leicestershire*
http://www.tccpublications.force9.co.uk/popup/index.html

1156. [Unidentified.] *World War II Evacuees Discussion Group*
http://groups.yahoo.com/group/Brit_WWII_Evacuees/

1157. [Various sources.] *World War II Newspapers* (selected articles; currently covers 1940-1944; eventually to encompass 1939-1945)
http://www.geocities.com/wwiinews/wwiinews.html

1158. Westall, Robert. *Westall's War: Air Raid Disaster in North Shields, 1941* (one of worst of war in UK; 103 killed; survivor and other accounts)
http://www.westallswar.org.uk/

HOLLAND (NETHERLANDS)

1159. Anderson, Anthony. *A Forgotten Chapter: Holland under the Third Reich* (detailed discussion)
http://www-lib.usc.edu/~anthonya/war/main.htm

1160. de Keizer, Madelon. *Het Parool* (major underground paper in Holland during the war)
http://www.hetillegaleparool.nl/summary.html

1161. Foundation Menno van Coehorn. *The Defence Line of Amsterdam*
http://www.stelling-amsterdam.org/engels/

1162. Houterman, Hans. *Atlantikwall, Zeeland, Wereldoorloz II* (Atlantic
Wall defenses in Holland and Holland during the war years; Dutch language site)
http://home.wxs.nl/~houte098/

1163. [Unidentified.] *The Dutch Interbellum and Occupation Bibliography*
http://www.geschiedenis.com/wo2/engels/indexeng.htm

1164. van der Heide, Albert. *Chronology of Dutch War-time History* (significant dates of entire war and occupation period)
http://www.godutch.com/herald/ww2/950323.htm

ITALY

1165. Department Special Collections, University of Wisconsin—Madi-
son. *Italian Life under Fascism*
http://www.library.wisc.edu/libraries/dpf/Fascism/

1166. [Unidentified.] *The Cinema and Mussolini*
http://ccat.sas.upenn.edu/italians/Amiciprize/1996/mussolini.html

LUXEMBOURG

1167. Dienhart, Daniel. *The Last Flight of Halifax No. W7677/102
Squadron* (crashed in Luxembourg September 1942)
http://www.geocities.com/Pentagon/Quarters/2284/HAL-RAM0.html

1168. [Unidentified.] *National Museum of Military History* (Diekirch, Luxembourg; has sections devoted to life during the occupation and to the
Battle of the Bulge)
http://www.luxembourg.co.uk/NMMH/

4

The European War: 1939–1945

The Anschluss with Austria

1169. Library of Congress. *Austria: A Country Study* (sections on the anschluss and the war)
http://memory.loc.gov/frd/cs/attoc.html

1170. [Unidentified.] *A.J.P. Taylor and the Anschluss*
http://history.acusd.edu/gen/WW2Timeline/Austria.html

1171. [Unidentified.] *History Maps* (ethnic maps of Austria and Czechoslovakia)
http://www2.bc.edu/~heineman/hs064maps.html

1172. [Unidentified.] *History Begins the Anschluss*
http://history.sandiego.edu/gen/WW2Timeline/step06.html

German Military and Navy

1173. Barmann, Lorenz. *German Night Fighters Resource Page*
http://www.csd.uwo.ca/~pettypi/elevon/baugher_other/fw190i.html

1174. Baugher, Joe. *Focke-Wulf Fw190*
http://www.fighter-planes.com/info/fw190.htm

1175. Bergstrom, Christer. *Adolf Galland and the Dramatic Air Combat July of 1941*
http://www.elknet.pl/acestory/galland/galland.htm

1176. Chavez, Rene. *Axis Military and Foreign Volunteer Legions*
http://axis101.bizland.com/

1177. Corridon, Raymond R. *Ray's Home Page: X-4 Missile* (experimental but workable air to air guided missile)
http://hometown.aol.com/rayeso/index.html/mainpage.html

1178. Denniston, Peter. *German Mountain Troops in World War II*
http://www.gebirgsjaeger.4mg.com/

1179. Emmerich, Michael. *German Kriegsmarine Encyclopedia*
http://www.german-navy.de/marine.htm

1180. Geipel, Barry L. *War Albums* (of two of his uncles: one served on the Eastern Front and one in the West)
http://www.geipelnet.com/war_albums/

1181. [German Government.] *Announcement of the Assumption of the Direct Command by Adolph Hitler with His Proclamation to the German Army (December 21, 1941)*
http://www.ibiblio.org/pha/policy/1941/411221a.html
http://www.sunsite.unc.edu/pha/policy/1941/411221a.html

1182. Heaton, Colin D. *Luftwaffe General Adolf Galland* (interview with)
http://www.military.com/Content/MoreContent?file=PRgalland

1183. Holm, Michael. *Luftwaffe: 1935-1944*
http://www.ww2.dk/

1184. Horta, Roy. *12 O'Clock High—Luftwaffe Page*
http://www.xs4all.nl/~rhorta/

1185. Jewell, Larry W. *H Class* (German planning of battleships that would have carried greater firepower than the *Bismarck*)
http://www.ibiblio.org/pub/academic/history/
marshall/military/wwii/German.navy/german_hclass_bat.txt

1186. Johnson, Dan. *Luft' 46* (proposed advanced experimental aircraft)
http://users.visi.net/~djohnson/luft46.html

1187. Johnson, David A. *Buzz Bomb Blasts Britain*
http://www.military.com/Content/MoreContent?file=PRbuzzbombf

1188. Klaussner, Sigmund H. *Hansgeorg Batcher: World War II Bomber Ace of Aces*
http://www.military.com/Content/MoreContent?file=PRbatcher

1189. Larroque, Paul. *An Unlucky Legend* (Messerschnitt Bf-109)
http://www.geocities.com/iturks/html/an_unlucky_legend.html

1190. Lavergne, Barbara. *The U-Boat Bases of La Rochelle–La Pallice*
http://perso.club-internet.fr/barbara9/anglais/

1191. Long, Jason, and Jim Broshot. *Heavy Tank Units of the Wehrmacht*
http://members.tripod.com/~Sturmvogel/tigers.html

1192. Long, Jason, and Jim Broshot. *Obscure Combat Formations of the Heer: Organizational Histories*
http://members.tripod.com/~Sturmvogel/heer-obscure.html

1193. Matthieu, Serra. *The U-Boat Bases* (in France)
http://www.uboat-bases.com/

1194. McSwiney, Michael. *Technical Virtue: Prototypes and Advanced Designs of the Wehrmacht, 1939-1945*
http://www.warlinks.com/cgi-bin/links/jump.cgi?ID=169

1195. Miller, Michael, and Jeff Chrisman. *Axis Biographical Research* (covers both the military and civilian leadership)
http://www.geocities.com/~orion47/

1196. Olsson, Kjell. *Orders, Medals, and Badges of the Third Reich*
http://home.swipnet.se/wehrwolf/index.htm

1197. Parada, George. *Vehicles of the Wehrmacht, 1939-1945*
http://www.geocities.com/Pentagon/3620/

1198. Parada, George. *Achtung Panzer* (details on German armor)
http://www.achtungpanzer.com/panzer.htm

1199. Pipes, Jason. *FeldGrau.com: A German Military History Research Site, 1919-1945*
http://www.feldgrau.com/

1200. Poyatos, Alvaro. *Waffen-SS in Pictures*
http://www.ctv.es/USERS/apf/home.htm

1201. Reinbold, Dan. *Das Reich 2nd SS Panzer Division*
http://www.dasreich.ca/dasreich.html

1202. Reits, Eric. *Panzer Page* (includes contemporary Germany propaganda glorifying their accomplishments)
http://www.geocities.com/Pentagon/Quarters/8662/home.htm

1203. Riva, Francesco. *"The Infantry of the Air:" The Life of German General Kurt Student and His Work for the Constitution and the War Use of a Paratroopers' Corps*
http://www.geocities.com/iturks/html/world_war_ii_3.html

1204. Schudak, Axel. *German Codenames of World War II*
http://worldatwar.net/article/germancode/index.html

1205. Sjodin, Michael. *Unterseebootwaffe: The German World War II Submarine Force*
http://www.dataphone.se/~ms/ubootw/welcom.htm

1206. Stahlbrant, Bo. *Unternehmen Moewe—The Secret German World War II Operations* (covert German operations behind the lines of its foes)
http://www.stahlbrandt.com/html/history/moewe.html

1207. Strobel, Warren P. *Absence of A-Bomb: Were the Nazis Duped—or Simply Dumb?*
http://www.usnews.com/usnews/doubleissue/mysteries/nazi.htm

1208. Thun, Rudolph E. *Rudolph E. Thun: Luftwaffe World War II Night Fighter*
http://www.geocities.com/Pentagon/7404/thun.html

1209. [Unidentified.] *Achtung Wuerger! The Comprehensive FW190 Site on the Internet*
http://home.earthlink.net/~poole124/

1210. [Unidentified.] *Adolf Galland (1912-1996): Pilot, Ace, General of the Luftwaffe* (pictures, obituaries, interviews with those who knew him
http://members.aol.com/geobat66/galland/galland.htm

1211. [Unidentified.] *A4/V2 Resource Site*
http://www.v2rocket.com/

1212. [Unidentified.] *An Overview of Third Reich Bunker Art* (such as camouflage patterns)
http://home.hetnet.nl/~thirdreich-bunkers/

1213. [Unidentified.] *Arsenal of Dictatorship: Online Encyclopedia* (description of Axis weapons, with photographs and diagrams)
http://www.geocities.com/pentagon/2833/

1214. [Unidentified.] *"Blood and Iron:" The Kriegsmarine, 1936-1945* (German navy)
http://www.geocities.com/Pentagon/2146/

1215. [Unidentified.] *German Aircraft Production during World War 2*
http://members.aol.com/forcountry/ww2/gma.htm

1216. [Unidentified.] *German and Italian Combat Casualties during World War 2*
http://members.aol.com/forcountry/ww2/gic.htm

1217. [Unidentified.] *German Experimental Aircraft* (in the FW190 series)
http://www.csd.uwo.ca/~pettypi/elevon/baugher_other/fw190i.html

1218. [Unidentified.] *German Nomenclature* (and the meaning in English)
http://www.geocities.com/Athens/Acropolis/3125/kgc/nomen.html

1219. [Unidentified.] *Great German Generals*
http://members.tripod.com/~SSPzComdr/index.html

1220. [Unidentified.] *JU-52* (German language site; English version available)
http://members.aol.com/igju52ev/ju52engl.htm

1221. [Unidentified.] *Luftwaffe Database*
http://users.aol.com/dheitm8612/index.htm

1222. [Unidentified.] *Luftwaffe Resource Center* (German planes from 1935 to today)
http://www.warbirdsresourcegroup.org/LRG/index.html

1223. [Unidentified.] *ME262: Technical Assessment* (German jet)
http://www.stormbirds.com/squadron/common/technical.htm

1224. [Unidentified.] *National Volunteer Formations in Wehrmacht and Waffen-SS* (available in Russian or English)
http://bka-roa.chat.ru/index.htm

1225. [Unidentified.] *Panzer Mk V: The Panther* (includes photographs and specifications)
http://www.panzerv-panther.fsnet.co.uk/

1226. [Unidentified.] *Panzer VI: The Tiger Tank* (includes photographs and specifications)
http://www.panzer-vi.fsnet.co.uk/

1227. [Unidentified.] *Panzergrenadier* (studies German motorcycle and motorized units)
http://www.geocities.com/Pentagon/6931/

1228. [Unidentified.] *Reichslieder* (German military and patriotic music from both world wars)
http://www.reichslieder.com/

1229. [Unidentified.] *SS Officer Computer Research* (data on ranks, authority, etc.)
http://members.rogers.com/ssocr/index_800.html

1230. [Unidentified.] *The Other Side of the Tracks* (German armored trains, 1939-1945)
http://www.geocities.com/mnrdunck/

1231. [Unidentified.] *The Panzer Divisions* (commanders and structure)
http://www.forces70.freeserve.co.uk/panzer%20divisions/pz-divtext.htm

1232. [Unidentified.] *Third Reich Command Centers in Former East Prussia*
http://www.geocities.com/bue02/index.html

1233. [Unidentified.] *12 SS-Pazerdivision "Hitlerjugend"* (designed to be composed strictly of Hitler Youth)
http://home.att.net/~SSPzHJ/Index.html

1234. [Unidentified.] *U-Boat Museums in Germany* (German language site)
http://www.juergenthuro.de/

1235. [Unidentified.] *Waffen SS in Austria* (studies 1 SS PzDv)
http://www.angelfire.com/sd/waffenss/

1236. [Unidentified.] *Waffen-SS Order of Battle*
http://www.wssob.com/

1237. [Unidentified.] *World War II Day by Day* (1939-1945, from the standpoint of German operations; only partly completed)
http://www.wwiidaybyday.com/

1238. Walden, Geoff. *Panzer Colors* (color photographs of the original paint schemes)
http://www.waldenarchives.simonides.org/pz/panzercolors.htm

1239. Warbirds Research Group. *Luftwaffe Research Center*
http://www.warbirdsresourcegroup.org/LRG/index.html

1240. Webster, G. A. *Jagdflieger: German VTO [Vertical Take-off] & Helicopter Projects of World War II*
http://www.germanvtol.com/

1241. Wiems, Gavin. *Formations of the Wehrmacht, 1935-1945*
http://www.expage.com/panzer

1242. Zuljan, Ralph. *Panzer War* (includes maps and other data)
http://www.geocities.com/~orion47/

Poland

1243. Blichasz, Michael. *Reflections on the 60th Anniversary of the Invasion of Poland and the Beginning of World War II*
http://www.polishamericancenter.com/60thAnniversary.htm

1244. Bostwick, Jr., Byron L. *Polish Armed Forces, 1939-1945*
http://www.geocities.com/byron_b86/

1245. Chamberlain, Neville. *Chamberlain Declares War* (sound recording)
http://www.otr.com/neville.html

1246. Chamberlain, Neville. *Some Documents Relevant to Great Britain's Response to the German Invasion of Poland* (September 1-3, 1939; three addresses by Prime Minister Chamberlain)
http://www.ibiblio.org/hyperwar/ETO/Dip/britain-39.html

1247. Chamberlain, Neville. *The Western Guarantee of Polish Independence (March 31, 1939)*
http://www.ibiblio.org/pha/policy/pre-war/390331a.html

1248. Copp, Terry. *Our Polish Comrades* (serving with the Allies in the West)
http://www.legionmagazine.com/features/canadianmilitaryhistory/00-01.asp

1249. Copp, Terry. *The Decision to Enter World War II* (the larger scope of interpreting underlying "causes" of the war)
http://www.legionmagazine.com/features/canadianmilitaryhistory/95-09.asp

1250. Fischer, Benjamin B. *The Katyn Controversy: Stalin's Killing Field*
http://www.cia.gov/csi/studies/winter99-00/art6.html

1251. Gladun, Leon. *A Katyn and World War II Diary, 1939-1951* (diary of a Polish officer, including his service in Italy)
http://www.geocities.com/chrisgladun/katyndiary.html

1252. [Great Britain and Poland.] *Anglo-Polish Agreement of 25 August 1939*
http://www.geocities.com/Athens/Troy/1791/anglopol.html

1253. Guttman, Jon. *Poland's Circus Master* (interview with Poland's fighter ace, Stanislaw Skalski)
http://www.military.com/Content/MoreContent?file=PRcircusf

1254. Jewell, Larry W. (compiler). *Some Documents Relevant to Germany's Invasion of Poland and Response to Great Britain's Ultimatum* (English translation)
http://wiretap.area.com/Gopher/Gov/US-History/WWII/german.39

1255. Kasprzyk, Mieczyslaw. *The History of Poland* (includes a chapter on World War Two)
http://www.kasprzyk.demon.co.uk/www/HistoryPolska.html

1256. Klukowski, Zygmunt. *The Nazi Occupation of Poland* (account by a Polish doctor)
http://www.ibiscom.com/poland.htm

1257. Lord Halifax. *Lord Halifax (Foreign Minister) on British Commitment to War* (sound recording)
http://www.otr.com/neville.html

1258. Lukas, Richard C. *Poland's Forgotten Holocaust* (stresses the large number of Gentiles systematically exterminated along with Jews)
http://holocaustforgotten.com/

1259. Malcher, George C. *Blank Pages: Soviet Genocide against the Polish People* (from 1939 to 1945)
http://www.pyrford.com/pp51.html

1260. Meirtchak, Benjamin. *Jewish Military Casualties in the Polish Armies in World War II*
http://www.geocities.com/Paris/Rue/4017/meirtchak/meirtchak.htm

1261. [Multi-sources.] *Some Documents Relevant to the French Response to the German Invasion of Poland* (September 2-3, 1939; two statements by Premier and a conversation with the French ambassador to Germany)
http://www.ibiblio.org/hyperwar/ETO/Dip/French-39.html

1262. [Multi-sources.] *Some Documents Relevant to the German Invasion of Poland and Response to Great Britain's Ultimatum* (September 1-3, 1939; three statements by Hitler and the official German response to the British protest)
http://www.ibiblio.org/hyperwar/ETO/Dip/german-39.html

1263. Nikor Project. *Individual Responsibility* (of specific German leaders for the outbreak of WWII; from *Nazi Conspiracy & Aggression*, volume 11, chapter 16)
http://www.nizkor.org/hweb/imt/nca/nca-02/nca-02-16-index.html

1264. Parada, George. *Bron Pancerna* (Polish tanks and tankettes in war against Germany)
http://www.mmpro.org/YD/dad's%20story.htm

1265. PIBWL [= in English, Private Land Army Research Institute]. *Polish Armour* (includes both tanks and armored trains)
http://republika.pl/derela/index.htm

1266. Postowicz, Robert. *Polish Aviation History* (World War Two era)
http://avstop.com/History/AroundTheWorld/Poland/main.html

1267. Ratuszynski, Wilhelm. *315 Polish Fighter Squadron* (year by year chronology of activities, beginning with 1941; list of reported kills)
http://www.geocities.com/CapeCanaveral/Lab/9431/

1268. Slizewski, Grzegorz. *1 September 1939 over Warsaw—the First Air Battle of World War 2*
http://www.elknet.pl/acestory/1sept/1sept.htm

1269. Swigart, Soren. *Blitzrieg: The Fall of Poland*
http://worldatwar.net/article/poland39/index.html

1270. [Unidentified.] *Hitler's Plans for Eastern Europe* (Jews, Polish, and Slavs in general)
http://www.dac.neu.edu/holocaust/Hitlers_Plans.htm

1271. [Unidentified.] *[Horse] Cavalry of the Second Polish Republic*
http://miasto.interia.pl/poptest.html?srv=kawaleria2rp.w.interia.pl

1272. [Unidentified.] *Katyn Forest Massacre: Polish Death at Soviet Hands*
http://www.geocities.com/Athens/Troy/1791/

1273. [Unidentified.] *Polish Fighter Aces*
http://members.tripod.com/adm/popup/roadmap.shtml?member_name
=marcin_w&path=index-paces.html&client_ip=152.163.189.132&ts=
1007624451&ad_type=POPUP&id=70e93303f6227f93910f3edcabb7aa50

1274. [Unidentified.] *Polish Maps and Bookstores—Sources* (maps of Poland throughout the centuries available on-line)
http://www.rootsweb.com/~polwgw/maps.html

1275. [Unidentified.] *Polish Navy* (covers 1918–1946)
http://info.fuw.edu.pl/~janbart/AB/Pln/Pln.html

1276. [Unidentified.] *Renault FT Tank* (available in English or Polish)
http://geocities.com/witekjl/

1277. [Unidentified.] *The Dawn of the Tragedy* (eruption of the war)
http://www.geocities.com/iturks/html/worldwarii1.html

1278. [Unidentified.] *The Polish Navy, 1918-1945*
http://republika.pl/zweglarz

1279. [Unidentified.] *The Polish Soldier* (investigating Polish units fighting in the East and in Italy)
http://www.pcdeal.com/polish/index.html

1280. [Unidentified.] *Virtual Museum of Mechanical Vehicles* (available in Polish or English)
http://gpz.prv.pl/

1281. [Unidentified.] *Wartime Losses of Polish Art* (confiscated by Germans and Soviets)
http://www.polamcon.org/lostart/001b.htm

1282. [Unidentified.] *World War II—My Dad's Story* (he served with the 7th Polish Horse Artillery Regiment)
http://www.accessweb.com/users/rbereznicki/index.html-ssi

1283. [U.S. Government.] *Formulation and Execution of the Plan to Invade Poland* (extract from *Nazi Conspiracy and Aggression*, volume one)
http://www.nizkor.org/hweb/people/h/hitler-adolf/hitler-and-poland.html

1284. Wesolowski, Zdzislaw P. *Hero to Two Nations: Stefan P. Wesolowski* (served on Polish, French, and American warships)
http://www.memoriesofwar.com/veterans/wesolowski/default.asp

The Phony War

1285. Simon Wisenthal Center. *"The Phony War:" October 1939–April 1940*
http://www.worldwar2database.com/html/phonywar.htm

1286. [Unidentified.] *Sitzrieg: The Phony War* (comments on researching a documentary on the subject)
http://www.secretsofwar.com/html/sitzkrieg_the_phony_war.html

1287. [Unidentified.] *The Phony War*
http://www-lib.usc.edu/~anthonya/war/phony.htm

The German Victory in the West

DENMARK

1288. Laursen, Gert. *Military History of Denmark* (Danish language site)
http://www.milhist.dk/

1289. [Unidentified.] *Forbidden Danish Publications during the Nazi Occupation (1940-1945)* (Danish language web site)
http://www.kb.dk/kultur/expo/illegale/index.htm

NETHERLANDS, BELGIUM, AND LUXEMBOURG

1290. Govaerts, Wim. *Bomber Command Losses, 1941-1945, Avro Manchester and Avro Lancaster Crashes in Belgium*
http://gallery.uunet.be/wim.govaerts/index.html

1291. McLeod, John C. *The Belgium Airforce in World War Two*
http://mercury.beseen.com/quizlet/s/29875/niblet.html

1292. Peeters, Rogier. *Royal Dutch Army Order of Battle, May 10, 1940*
http://www.geocities.com/Pentagon/Barracks/1247/

1293. Peeters, Rogier. *Royal Netherlands Brigade Princess Irene and the Guards Regiment Fusiliers Princess Irene* (Dutch units fighting against Axis after their country surrendered)
http://home.wxs.nl/~sonne005/history-eng.htm

1294. Ragas, Ed. *Research Group Air War, 1939-1945* (with an emphasis on the Netherlands)
http://www.airwar-europe.yucom.be/AirwarStudygroup.html

1295. Regter, Almer. *Hugh Godefroy—Dutch Ace* (with the RAF)
http://www.elknet.pl/acestory/godef/godef.htm

1296. [Unidentified.] *Dutch Submarines*
http://www.warlinks.com/cgi-bin/links/jump.cgi?ID=130

1297. [Unidentified.] *Netherlands Institute for War Documentation* (only a little available yet on the internet itself)
http://www.oorlogsdoc.knaw.nl/engels/english.html

1298. [Unidentified.] *Royal Netherlands Navy Warships of World War II*
http://leden.tref.nl/~jviss000/Default.htm

1299. [Unidentified.] *The Hins' Homepage: Canadian Army, 1940-1945* (with emphasis on liberation of the Netherlands)
http://www.homepages.hetnet.nl/~pa3geg/Index2.html

1300. [Unidentified.] *The History of the Belgian Air Force during World War II*
http://mercury.beseen.com/quizlet/s/29875/niblet.html

1301. Vanderheyden, Kees. *Memories of a Dutch Schoolboy* (four short stories of life under occupation and during the liberation)
http://atschool.eduweb.co.uk/chatback/english/memories/~kees.html

1302. van Faassen, Dick. *Air Battle over Holland in May 1940* (role of the local air force in opposing the Germans)
http://members.tripod.lycos.nl/DeeJay/luvaeng.html

BATTLE OF FRANCE

1303. Carrey, Michael J. *France and the Origins of the Second World War* (book review)
http://www2.h-net.msu.edu/reviews/showrev.cgi?path=10472882816952

1304. Compen, Niels. *Blitzrieg in Europe*
http://worldwar2.spydar.com/

1305. Copp, Terry. *The Fall of France* (involvement of Canadian troops with the Allies)
http://www.legionmagazine.com/features/canadianmilitaryhistory/
95-10.asp

1306. Daladier, Edouard (Premier of France). *"Nazis Aim for Slavery"* (29 January 1940 radio address, English translation)
http://www.historyplace.com/speeches/daladier.htm

1307. Doody, Richard. *Brittany from the Great War to [Second World War] Liberation*
http://worldatwar.net/article/brittany/index.html

1308. Gill, Pete. *The Destruction of [British] 12th Division, 20th May 1940*
http://www.magweb.com/sample/ssotcw/sso2512.htm

1309. Kirkland, Faris R. *The French Air Force in 1940: Was It Defeated by the Luftwaffe or by Politics?*
http://www.airpower.maxwell.af.mil/
airchronicles/aureview/1985/sep-oct/kirkland.html

1310. Marks, Sally. *The French Defeat of 1940: Reassessments* (evaluation of this book; click on "message message ... thread" and that will take you do six additional evaluations of the book's views and arguments)
http://h-net.msu.edu/cgi-bin/logbrowse.pl?trx=vx&list
=h-diplo&month=0010&week=a&msg=dMdoiEad/txDYk9fxxcfqw&
user=&pw=

1311. McDonald, Alexi. *A Travesty of an Armoured Division* (1st [UK] Armoured, in France 1940)
http://www.geocities.com/area51/vault/3272/

1312. [Unidentified.] *Chars et blinds Francais* (models and photos of French armored vehicles)
http://www.info-micro.com/engins/index.htm

1313. [Unidentified.] *France 1940* (chronology of collapse)
http://history.sandiego.edu/gen/WW2Timeline/step08.html

1314. [Unidentified.] *France 1940* (expanding range with goal of 1945; French and English versions)
http://france1940.free.fr/

1315. [Unidentified.] *French Aces of World War Two* (five or more kills; French language site)
http://frenchaces.free.fr/

1316. [Unidentified.] *French Navy's Submarines in July 1939*
http://perso.wanadoo.fr/bertrand.daubigny/FSS39uk.htm

1317. [Unidentified.] *Maginot Line*
http://www.ifrance.com/letunnel/Maginot/history.html

1318. [Unidentified.] *Maginot Line*
http://www.geocities.com/maginot.geo/

DUNKIRK

1319. Quittenton, Richard G. *Evacuation: Diary of One Man's Experience*
http://website.lineone.net/~heathq/

1320. Riva, Francesco. *A Defeat Transformed in Victory*
http://www.geocities.com/iturks/html/an_unlucky_legend.html

1321. Sopel, Jon. *Dunkirk Spirits Gets Lost in Translation* (French reaction to the withdrawal)
http://news.bbc.co.uk/hi/english/world/europe/newsid_774000/774678.stm

1322. [Unidentified.] *Behind Dunkirk: Harry Thomas Munn, 1916–1997* (includes Mann's account of the rear-guard action his unit fought to make possible the successful withdrawal of forces from Dunkirk)
http://www.warlinks.com/cgi-bin/links/jump.cgi?ID=48

1323. [Unidentified.] *Dunkirk: The Propaganda War*
http://news.bbc.co.uk/hi/english/in_depth/uk/2000/dunkirk/newsid_774000/774417.stm

German Alliances and Triumphs in the East

BULGARIA

1324. Dimitrov, Bojidar. *Bulgaria during World War II*
http://www.bulgaria.com/history/bulgaria/war2.html

1325. Library of Congress. *Bulgaria: A Country Study* (several sections on the war)
http://memory.loc.gov/frd/cs/bgtoc.html

1326. Stoyanov, Mr. *Stoyan Stoyanov—the Bulgarian Top Ace*
http://www.elknet.pl/acestory/stojanov/stojanov.htm

HUNGARY

1327. Baross, G. *Hungary and Hitler* (select from "Hungarian History" list; 115 K)
http://www.hungary.com/corvinus/lib/hung2.htm

1328. Becze, Csaba. *Gyorgy Debrody—the Survivor* (survived combat with both Russian and western pilots)
http://www.elknet.pl/acestory/debrody/debrody.htm

1329. Chaszar, E. *The Czechoslovak-Hungarian Border Dispute of 1938* (listed under "Czeho-Slovakian-Hungarian Affairs;" 153 K)
http://www.hungary.com/corvinus/lib/cze.htm

1330. Horthy, Miklos (Admiral). *The annotated Memoirs* (select from "Hungarian History" list; 1.10 M)
http://www.hungary.com/corvinus/lib/hung2.htm

1331. Kapronczay, Karoly. *Refugees in Hungary: Shelter from Storm during World War II* (select from under "Autonomy and minorities;" downloadable, 546 K)
http://www.hungary.com/corvinus/lib/auto.htm

1332. Long, Jason. *The Hungarian 2 Army in Russia: Structure and Equipment, Summer 1942*
http://members.tripod.com/~Sturmvogel/Hung2Army.html

1333. Long, Jason. *The Hungarians in Barbarossa*
http://www.geocities.com/CapeCanaveral/2072/hung_tw.html

1334. Major, Mark J. *American-Hungarian Relations, 1918-1944* (select

from short list of materials discussing "USA and Hungary;" downloadable, 220 K)
http://www.hungary.com/corvinus/lib/usa.htm

1335. Romsics, Ignac. *Wartime American Plans for a New Hungary* (on
short list of materials discussing "USA and Hungary;" downloadable, 238
K)
http://www.hungary.com/corvinus/lib/usa.htm

1336. Veress, Laura-Louis. *Clear the Line—Hungary's Struggle to Leave the
Axis during the Second World War* (last item on a list of varied historical
studies; uses Adobe Acrobat; also downloadable, 716 K)
http://www.hungary.com/corvinus/lib/twenty.htm

ROMANIA

1337. Kelley, Greg, with Jason Long. *Romanian Armour in World War Two*
http://members.tripod.com/~Sturmvogel/romafv.html

1338. Nitu, V. *Operation "Tidal Wave"* (Romanian effort to impede western bombings of Polesti)
http://www.elknet.pl/acestory/tidalwave/tidalwave.htm

1339. Nitu, V. *The First Day of War of the APR* (the Romanian air force
role in the assault on the Soviet Union)
http://www.elknet.pl/acestory/firstdayarr/firstdayarr.htm

1340. Nitu, Victor, and George Florea. *Romanian Army in World War II*
(includes documents translated from Romanian)
http://www.wwii.home.ro/men.htm

1341. Patrick, Bethanne K. *Col. Leon William Johnson* (his role in the
Romanian oilfield strikes)
http://www.military.com/Content/MoreContent?file=ML_ljohnson_bkp

1342. Pusia, Dragon. *The Dutch Helmet—Romanian Army in World War
II*
http://www.armata.home.ro/

1343. [Unidentified.] *Black Sunday* (major bomber raid on Ploesti on
August 1, 1943, with resulting huge Allied losses)
http://members.aol.com/BlndBat/Ploesti.html

SLOVAKIA

1344. Long, Jason. *Disposition of Czech AFVs [Armoured Fighting Vehicles]*

(includes those produced after creation of Slovakia and sent by Germany to her allies)
http://members.tripod.com/~Sturmvogel/CzechAFV.html#CzechExports

1345. Long, Jason. *Slovak Use of AFVs [Armoured Fighting Vehicles]*
http://members.tripod.com/~Sturmvogel/SlovakAFVs.html

Northwestern Europe

NORWAY

1346. Hubel, Andreas. *World War II in our Family* (narrative of her grandfather's service in the German Army in Norway)
http://atschool.eduweb.co.uk/chatback/english/memories/~andreas.html

1347. Lee, Eric. *Stalin's Secrets Wars in Norway* (the Communist's Party's collaboration with the Nazi take-over)
http://www.geocities.com/CapitolHill/2808/norway.html

1348. Monsen, Kurt. *Norway in World War Two* (site available in English or Norwegian)
http://www.nuav.net/

1349. Pelizza, Simone. *The Invasion of Norway* (also treats Britain's invasion plans)
http://www.geocities.com/iturks/html/world_war_ii_4.html

1350. Ratuszynski, Wilhelm, and Dariusz Tyminski. *Michal Cwynar: In Battle over Norway Fiords* (Cwynar was a Polish pilot)
http://www.elknet.pl/acestory/cwynar/cwynar.htm

FINLAND

1351. Finnish Defense Forces. *The Winter War, 1939-1940*
http://www.mil.fi/tiedotus/talvisota_eng/index.html

1352. Hyry, Matti. *An Interview of Matti Hyruy* (concerning the war with Russia; at top of screen click on "H-L;" pick this person's name from list on left screen; text appears to right)
http://www.warlinks.com/memories/index.html

1353. Jarvinen, Jyri-Pekka. *Allied Planes in Finish Air Force in World War II*
http://hkkk.fi/~yrjola/war/faf/allied.html

1354. Juntunen, Ossi. *Adventure of DN-52 "Oaku"—Bombed [by Its Own Airforce] in Mid-Air*
http://www.elknet.pl/acestory/osku/osku.htm

1355. Juntunen, Ossi. *"Illu" Juutilanen—the Top [Finish] Ace*
http://www.elknet.pl/acestory/juuti/juuti1.htm

1356. Korhonen, Sami. *The Battles of the Winter War*
http://www.winterwar.com/

1357. Kruhuse, Pauli. *A Selection of Events and Documents on the History of Finland* (links to document texts from early 1800s through World War II)
http://www.pp.clinet.fi/~pkr01/historia/history.html

1358. Kuoppamaki, Pasi. *Three Finish Wars of World War II, 1939-1945*
http://ky.hkkk.fi/~k21206/finhist.html#war

1359. Perttula, Pentti. *Finish Air Force Aircraft in World War II*
http://www.sci.fi/~ambush/faf/faf.html

1360. Ries, Thomas. *Lessons from the Winter War*
http://virtual.finland.fi/finfo/english/war1.html

1361. [Unidentified.] *Air Raids on Helsinki in February 1944*
http://personal.inet.fi/koti/pauli.kruhse/lauttasaari/airraid.htm

1362. [Unidentified.] *Battle of the Raattee Road* (prominent Finnish victory)
http://www.lukio.palkane.fi/raate/raate.html

1363. [Unidentified.] *Finnish Air Force "Aces"*
http://hkkk.fi/~yrjola/war/faf/ww2aces.htmlJanuary 1, 1990

1364. [Unidentified.] *Pictures from Wars during Finland's Independence* (stress on the 1939-45 series of conflicts)
http://koti.mbnet.fi/~avalpas/

1365. [Unidentified.] *Stalin's Plan to Bisect Finland*
http://www.publiscan.fi/sc20e-0.htm

1366. Valdre, Andres. *Soviet Air Raids on Helsinki in February 1944*
http://www.hut.fi/~andres/m44/m44hki.htm

1367. Vihavainen, Timo. *Before the War: Finland, Stalin and Germany in the 1930s*
http://www.finland.org/before.html

Southeastern Europe

ALBANIA

1368. Library of Congress. *Albania: A Country Study* (several chapters deal with the World War II era)
http://memory.loc.gov/frd/cs/altoc.html

1369. [Unidentified.] *Albania and the Second World War*
http://www.spartacus.schoolnet.co.uk/2WWalbania.htm

1370. [Unidentified.] *History: World War II*
http://www.albanian.com/main/history/worldwarii.html

CRETE

1371. Denniston, Peter. *Operation Merker: Invasion of Crete*
http://www.geocities.com/CapeCanaveral/Hangar/4602/kreta.htm

1372. Edwards, Geoff. *Geoff Edwards Story* (also has an extract on a successful escape from the island)
http://www.explorecrete.com/preveli/story.html

1373. Myles, Gerry. *H.M.S. Fiji Association* (cruiser sunk during the Battle of Crete; includes a survivor's account)
http://hmsfiji.onweb.cx/

1374. Tsouderos, Emmanuel. *Message to the Greeks Broadcast by Greek Premier, Emmanuel Tsouderos* (upon the fall of Crete)
http://www.ibiblio.org/pha/policy/1941/410605a.html

1375. [Unidentified.] *Battle of Crete* (predominantly Greek language site)
http://www.cyberpoint.gr/battleofcrete/

1376. [Unidentified.] *Escape by Submarine from Preveli*
http://www.explorecrete.com/preveli/submarine.html

1377. [Unidentified.] *The Battle of Crete*
http://www.explorecrete.com/preveli/battle-of-crete.html

1378. Walker, C. *A Sailor's Story—The Battle of Crete* (at top of screen click on "R-Z;" pick "Seaman Walker" from list on left screen; text appears to right)
http://www.warlinks.com/memories/tenny/index.html

GREECE

1379. Hitler, Adolph. *Adolf Hitler's Order of the Day Calling for Invasion of Yugoslavia and Greece (Berlin, April 6, 1941)* (explaining and justifying the decision)
http://www.sunsite.unc.edu/pha/policy/1941/410406a.html

1380. Jebeyan, Rouben. *History of the Hellenic Navy in 19th-20th Centuries: Online Encyclopedia*
http://www.geocities.com/grbattlesships/index.html

1381. Roosevelt, Franklin D. *President Franklin D. Roosevelt's Statement on the War in Greece (April 25, 1941)*
http://www.ibiblio.org/pha/policy/1941/410425a.html

1382. Taylor, Barry M. *Civil War of Passion* (war-time guerrilla factions and the problems they caused when liberation occurred)
http://www.military.com/Content/MoreContent?file=PRpassion

1383. [Unidentified.] *History of the Greek Navy during the Second World War*
http://www.warlinks.com/cgi-bin/links/jump.cgi?ID=142

1384. Watkins, [Chief Signal Yeoman]. *HMAS Stuart: Battle of Matapan* (combat with the Italian Navy; click on this title way down left hand list; text appears on right hand side)
http://www.gunplot.net/

YUGOSLAVIA

1385. Blau, George E. *The German Campaigns in the Balkans, Spring 1941* (Department of the Army, 1953; first issued as a "restricted" use document)
http://www.ibiblio.org/hyperwar/ETO/East/Balkans/Campaigns/index.html

1386. Kennedy, Robert M. *German Anti-Guerrilla Operations in the Balkans (1941-1944)* (CMH Publication 104-18)
http://www.ibiblio.org/hyperwar/ETO/East/Balkans/Campaigns/index.html
http://www.army.mil/cmh-pg/books/wwii/antiguer-ops/AG-BALKAN.HTM

1387. Knez, Saso. *Dogfights over Belgrade [during the German Invasion]— the First Day*
http://www.elknet.pl/acestory/belgra/belgra.htm

1388. Knez, Saso. *Dogfights over Belgrade [during the German Invasion]— the Second Day*
http://www.elknet.pl/acestory/belgra/belgra1.htm

1389. Knez, Saso. *Dogfights over Belgrade [during the German invasion]—the Last Free Days*
http://www.elknet.pl/acestory/belgra/belgra2.htm

1390. Mreza, Srpska. *Yugoslavia during World War II* (a vigorous pro-Serb/anti-Croat reading)
http://www.srpska-mreza.com/library/facts/ww2.html

1391. Rossos, Andrew. *The British Foreign Office and Macedonian National Identity, 1918-1941*
http://www.gate.net/~mango/Rossos_British_FO.htm

1392. Springer, Zvonko. *Memories of a Croatian Soldier*
http://atschool.eduweb.co.uk/chatback/english/memories/~zvonko.html

1393. [Unidentified.] *Invasion of Yugoslavia, 1941: Report by a German General (1947)*
http://carlisle-www.army.mil/cgi-bin/usamhi/DL/showdoc.pl?docnum=396

1394. [Unidentified.] *Partisan Warfare in the Balkans, 1944—Report by a German General, 1953*
http://carlisle-www.army.mil/cgi-bin/usamhi/DL/showdoc.pl?docnum=397

1395. [Unidentified.] *World War 2 in Yugoslavia* (designed specially for "gamers" recreating scenarios of what could have happened)
http://www.inet.hr/steelpanthers/ww2/index.htm

1396. [Unidentified,] Klemen. *Slovenian Axis Forces, 1941-1945*
http://www.geocities.com/Pentagon/Quarters/5814/

1397. U.S. Department of the Army. *Yugoslavia in World War II (1941-1945)* (a chapter of the *Army Area Handbook* on Yugoslavia)
gopher://gopher.umsl.edu/00/library/govdocs/armyahbs/aahb2/aahb0148

1398. [U.S.S.R. and Yugoslavia.] *Treaty between U.S.S.R. and Yugoslavia (April 11, 1945)*
http://www.sunsite.unc.edu/pha/policy/1945/450411a.html

Vichy France

1399. Bell, Kelly. *Death of a Double Dealer* (assassination of Admiral Darlan in North Africa)
http://www.military.com/Content/MoreContent?file=PRdarlan

1400. Darlan, Jean Francois [Vice Premier]. *Broadcast to the French People (Vichy, France, May 23, 1941)*
http://www.ibiblio.org/pha/policy/1941/410523a.html

1401. Darlan, Jean Francois [Vice Premier]. *Speech to the French People (Vichy, France, June 10, 1941)*
http://www.sunsite.unc.edu/pha/policy/1941/410610a.html

1402. Doody, Richard. *French Empire Timeline, 1940-1945: The Second World War in the French Overseas Empire*
http://worldatwar.net/timeline/france/empire40-45.html

1403. Doody, Richard. *"Over for Christmas"—The Liberation of St. Pierre and Miquelon* (the Free French seizure and the Vichy French opposition)
http://worldatwar.net/article/miquelon/index.html

1404. Hitler, Adolph. *Chancellor Adolf Hitler's Appeal to the French on the Entry of German Troops into Unoccupied France (November 10, 1942)*
http://www.sunsite.unc.edu/pha/policy/1942/421110c.html

1405. Hitler, Adolph. *Chancellor Adolf Hitler's Letter to Marshal Petain Announcing Complete German Occupation of France (November 11, 1942)*
http://www.sunsite.unc.edu/pha/policy/1942/421111a.html

1406. Hitler, Adolph. *Chancellor Adolf Hitler's Letter to Marshal Petain Announcing Decision to Occupy Toulon (November 27, 1942)*
http://www.sunsite.unc.edu/pha/policy/1942/421127a.html

1407. Hull, Cordell. *Memorandum by the Secretary of State Regarding a Conversation with the French Ambassador [Henry-Haye] (4 November 1940)*
http://www.mtholyoke.edu/acad/intrel/WorldWar2/hull20.htm

1408. Hull, Cordell. *Refugee Problem in France: A Note Sent by Secretary of State Cordell Hull to Gaston Henry-Haye, French Ambassador (January 9, 1941)*
http://www.sunsite.unc.edu/pha/policy/1941/410109a.html

1409. Hull, Cordell. *Secretary of State Cordell Hull's Statement on Franco-German Collaboration (June 13, 1941)*
http://www.ibiblio.org/pha/policy/1941/410613a.html

1410. Labayle, Eric. *Cherchell-Mediouna French Cadet Officers Academy (1942-1945)* (site available in French and English)
http://perso.club-internet.fr/scandel/

1411. Petain, Henri [Marshal]. *Address to the French People (Vichy, France, August 12, 1941)*
http://www.ibiblio.org/pha/policy/1941/410812a.html

1412. Petain, Henri [Marshal]. *Reply to President Roosevelt's Note of November 8, 1942*
http://www.sunsite.unc.edu/pha/policy/1942/421108d.html

1413. Petain, Henri [Marshal]. *Speech to the French People* (Vichy, France, May 15, 1941)
http://www.ibiblio.org/pha/policy/1941/410515b.html

1414. Ribbentrop (Ministry of Foreign Affairs). *Authority of Nazi Ambassador to Vichy France* (August 3, 1940)
http://www.ibiblio.org/pha/policy/1940/400803a.html

1415. Roosevelt, Franklin D. *Message to Marshal Henri Petain (November 8, 1942)*
http://www.sunsite.unc.edu/pha/policy/1942/421108c.html

1416. Roosevelt, Franklin D. *Statement on the United States Policy toward the French Republic (May 15, 1941)*
http://www.ibiblio.org/pha/policy/1941/410515a.html

1417. Roosevelt, Franklin D. *Statement upon Termination of Diplomatic Relations with the Vichy Government (November 9, 1942)*
http://www.sunsite.unc.edu/pha/policy/1942/421109c.html

1418. Ryan, Donna F. *Politics, Society and Church in Vichy France* (extended book review)
http://www.amgot.org/hall.htm

1419. [Unidentified.] *July 10: Vichy Government Formed*
http://www.yad-vashem.org.il/about_holocaust/chronology/
1939-1941/1940/chronology_1940_12.html

1420. [Unidentified.] *Not the Germans Alone* (links to additional sources showing French co-operation in vigorous anti-Jewish policies)
http://home.sprynet.com/~levendel/index.html

1421. [Unidentified.] *Occupied France* (much of the article is actually concerned with the collaboration of Vichy with the Germans)
http://www.sunderland.ac.uk/~os0tmc/occupied/collab.htm

1422. [Unidentified.] *U.S. and French Diplomatic Relations*
http://www.acusd.edu/~mphelps/

1423. [U.S. Acting Secretary of State.] *United States Policy toward France and the French People* (diplomatic note to the French Ambassador, dated April 13, 1942)
http://www.sunsite.unc.edu/pha/policy/1942/420413a.html
http://www.ibiblio.org/pha/policy/1942/420413a.html

1424. [U.S. State Department.] *The Charge in France [Matthews] to the Secretary of State on Petain's View of the French Fleet (1 November 1940)*
http://www.mtholyoke.edu/acad/intrel/WorldWar2/petain.htm

1425. Welles, Sumner. *Relations with the French Government at Vichy* (statement read to the press on February 27, 1942)
http://www.sunsite.unc.edu/pha/policy/1942/420227a.html

Non-Belligerents

Eire (Ireland)

1426. Burke, Dennis. *The War Room, Ireland*
http://www.generals.dk/

1427. de Valera, Eamon. *Speech on Eire Neutrality, Cork, Ireland (December 12, 1941)*
http://www.sunsite.unc.edu/pha/policy/1941/411212a.html

1428. [Unidentified.] *Ireland in World War Two*
http://www.csn.ul.ie/~dan/war/eire.htm

1429. [Unidentified.] *Ireland's Involvement in the Second World War*
http://www.csn.ul.ie/~dan/war/involvement.htm

Iceland

1430. Churchill, Winston. *Prime Minister, Winston Churchill in House of Commons on U.S. Troops in Iceland (July 9, 1941)*
http://www.ibiblio.org/pha/policy/1941/410709a.html

1431. Donovan, James A. *Outpost in the North Atlantic: Marines in the Defense of Iceland* (1991; in the "Marines in World War II Commemorative Series")
http://www.ibiblio.org/hyperwar/USMC/USMC-C-Iceland.html

1432. Iceland National web site. *Iceland in World War II* (on American seizure and control)
http://www.hugvit.is/interpro/islandia/islandia.nsf/0000/ef7383834183146d00256603005aa493?OpenDocument

1433. Roosevelt, Franklin D. *Franklin D. Roosevelt's Message to Congress on U.S. Occupation of Iceland (July 7, 1941)* (actually an exchange between Roosevelt and the Prime Minister of Iceland)
http://www.sunsite.unc.edu/pha/policy/1941/410707a.html

1434. Roosevelt, Franklin D. *Message of President Roosevelt to the Congress on [the Occupation of] Iceland (July 7, 1941)*
http://www.mtholyoke.edu/acad/intrel/WorldWar2/iceland.htm

PORTUGAL

1435. Contemporary Portuguese Politics & History Research Centre. *New State, 1933-1974* (includes a dozen English translations, including the Constitution and other materials from the 1930s)
http://www.cphrc.org.uk/sources/so-ns/so-ns-p1.htm

1436. [Unidentified.] *Portugal and the Second World War*
http://www.spartacus.schoolnet.co.uk/2WWportugal.htm

SPAIN

1437. Flores, Santiago. *Angel Salas Larrazabal—A Fighter Ace in Two Wars* (only Spaniard to be ranked an "ace" in the Spanish Civil War and in service with the Spanish air wing fighting the Russians on the Eastern Front)
http://www.elknet.pl/acestory/larrazabal/larrazabal.htm

1438. Franco, Francisco. *Speech to Falangist Party Council Praising German, Italian, and Spanish Fascism (December 8, 1942)*
http://www.sunsite.unc.edu/pha/policy/1942/421208a.html

1439. Roosevelt, Franklin D. *President Franklin D. Roosevelt's Message to General Francisco Franco Bahamonde, Head of the Spanish State (November 8, 1942)* (concerning U.S. intent to intervene in French North Africa to forestall a German intervention)
http://www.sunsite.unc.edu/pha/policy/1942/421108e.html

1440. [Spanish and German Governments]. *The Spanish Government and the Axis* (a collection of contemporary documents)
http://www.yale.edu/lawweb/avalon/wwii/spain/spmenu.htm

1441. [Unidentified.] *Spanish Civil War* (how the fascists came to power in the 1930s)
http://history.sandiego.edu/gen/WW2Timeline/step04.html

1442. [Unidentified.] *Spanish Volunteers in the Third Reich* (Spanish language site)
http://www.geocities.com/visantain/

1443. [Unidentified.] *The Battle of the Thompson Gun: Resistance to Franco, 1939-1952*
http://www.geocities.com/CapitolHill/Senate/5602/scwar6.html

SWEDEN

1444. Floriante, Jari. *Opportunity and Constraint in the Game for Public Goods: The Political Economy of Military Spending in Finland and Sweden, 1920-1938* (in Adobe Acrobat)
http://www.cc.jyu.fi/~pete/SWEFINCOMPARISON.pdf

1445. Svensson, John. *Sweden in the Second World War, 1939-1945* (in Swedish)
http://home.swipnet.se/Sverige_under_kriget/

SWITZERLAND

1446. Cassidy, Charles. *Charles Cassidy: 303rd Bombardment Group (Hells Angels), 360th Bombardment Squadron* (his damaged plane landed in Switzerland and the crew was interned)
http://www.west.net/~macpuzl/internee.html

1447. Federal Department of Foreign Affairs (Switzerland). *Documentation on Switzerland during World War Two* (with emphasis on degree of liability for assets seized by Nazis)
http://www.switzerland.taskforce.ch/start/script.htm

1448. Rathje, Ed. *The Story of "Baby:" A B-17 and Her Crew [Interned] in Switzerland*
http://www.jmi.com/WWII/

Battle of Britain and Operation Sea Lion

BATTLE OF BRITAIN

1449. Ainsbury, Frank. *The Catastrophe of Coventry* (an eyewitness; at top of screen click on "A-G;" pick this person's name from list on left screen; text appears to right)
http://www.warlinks.com/memories/index.html

1450. American War Library. *Tonnage Lost during the Battle of Britain*
http://members.aol.com/forcountry/ww2/tlb.htm

1451. Auckland, Margaret. *A "Doodlebug" Hits a School* (a youngster recalls what it was like to be in a bombed school)
http://atschool.eduweb.co.uk/chatback/english/memories/~margare.html

1452. Battle of Britain Press. *Battle of Britain Press* (narratives from pilots, nurses, and civilians)
http://www.acseac.co.uk/

1453. Beard, John. *Air Battle over London, 1940* (Beard was a RAF Hurricane pilot)
http://www.ibiscom.com/airbattle.htm

1454. Bogomolny, Eric. *Douglas Bader*
http://www.elknet.pl/acestory/bader/bader.htm

1455. Brockington, Kath. *Bombed in the London Blitz*
http://atschool.eduweb.co.uk/chatback/english/memories/blitz.html

1456. Bryant, Melrose M. *Battle of Britain, Summer 1940* (a bibliography)
http://www.au.af.mil/au/aul/bibs/britain/brit.htm

1457. Burgess, Kris. *Their Finest Hour* (includes bibliography)
http://www.geocities.com/Athens/Forum/8723/index1.html

1458. Callewaert, Jan. *Aircraft in the Battle of Britain* (study of the various types of planes)
http://www.geocities.com/CapeCanaveral/Runway/8420/mainpage.html

1459. Churchill, Winston. *Churchill Anticipates Battle of Britain* (speech to House of Commons, June 18, 1940; audio)
http://www.rjgeib.com/thoughts/britain/britain.html

1460. Copp, Terry. *Standing Up to the Blitz*
http://www.legionmagazine.com/features/canadianmilitaryhistory/96-01.asp

1461. Copp, Terry. *The Battle over Britain*
http://www.legionmagazine.com/features/canadianmilitaryhistory/95-11.asp

1462. Harrison, Nigel, and Andy Jackson. *Battle of Britain: Compendium of Information* (poetry, stories, etc.)
http://www.battle-of-britain.com/

1463. Matusek, David. *Battle of Britain* (photographs, information on pilots, etc.)
http://www.geocities.com/Pentagon/4143/

1464. Merritt, C. C. I. *South of England—August 1940* (a Canadian officer's description of an aerial battle he observed)
http://cap.estevan.sk.ca/ssr/documents/south.html

1465. Methes, Paul. *Remembering the Battle of Britain* (Methes flew for the Luftwaffe Air-Sea Rescue Service)
http://www.battleofbritainpress.co.uk/memories/List/0004.html

1466. Olejnik, Robert. *Remembering the Battle of Britain* (Olejnik was a Luftwaffe pilot)
http://www.battleofbritainpress.co.uk/memories/List/0003.html

1467. Putland, Alan L. *Royal Air Force Fighter Command, Battle of Britain —1940* (chronology, information on airfields and other aspects of the conflict)
http://www.battleofbritain.net/contents.html

1468. Pyle, Ernie. *The London Blitz, 1940* (one's night's bombing as recorded by one of the most respected correspondents of the war)
http://www.ibiscom.com/airbattle.htm

1469. Richardson, John. *Pom Pom Guns and Scarlet Corpses* (what it was like for a young boy to be in the hospital in Coventry while it was being bombed)
http://atschool.eduweb.co.uk/chatback/english/memories/~johnr.html

1470. Richardson, Mary. *An Air Raid Warden in Coventry*
http://atschool.eduweb.co.uk/chatback/english/memories/~maryr1.html

1471. [Unidentified.] *Battle of Britain* (sound recordings of daily events as well as print material on various aspects of the battle)
http://www.raf.mod.uk/bob1940/bobhome.html

1472. [Unidentified.] *Battle of Britain*
http://www.geocities.com/Broadway/Alley/5443/bofb1.htm

1473. [Unidentified.] *Battle of Britain—1940*
http://www.geocities.com/athens/7607/

1474. [Unidentified.] *Battle of Britain—1940* (and events in other areas occurring in the same time frame)
http://history.sandiego.edu/gen/WW2Timeline/step09.html

1475. [Unidentified.] *Pilots' Perspectives* (brief German and English pilots' descriptions of various parts of the battle)
http://www.geocities.com/Athens/Forum/8723/Intro.html

1476. [Unidentified.] *The Battle of Britain Press* (profiles of participants and accounts of what they did)
http://www.battleofbritainpress.co.uk/home/home.html

1477. [Unidentified.] *Westall's War: Air Raid Disaster, North Shields: May 3rd, 1941* (one bomb hits an air raid shelter and kills 103 people)
http://www.westallswar.org.uk/

1478. Whitehead, Christopher. *The Spitfire—An Operational History* (year by year links)
http://www.deltaweb.co.uk/spitfire/into_svc.htm

OPERATION SEA LION

1479. Brooks, Alison, and David Flin. *Why Sealion Is Not an Option for Hitler to Win the War* (detailed critique that Sealion was fatally flawed and could not have been successfully carried out)
http://www.flin.demon.co.uk/althist/seal1.htm

1480. Montgomerie, Ian. *Why Operation Sealion Wouldn't Work*
http://gateway.alternatehistory.com/essays/Sealion.html

LAND DEFENSES

1481. Ashwood, David T. *Codeword Cromwell: English Invasion Defences*
http://www.geocities.com/thedashman_99/frontpage.html

1482. Barnes, Russell W. *20th Century Defence Architecture in Cumbria*
http://www.users.globalnet.co.uk/~rwbarnes

1483. Bray, John. *Fortress UK* (from Tudor to modern era)
http://www.aberdeenshire.gov.uk/archaeology/
defencescotland/defenceofscotland.pdf

1484. Carter, Timothy. *Pillboxes* (types, design, etc.)
http://www.geocities.com/pentagon/camp/3224/

1485. Lewis, Rebecca. *British Home Front Propaganda Posters*
http://www.wkac.ac.uk/hss/rlewi/docs/web/WW2Index.htm

1486. Matthews, Graham, and John Hellis. *Architecture of Aggression: Westcounty Wartime Defence Structures*
http://www.architecture-of-aggression.com/

1487. [Unidentified.] *Auxunit News: Record of the Auxiliary Units, 1940–1944* (home guard units designed to go underground if Germans invaded and to function as resistance centers)
http://www.auxunit.org.uk/

1488. [Unidentified.] *Defence of Britain Project*
http://www.britarch.ac.uk/projects/dob/index.html

1489. [Unidentified.] *English Invasion Defenses*
http://www.geocities.com/thedashman_99/frontpage.html

1490. [Unidentified.] *White Cliffs Underground* (Dover region)
http://www.castlekas.freeserve.co.uk/

Battle of the Atlantic and Atlantic Submarine Warfare

1491. American War Library. *Numbers of Axis Submarines Destroyed* (by
nationality)
http://members.aol.com/forcountry/ww2/sub.htm

1492. Asmussen, John. *Bismarck & Tirpitz*
http://www.bismarck-class.dk/

1493. Asmussen, John. *Schornhorst & Gneisenau* (details on the two battleships)
http://www.scharnhorst-class.dk/

1494. Bell, Sheridan. *Sinking of U-233* (July 5, 1944; Bell was Chaplain
on board one of the attacking vessels)
http://www.history.navy.mil/faqs/faq87-3o.htm

1495. Bradshaw, Harold G. *Sinking of U-172* (Bradshaw flew an "Avenger"
torpedo-bomber on the *USS Bogue*)
http://www.history.navy.mil/faqs/faq87-3k.htm

1496. Copp, Terry. *[Canadian] Achievement on the Atlantic*
http://www.legionmagazine.com/features/canadianmilitaryhistory/96-
02.asp

1497. DeNardo, Frank P. *Capture of the U-505: A First Person Account*
http://u505.dnsdata.com/

1498. Eisner, Adam. *War Stories: The Life and Experiences of Arnold Spring*
(a major emphasis is his anti-sub patrolling)
http://www.geocities.com/Pentagon/Camp/2501/story.html

1499. Gilbey, Joseph. *Langsdorff of the "Graf Spee"*
http://www.grafspee.com/

1500. Izzi, Basil D. *Recollections* (an Armed Guard on board a Dutch mer-
chantman, the vessel was torpedoed in November 1942 and Izzi survived 83 days adrift)
http://www.history.navy.mil/faqs/faq87-3j.htm

1501. Knox, Dudley S. *Sinking of U-515 and U-68* (April 1944; Dudley was serving on the *USS Chatelain* at the time)
http://www.history.navy.mil/faqs/faq87-3n.htm

1502. Mason, Jerry. *U-Boat Archive*
http://uboatarchive.net/

1503. Mifflin, Fred J. *Battle of the Atlantic*
http://www.vac-acc.gc.ca/general/sub.cfm?source=history/secondwar/atlantic

1504. Naval Historical Center. *Capture of U-505 on 4 June 1944* (first ship captured at sea in combat by the U.S. Navy since 1800s)
http://www.history.navy.mil/faqs/faq91-1.htm

1505. Naval Historical Center. *Q-Ships (Anti-Submarine Vessels Disguised as Merchant Vessels)*
http://www.history.navy.mil/docs/wwii/Q-ships.htm

1506. Naval Historical Center. *U-571, World War II German Submarine* (discusses various subs boarded by U.S. or Britain during the war)
http://www.history.navy.mil/faqs/faq97-1.htm

1507. Naval Historical Center. *U-1105* (advanced German submarine design introduced in 1944)
http://www.history.navy.mil/branches/org12-5.htm

1508. Patrick, Bethanne K. *Lt. j.g. Albert L. David* (led the boarding party seizing the U-505)
http://www.military.com/Content/MoreContent?file=ML_david_bkp

1509. Purnell, [? .] *Canonesa, Convoy HX72 & U-100* (September 1940 convoy attack)
http://www.canonesa.co.uk/

1510. Rico, Jose M. *Battleship Schornhorst* (history of vessel; drawings)
http://idd007xs.eresmas.net/scharnhorst.html

1511. Reedy, Jr., James R. *Coast Guard Sinking of U-352*
http://www.military.com/Content/MoreContent?file=PRicarus

1512. Russell, Jerry C. *Ultra and the Campaign against the U-Boats in World War II* (Studies in Cryptology, NSA, Document SRH-142)
http://metalab.unc.edu/pha/ultra/navy-1.html

1513. Sarty, Roger. *The Royal Canadian Navy and the Battle of the Atlantic*
http://www.warmuseum.ca/cwm/disp/dis007_e.html

1514. Smith, Larry. *War on Their Minds* (interview; stationed in Newfoundland during the war with the Army Air Force)
http://www.whshistoryproject.org/ww2/Interviews/mr_rockett.html

1515. Tucker, Richard A. *The S Boats: Gallant Ladies of the Past* (a few of these pre-WW2 submarines saw service during that war as well)
http://thesaltysailor.com/s-boats/

1516. [Unidentified.] *Battle of the Atlantic* (by phases and with key dates)
http://history.acusd.edu/gen/WW2Timeline/atlantic.html

1517. [Unidentified.] *Bismarck Legend Lives*
http://www.geocities.com/pentagon/barracks/5684/

1518. [Unidentified.] *Canonesa: Convoy HX72 and U-100*
http://home.onet.co.uk/~canonesa/

1519. [Unidentified.] *H.M.S. Hood*
http://www.voodoo.cz/hood/

1520. [Unidentified.] *Tenth Fleet* (as a fleet it actually never existed, but was a group of 50 men who coordinated the submarine hunting efforts of all existing available naval resources)
http://uboat.net/allies/ships/us_10thfleet.htm

1521. [Unidentified.] *The Commander Interviews* (audio interviews with four U-boat commanders)
http://uboat.net/men/interviews/index.html

1522. [Unidentified.] *The U Web: The U Boat War, 1939-1945* (articles on boats, personnel, etc.)
http://uboat.net/

1523. United States Air Force Museum. *Antisubmarine Warfare*
http://www.wpafb.af.mil/museum/history/wwii/asw.htm

1524. Vanzo, John P. *Saga of U-505* (captured at sea by U.S. Navy; story told from standpoint of Hans Goebeler of its crew)
http://www.military.com/Content/MoreContent?file=PRu505

1525. von Hartmut, Gunther. *Marine Homepage* (German language site on German submarines)
http://www.warlinks.com/cgi-bin/links/jump.cgi?ID=450

Allied Bombing Campaigns Against Occupied Europe

1526. Anderson, P. *A Raid on Munich* (his father's account of an RAF raid on Munich and his imprisonment as a POW after his plane was shot down)
http://www.camomilesworld.com/raid/

1527. Baxter, Bob. *Bomber Command* (goal: to document all operations from 1939 to 1945)
http://www.bomber-command.info/

1528. Belli, Tony. *B-17 Missions of Tony Belli* (B-17 pilot at a time he did not yet have a driver's license!)
(part 1:) http://www.ratol.fi/~tmannine/b-17/b-17_stories_belli.htm
(part 2:) http://www.ratol.fi/~tmannine/b-17/b-17_stories_belli2.htm

1529. Blair, Dale V. *We're Going to Ditch* (ditching in the North Sea after an April 1944 raid on outskirts of Berlin)
http://www.geocities.com/b24gunr2000/Ditching1.html

1530. Buckingham, David. *The Effect of the North American P-51 Mustang on the Air War in Europe*
http://cpcug.org/user/billb/mustang.html

1531. Cadden, John. *Interview* (radio operator; crash landed in England after the September 1944 raid on Kassel, Germany)
http://www.tankbooks.com/intviews/cadden/cadden1.htm

1532. Copp, Terry. *The Bomber Command Offensive*
http://www.legionmagazine.com/features/canadianmilitaryhistory/96-09.asp

1533. Correia, Louis. *Our Greatest Fear (Story of October 26, 1944)* (Correia, a tail gunner, was one of the two survivors of this mid-air collision)
http://www.missingplanes.com/stexcerpt.htm

1534. Darilek, Victor. *Log Book* (nose-gunner on a B-24 Liberator; kept short notes on each combat mission)
http://www.wf.net/~darilek/dar1.htm

1535. EAA Aviation Foundation. *B-17 Tour* (video and other resources)
http://www.b17.org/

1536. Feise, Tom. *U.S. 8th and 9th Army Air Force in East Anglia* (location of bases and other information)
http://www.455th.ukpc.net/tomfeise/8thusaaf/index.htm

1537. Flatley, Teresa K. *Bizarre Collision over North Sea* (2 B-17s collide, one ramming and locking into the bottom of the other)
http://www.military.com/Content/MoreContent?file=PRdragonflies

1538. Fowler, George. *Holocaust at Dresden*
http://www.melvig.org/files/dresden.html

1539. Green, Daniel. *War in the West* (air power as used by the Axis and Allies)
http://www.danshistory.com/ww2/west.html

1540. Harwood, Raymond. *9th U.S. Air Force, Order of Battle* (first link on page)
http://www.harwood.plus.com/

1541. Heinrichs, Edward T. *Missing Planes of the 452nd Bomber Group* (description of flight mission; list of personnel; selected examples from a book length analysis)
http://www.missingplanes.com/mp1.htm

1542. Hoffman, Wally. *From Fantasy to Reality: B-17 Mission to Schweinfurt, 1943*
http://www.magweb.com/sample/ww2/wl003sch.htm

1543. Hoffman, Walley. *We Get Our Feet Wet* (ditched in English Channel on return from bombing raid)
http://www.tankbooks.com/stories/story94.htm
http://www.magweb.com/sample/ww2/wl004ger.htm

1544. Lynch, J. J. *Bomber Harris Trust* (various materials defending the massive bombing campaign against Germany in response to its critics)
http://www.blvl.igs.net/~jlynch/

1545. Metzger, Lothar. *The Fire-Bombing of Dresden* (the writer was nine years old at the time of the massive attack)
http://atschool.eduweb.co.uk/chatback/english/memories/~lothar.html

1546. Moncur, Vern L. *Mission Journal* (kept by Captain of a B-17 in 1944)
http://www.303rdbga.com/thunderbird/vlm-journal.html

1547. Morgan, Robert, and Linda Morgan. *B-17 Memphis Belle and B-29 Dauntless Dotty*
http://www.memphis-belle.com/

1548. Rapp, Don. *306th Bombardment Group: "First over Germany"* (8th Air Force)
http://www.the-old-reliable-rapp-house.org/306BG%20Base.htm

1549. Rockett, Maurice. *War on Their Minds* (interview; flew in B-17s)
http://www.whshistoryproject.org/ww2/Interviews/mr_rockett.html

1550. Stelzriede, Marshall. *Marshall Stelzriede's Wartime Story: The Experiences of a B-17 Navigator during World War II*
http://members.loop.com/~tstel/marshw.htm

1551. Uebelhoer, Web. *Interview* (on one of only four planes to survive a major 1944 raid on Kessel, Germany)
http://www.tankbooks.com/intviews/uebelhoer/uebelhoer1.htm

1552. [Unidentified.] *A Brief Outline of the 410th Bomber Group*
http://members.aol.com/famjustin/410th1.html

1553. [Unidentified.] *Air Battle of the Ruhr, 1939-1945* (German and English versions)
http://www.hco.hagen.de/ruhr/index.html

1554. [Unidentified.] *Air Target Statistics over Germany*
http://members.aol.com/forcountry/ww2/awg.htm

1555. [Unidentified.] *Air War Statistics in the European Theater, 1942-1944*
http://members.aol.com/forcountry/ww2/aws.htm

1556. [Unidentified.] *Bomber Command: Death by Moonlight* (19 brief accounts—nearly all by those being bombed—of what the massive firebombing campaigns were like)
http://www.valourandhorror.com/BC/Stories/Home.htm

1557. [Unidentified.] *Combined Bomber Offensive*
http://history.sandiego.edu/gen/WW2Timeline/Europe06.html

1558. [Unidentified.] *150 Squadron [Bomber] Royal Air Force* (emphasis on Tunisia and Italy)
http://www.perth.igs.net/~long/

1559. [Unidentified.] *RAF Liberator Squadrons of 205 Group, the SEAC, Bomber Command and Coastal Command* (B24 Liberators)
http://www.acseac.co.uk/

1560. [Unidentified.] *The Carpetbagger Complex: 801st/492nd Bombardment Group; Station 179—8th Air Force, United Kingdom* (Air Force special operations)
http://www.fortunecity.com/meltingpot/roberts/38/

1561. van Gelderen, Peter. *RAF Short Stirling Bomber Homepage* (details on the craft and its many missions)
http://www.box.nl/~stirling/home.htm

1562. Weir, Gordon W. *Navigating through World War II: A Memoir of the War Years* (B-17 navigator)
http://www.geocities.com/gordonWW/

1563. Yeager, Chuck. *Shot Down over France, [March] 1944* (Yeager's account of the downing and how the Resistance assisted him to reach Gibraltar)
http://www.ibiscom.com/shot.htm

The Soviet Union

THE WAR OVERALL

1564. Bergstrom, Christer. *Erich Hartmann—the [German] Ace of Aces*
http://www.elknet.pl/acestory/hartm/hartm1.htm

1565. Bergstrom, Christer. *JG54 versus Soviet Aces: A Comparison of Sources* (through links reprints an English translation of V. Dymich's study and makes comments on what he regards to be its strengths and weaknesses)
http://www.blackcross-redstar.com/dymich.html

1566. Bergstrom, Christer. *German and Soviet Bombers on the Eastern Front in 1942: A Comparison*
http://www.blackcross-redstar.com/bomber.htm

1567. Bergstrom, Christer. *The First Aerial Combat on the Eastern Front*
http://www.elknet.pl/acestory/rubstov/rubstov.htm

1568. Bergstrom, Christer, and Andrey Mikhailov. *German and Soviet Fighter Aces: A Comparison*
http://www.blackcross-redstar.com/text.html

1569. Bergstrom, Christer, and Andrey Mikhailov. *Soviet Aircraft Losses in World War II*
http://www.blackcross-redstar.com/sovair.html

1570. Bessonov, Evgenii B. *Memoirs* (he served as a *tankodesantnik* platoon commander)
http://history.vif2.ru/atwar/infantry/bessonov/bessonov.htm

1571. [Britain and U.S.S.R. Governments.] *Agreement between the United Kingdom and the Union of Soviet Socialistic Republics (Moscow, July 12, 1941)*
http://www.ibiblio.org/pha/policy/1941/410712a.html

1572. Bukovsky, Vladimir. *Soviet Archives* (Russian language documents from U.S.S.R. government, agencies, and Communist Party; primarily post-war)
http://psi.ece.jhu.edu/~kaplan/IRUSS/BUK/GBARC/buk.html

1573. Churchill, Winston. *Broadcast on the Soviet-German War (London, June 22, 1941)*
http://www.ibiblio.org/pha/policy/1941/410622d.html

1574. Denkhaus, Raymond A. *Death of Convoy PQ-17* (bringing war supplies to the U.S.S.R.)
http://www.military.com/Content/MoreContent?file=PRpq17

1575. Denniston, Peter. *A Brief History of the 5th Gebirgsjaeger 100th Regiment, 1941-1945* (fought in Crete and Russian front)
http://www.geocities.com/CapeCanaveral/Hangar/4602/Gebirgs2.htm

1576. Drabkin, Artem, and Oleg Sheremet. *Soldiers at War* (first hand narratives by Russian veterans)
http://history.vif2.ru/atwar/index.html

1577. Dubov, Alexander. *Russian Liberation Army* (a Russian/English site defending Vlasov's raising an Army to fight the Russian Communists during the war)
http://www.ukma.kiev.ua/~holod/roa/index_e.htm

1578. Fernandez, J. A. *Operation Barbarossa: Eastern Front Combat History, 1941-1945*
http://www.geocities.com/Area51/Cavern/2941/

1579. Germinsky, Robert A. *World War II Convoys: The Run to Russia*
http://www.chinfo.navy.mil/navpalib/wwii/facts/convoys.txt

1580. [High Command of Wehrmacht.] *Commissar's Order for "Operation Barbarossa"* (June 6, 1940; ordering immediate execution of all Communist commissars)
http://www.yadvashem.org/about_holocaust/documents/part3/doc170.html

1581. Himmler, Heinrich. *Speech of Reichsfuhrer-SS Heinrich Himmler at Posesn (4 October 1943)* (translated by Carlos Porter; on past progress of the Russian war and future prospects)
http://www.codoh.com/incon/inconhh.html

1582. Hitler, Adolph. *Hitler's Explanation of the Soviet Invasion (June 21, 1941)* (letter to Mussolini)
http://www.ibiblio.org/pha/policy/1941/410621a.html

1583. Ioffe, Emmanuel. *How Many Belrussians Perished during the War?*
http://www.open.by/belarus-now/cont/1998/0630/politics/bg2-pol.html

1584. Johmann, Kurt. *Operation Barbarossa: Why?*
http://www.johmann.net/commentary/barbarossa.html

1585. Kolesnik, Nikolai T. *Memoirs* (served as an artilleryman in the Soviet Army)
http://history.vif2.ru/atwar/artillerymen/kolesnik/kolesnik.html

1586. Library of Congress. *Revelations from the Russian Archives* (on different aspects of Soviet era internal and external policies)
http://lcweb.loc.gov/exhibits/archives/intro.html

1587. Michaels, Daniel W. *New Evidence on the 1941 "Barbarossa" Attack: Why Hitler Attacked Soviet Russia When He Did*
http://ihr.org/jhr/v18/v18n3p40_Michaels.html

1588. Molotov, Vyacheslav. *Molotov on the Nazi Invasion of Russia* (22 June 1941; English translation)
http://www.historyplace.com/speeches/molotov.htm
http://www.fordham.edu/halsall/mod/1941molotov.html

1589. Noyes, III, Harry F. *Sergeant's Odyssey* (a young German-American drafted into the German army and serving on the Russian front)
http://www.military.com/Content/MoreContent?file=PRsarge

1590. Olsson, Thorlief. *Red Steel* (Soviet armor)
http://www.algonet.se/~toriert/

1591. Rempel, Gerhard. *Stalin as Warlord*
http://mars.acnet.wnec.edu/~grempel/courses/stalin/lectures/Warlord.html

1592. Soviet Government and Agencies. *Archival Stuff* (military orders; test results on weapons systems; pre-war intelligence evaluations on German preparations for invasion [in Russian])
http://history.vif2.ru/library/archives/index.html

1593. Stackton, Harold, Dariusz Tyminski, and Christer Bergstrom. *Marina Raskova and Soviet Female Pilots*
http://www.elknet.pl/acestory/raskov/raskov.htm

1594. Stainforth, Thorfinn. *Why Did Hitler's Campaign in the Soviet Union Fail?* (also has a link to the same author's discussion of *Why Hitler Lost the Second World War*)
http://www.geocities.com/t_stainforth/barbarossa.html

1595. Stalin, Joseph. *Broadcast to the People of the Soviet Union (July 3, 1941)*
http://www.ibiblio.org/pha/policy/1941/410703a.html

1596. Stalin, Joseph. *Joseph Stalin's Speech on Red Square on Anniversary Celebration of the October Revolution (November 7, 1941)* (assuring the audience of the inevitability of Russian victory)
http://www.ibiblio.org/pha/policy/1941/411107a.html

1597. Starostin, Serge. *Soviet Guns 1920-1945* (types of artillery, ammunition, etc.)
http://history.vif2.ru/guns/index.html

1598. Stolfi, Russel H. S. *Lightning Eastern Front Offensive*
http://www.military.com/Content/MoreContent?file=PRpanzer

1599. Toppe, Alfred (General) et al. *Night Combat* (comparative study of German and Russian techniques and styles; 1982, 1986; CMH Publication 104-3; revision of an earlier study)
http://www.army.mil/cmh-pg/books/wwii/104-3/fm.htm

1600. Tyminski, Dariusz. *Ivan Kozhedub—Top Soviet Ace*
http://www.elknet.pl/acestory/kozedub/kozedub.htm

1601. [Unidentified.] *Battle of Minsk—1941*
http://www.shortway.to/1941/eminsk.htm

1602. [Unidentified.] *Civil and Political Events [in the Soviet Union] during the Great Patriotic War (1941-1945)*
http://www.geocities.com/nkvdman/1941polit_history.htm

1603. [Unidentified.] *Equipment Lend-Leased to the USSR* (by type of product)
http://members.aol.com/forcountry/ww2/lus.htm

1604. [Unidentified.] *German Order of Battle, 22 June 1941* (at time invasion began; detailed but not fully complete)
http://members.tripod.com/~Sturmvogel/BarbarossaOB.html

1605. [Unidentified.] *Great Patriotic War* (discussion of material available in Bularusian archives)
http://www.president.gov.by/gosarchives/evov/evov.htm

1606. [Unidentified.] *Military Maps of World War II* (of Russian front; available in English or Russian)
http://mapww2.narod.ru/

1607. [Unidentified.] *1941: Russian-German Front* (available in Russian or English)
http://www.shortway.to/1941/

1608. [Unidentified.] *Relevant Soviet Aircraft*
http://pratt.edu/~rsilva/aircraft.htm

1609. [Unidentified.] *Soviet Women Pilots· in the Great Patriotic War* (including discussion of specific individuals)
http://pratt.edu/%7Ersilva/sovwomen.htm

1610. [Unidentified.] *The Defense of the Brest Fortress* (prime initial target of Army Group Centre)
http://city.bresttelecom.by/ct/page3e.html

1611. [Unidentified.] *Velikaja Otechestvennaja (Great Patriotic War)* (Russian language site)
http://gpw.tellur.ru/

1612. [Unidentified.] *Yakovlev Fighters of the Great Patriotic War*
http://home.att.net/~historyzone/Yakovlev.html

1613. [Unidentified,] Otto. *The Russian Campaign, 1941-1945: A Photo Diary*
http://www.geipelnet.com/war_albums/otto/ow_011.html

1614. [Unidentified American.] *Attack on an Arctic Convoy [Carrying War Goods to Russia], 1942* (describing a Nazi aerial attack)
http://www.ibiscom.com/convoy.htm

1615. Victor, Kisly. *Rare Photos of Bagration Operation (Belorussia 1944)* (two galleries)
http://br.by/ironage/tanks/Photos/photos.htm

1616. von Reichenau, Walter. *A German Field Marshall Instructs the Wehrmacht on Its Role in USSR* (stresses the historic opportunity to crush Communism and Russian jewry; has link to German language original as well)
http://www2.h-net.msu.edu/~german/gtext/nazi/reichenau-english.html

1617. Webb, William A. *Surrounded in the Snow* (high price Soviets paid to retake Velikiye Luki)
http://www.military.com/Content/MoreContent?file=PRsovietf

1618. Wendel, Marcus. *Soviet Union Factbook*
http://www.skalman.nu/soviet/

1619. Zimakov, Vladimir M. *Memoirs* (served as scout and anti-tank weapons man)
http://history.vif2.ru/atwar/infantry/zimakov/zim1.htm

1620. Zuljan, Ralph. *Documents Online from the Fuhrer Headquarters* (Hitler orders dealing with the war in the East; a growing collection of material)
http://www.geocities.com/Pentagon/1084/fuehrer_directives.htm

BALTIC COUNTRIES: ESTONIA, LATVIA, LITHUANIA

1621. Cerskus, Leonas. *Leonas Cerskus: The Story of a Lithuanian Soldier*
http://www.angelfire.com/de/Cerskus/

1622. Maslaiskaute, Daina. *Daiana's Grandmother's Story: Lithuania under the Occupation*
http://atschool.eduweb.co.uk/chatback/english/memories/~daina.html

UKRAINE

1623. Gregorovich, Andrew. *World War II in Ukraine: The Ukrainian Experience in World War II with a Brief Survey of Ukraine's Population Loss of Ten Million*
http://www.infoukes.com/history/ww2/

1624. Potichnyj, Peter J. *Ukrainians in World War II Military Formations: An Overview*
http://www.infoukes.com/upa/related/military.html

1625. [Unidentified.] *Chronicle of the Ukrainian Insurgent Army* (source materials and analyses; fought with the Germans as a means of liberating Ukraine from the Communists)
http://www.infoukes.com/upa/

RUSSIAN CITIES

1626. [Unidentified. *German Order of Battle at Kursk*
http://members.tripod.com/~Sturmvogel/SouthKursk.html

1627. [Unidentified.] *Tank Strengths before Kursk, 1 July 1943*
http://members.tripod.com/~Sturmvogel/kursktanks.html

1628. Wilson, Alan. *Kursk—July 1943* (daily accounts, order of battle, photos, etc.)
http://dspace.dial.pipex.com/town/avenue/vy75/kursk.htm
(map page:. January 1, 1990http://ds.dial.pipex.com/town/avenue/vy75/maps.htm

1629. [Unidentified.] *Battle of Leningrad* (available in English or Russian)
http://www.lenbat.narod.ru/

1630. Bergstrom, Christer, and Andrey Mikhailov. *Zerstorer versus Soviet Airborne Operations* (major Russian parachute drop as part of effort to force Germans further from Moscow)
http://www.blackcross-redstar.com/Zerst.htm

1631. [Unidentified.] *Battle of Moscow* (available in English or Russian)
http://www.serpukhov.su/dima/war/eng/eindex.htm

1632. Tyminski, Dariusz. *Lilya Litvak—the "White Rose" of Stalingrad*
http://www.elknet.pl/acestory/litvak/litvak.htm

1633. [Unidentified.] *Battle for Stalingrad* (hundreds of pages of data)
http://users.pandora.be/stalingrad/

1634. [Unidentified.] *Stalingrad: History of the Great Battle* (materials from various scholars and close students available by intra-site links)
http://www.stalingrad.com.ru/history/history.htm

1635. [Unidentified.] *Stalingrad Military-Historical Club* (in English and Russian versions)
http://stalingrad.ic.ru/

1636. [Unidentified.] *Stalingrad Maps*
http://users.compaqnet.be/cn002816/

1637. Wijer, Hans. *The Battle for Stalingrad* (includes first hand accounts)
http://home.planet.nl/~wijer037/HansW.html

Normandy Invasion

LAND AND AIR OPERATIONS

1638. Austra, Kevin R. *Desperate Hours on Omaha Beach*
http://www.military.com/Content/MoreContent?file=PRomaha

1639. Boccafogli, Ed. *Interview* (paratrooper in the 82nd Airborne Division)
http://www.tankbooks.com/intviews/boccafog/boccafogli1.htm

1640. Boyer, Fred. *Omaha Beach Intelligence Assault Map*
http://www.ww2omahabeach.com/

1641. Britannica Online. *Normandy: 1944—Maps*
http://normandy.eb.com/normandy/maps.html

1642. Brown, Arnold. *Interview* (company commander, 90th Infantry Division; sent in as a replacement post D-Day)
http://www.tankbooks.com/intviews/brown/brown1.htm

1643. Burkhalter, John G. *God Was on the Beach on D-Day: Chaplain Burkhalter Tells Power of Prayers* (letter describing Omaha beachhead with assorted other materials)
http://www.highrock.com/JohnGBurkhalter/D-day.html

1644. Combined Chiefs of Staff. *CCS Directive for Overlord*
http://www.ibiblio.org/hyperwar/ETO/Overlord/Overlord-CCS-Dir.html

1645. Copp, Terry. *Allied Bombing in Normandy*
http://www.legionmagazine.com/features/canadianmilitaryhistory/98-11.asp

1646. Copp, Terry. *TAF [Tactical Air Force] over Normandy*
http://www.legionmagazine.com/features/canadianmilitaryhistory/99-01.asp

1647. Copp, Terry. *The [Canadian] Airborne on D-Day*
http://www.legionmagazine.com/features/canadianmilitaryhistory/98-04.asp

1648. Copp, Terry. *The Normandy Battle of Attrition*
http://www.legionmagazine.com/features/canadianmilitaryhistory/98-09.asp

1649. Corry, A. L. *Voices of D-Day* (from a bombardier)
http://www.pbs.org/wgbh/amex/guts/sfeature/voices_corry.html

1650. Doody, Richard. *Operation Overlord* (a chronology of the time datable events of the immediate invasion)
http://worldatwar.net/article/overlord/index.html

1651. Elie, Patrick. *D-Day* (French language site)
http://www.6juin1944.com/

1652. Encyclopedia Britannica. *Normandy*
http://normandy.eb.com/

1653. Gibbons, Joseph H. *Oral History—Invasion of Normandy, 6-25 June 1944* (during this time Gibbons was Commanding Officer of Navy Combat Demolition Units at Omaha Beach)
http://www.history.navy.mil/faqs/faq87-3p.htm

1654. Greenip, [?]. *[Resupply of Forces under German Attack]*
http://www.military.com/Content/MoreContent?file=vetstory_wwii_greenip

1655. Hall, Wayne V. *A Tree Marks the Start of One Soldier's War* (101st Airborne)
http://www.odedodea.edu/k-12/D-Day/Stars_and_stripes/Articles/A_TREE_MARKS_THE_START/index.htm

1656. Hallion, Richard P. *The U.S. Army Air Forces in World War II: D Day 1944—Air Power over the Normandy Beaches and Beyond*
http://www.aero-web.org/history/wwii/d-day/toc.htm

1657. Hammond, William M. *U.S. Army Campaigns of World War II: Normandy* (CMH Publication 72-18)
http://www.army.mil/cmh-pg/brochures/normandy/nor-pam.htm

1658. Harrison, Gordon A. *U. S. Army in World War II (European Theater of Operations): Cross-Channel Attack* (1951; CMH 7-4)
http://www.army.mil/cmh-pg/books/wwii/7-4/7-4_cont.htm

1659. Harris, Gilian. *Final Fling for D-Day Kilted Piper*
http://www.thetimes.co.uk/article/0,,2-69190,00.html

1660. Hillman, Elizabeth. *Interview with Elizabeth Hillman, World War II Army Nurse* (nurse at Normandy and other places in France)
http://www.normandyallies.org/aeh97.htm

1661. Hinton, John D. *The D-Day Invasion* (Omaha Beach)
http://www.memoriesofwar.com/veterans/hinton.asp

1662. Historical Section, European Theater of Operations. *506 Parachute Infantry Regiment in Normandy Drop* (Regimental Unity Study No. 3)
http://www.army.mil/cmh-pg/documents/WWII/506-Nor/506-nor.htm

1663. History Place. *D-Day Photos*
http://www.historyplace.com/worldwar2/timeline/dday.htm

1664. Hurlbut, Chuck. *Interview* (Hurlbut was a combat engineer at Omaha Beach)
http://www.tankbooks.com/intviews/hurlbut/hurlbut1.htm

1665. Isbill, [? .] *29th Infantry Division 175th Infantry Normandy, July 1944* (includes history of division and its role on D-Day and shortly thereafter involvement in the battles)
http://isbills.tripod.com/normandy/normandy.htm

1666. Jennys, David R. *D-Day's Mighty Host*
http://www.military.com/Content/MoreContent?file=PRhost

1667. Johnson, Paul. *2nd Tactical Air Force and the Normandy Campaign* (MA thesis)
http://home.istar.ca/~johnstns/tacair/tacair.html

1668. Karoly, Steve. *The 25th NCR at Normandy* (Seabees)
http://www.seabeecook.com/history/25th_ncr/the_25th_ncr_at_normandy.htm

1669. Lane, Larry. *Back to Normandy* (veterans return to the battlefield)
http://www.dtic.mil/soldiers/august94/p18.html

1670. Lomell, Leonard. *Voices of D-Day* (beachhead experiences)
http://www.pbs.org/wgbh/amex/guts/sfeature/voices_lomell.html

1671. Martin, Craig. *"Seasoned GIs Survived, Vets Say"*
http://www.odedodea.edu/k-12/D-Day/Stars_and_stripes/
Articles/Seasoned_GIs_Survived.html

1672. McKay, Alasdair. *Ham N Jam: 26 Minutes Which Changed the World*
(the coup de main at the Orne bridges)
http://www.users.globalnet.co.uk/~njmckay/.htm

1673. McKinney, Mike. *Interview* (one of first men landing on Omaha
Beach)
http://www.tankbooks.com/intviews/mckinney/mckinney1.htm

1674. Merrill, Clifford. *Interview* (served in 712th Tank Battalion;
wounded in Normandy and, ironically, decades later in Vietnam as well)
http://www.tankbooks.com/intviews/merrill/merrill1.htm

1675. Morss, Robert. *59th Division* (British)
http://www.morssweb.com/59div/

1676. Nando Times. *The Fiftieth Anniversary of D-Day*
http://archive.nandotimes.com/sproject/dday/dday.html

1677. National D-Day Museum. *National D-Day Museum Website* (New
Orleans)
http://www.ddaymuseum.org/intropage.htm

1678. Osmont, Marie-Louise. *Invasion of Normandy, June 6, 1944* (from
her diary; lived at Sword Beach)
http://www.ibiscom.com/dday.htm

1679. Patrick, Bethanne K. *Capt. Quentin R. Walsh* (by ruse, Walsh captured
the fort that maintained effective German control over port of
Cherbourg)
http://www.military.com/Content/MoreContent?file=ML_walsh_bkp

1680. Patrick, Bethanne K. *Gen. Elwood "Pete" Quesada* (established his air
command headquarters at the Normandy beachhead on D-Day plus one)
http://www.military.com/Content/MoreContent?file=ML_quesada_bkp

1681. Patrick, Bethanne K. *Mjr. Gen. Norman "Dutch" Cota* (Omaha Beach)
http://www.military.com/Content/MoreContent?file=ML_cota_bkp

1682. Patterson, Grace C. *Nurses' Tales* (nurse at Utah Beach and inland locations)
http://www.pbs.org/wgbh/amex/guts/sfeature/nurses_grace.html

1683. Pavlovsky, Helen, and Sara Marcum. *Support for Normandy Invasion, June 1944* (the two were nurses at Navy Base Hospital 12 [= Royal Hospital], Netley, England)
http://www.history.navy.mil/faqs/faq87-3e.htm

1684. Perkins, Bradford. *Oral History* (fought in Normandy among other battles)
http://www-personal.umich.edu/~amnornes/Glass.html

1685. Perry, Tenna. *D-Day Beaches*
http://txtx.essortment.com/ddaybeaches_rjse.htm

1686. Public Broadcasting System. *Guts and Glory* (includes film of the invasion)
http://www.pbs.org/wgbh/amex/guts/index.html

1687. Reagan, Ronald. *President Reagan's Address at the U.S.-French Ceremony at Omaha Beach* (June 6, 1984; 40th anniversary of the invasion)
http://www.townhall.com/hall_of_fame/reagan/speech/omaha.html

1688. Reagan, Ronald. *President Reagan's Speech at Pointe de Hock* (June 6, 1984; 40th anniversary of the invasion)
http://www.townhall.com/hall_of_fame/reagan/speech/normandy.html

1689. Sedler, Aryn. *D-Day: What an Invasion!*
http://www.utexas.edu/projects/latinoarchives/
narratives/vol1no2/D_day/D_DAY.HTML

1690. Stanley, William J. *Perpetuation of Testimony* (Omaha Beach survivor)
http://www.military.com/Content/MoreContent?file=stanley01

1691. Tomalin, Roy. *Roy Tomalin* (tank driver at Normandy)
http://freespace.virgin.net/susan.tomalin/nva/roy.htm

1692. [Unidentified.] *Canadian Beach Juno*
http://www.stormpages.com/junobeach/

1693. [Unidentified.] *Cassidy's Battalion* ("Battalion and Small Unit Study No. 9"—detailed study of an airborne battalion)
http://www.army.mil/cmh-pg/documents/WWII/Cassidy/cassidy.htm

1694. [Unidentified.] *D-Day, June 6 1944*
http://www.geocities.com/paddyjoe_m/index.html

1695. [Unidentified.] *D-Day, 6th June 1944* ("virtual tour" of the battlefields)
http://www.dday.co.uk/

1696. [Unidentified.] *Debriefing Conference on D-Day: 82nd Airborne Division Report (August 1944)*
http://carlisle-www.army.mil/cgi-bin/usamhi/DL/showdoc.pl?docnum=32

1697. [Unidentified.] *421 RCAF Squadron and Allied Air Supremacy in the Normandy Campaign*
http://home.istar.ca/~421sqadn/

1698. [Unidentified.] *Hill 112* (considered by Rommel the one essential location that had to be held to hold France against the invasion)
http://www.hill112.com/

1699. [Unidentified.] *In Desperate Battle: Normandy, 1944* (Canadian role; maps and accounts and other resources)
http://www.valourandhorror.com/DB/home.htm

1700. [Unidentified.] *Normandy: The Great Crusade Online*
http://www.m-2k.com/cdjg/normandy/

1701. [Unidentified.] *Omaha Beachhead (6 June-13 June 1944)* (facsimile reprint, 1984; in the "American Forces in Action Series;" CMH Publication 100-11)
http://www.army.mil/cmh-pg/books/wwii/100-11/100-11.htm
http://www.shsu.edu/~his_ncp/Omaha.html (lengthy extract.

1702. [Unidentified.] *Outline of Operation Overlord* (manuscript history prepared by Army historians in the European Theater of Operations)
http://www.army.mil/cmh-pg/documents/wwii/g4-OL/g4-OL.htm

1703. [Unidentified.] *Rob's 101st and 82nd Airborne Homepage* (dedicated to the Normandy assault)
http://members.tripod.com/~Rob101st/index.html

1704. [Unidentified.] *St-Lo (7 July-19 July 1944)* (1983 reprint; in the "American Forces in Action Series")
http://www.army.mil/cmh-pg/books/wwii/100-13/st-lo_0.htm

1705. [Unidentified.] *Thames Barges at War in Time for D-Day*
http://www.naval-history.net/WW2RNLandingBarges.htm

1706. [Unidentified.] *The Fight at the Lock* (Regimental Unit Study Num-

ber 2; postwar manuscript history of this action by the 501st Parachute Infantry Regiment)
http://www.army.mil/cmh-pg/documents/WWII/Lock/lock.htm

1707. [Unidentified.] *The Forcing of the Merderet Causeway at La Fiere, France—An Action by the Third Battalion, 325th Glider Infantry* ("Regimental Unity Study Number 4"; manuscript written 1944-1945)
http://www.army.mil/cmh-pg/documents/wwii/lafiere/325-LaF.htm

1708. [Unidentified.] *The German Atlantikwall* (originally a Dutch site; being transformed into an English language one)
http://www.atlantikwall.net/

1709. [Unidentified.] *The Normandy Invasion*
http://www.army.mil/cmh-pg/reference/normandy/normandy.htm

1710. [Unidentified.] *UN Command Structure for Overlord*
http://www.ibiblio.org/hyperwar/ETO/Overlord/img/Overlord-Command.gif

1711. [Unidentified.] *Utah Beach to Cherbourg (6 June-27 June 1944)* (1947; in the "American Forces in Action Series")
http://www.army.mil/cmh-pg/books/wwii/utah/utah.htm

1712. Valence, Thomas. *Voices of D-Day* (beach landing experiences)
http://www.pbs.org/wgbh/amex/guts/sfeature/voices_valence.html

1713. Wiley, Judd. *Seven Dead Germans* (autobigoraphical account)
http://www.tankbooks.com/stories/story99.htm

1714. Wilkins, Jim. *D-Day Recollections* (Canadian)
http://users.erols.com/wolfy/qor/html/body_wilkins.html

NAVAL OPERATIONS

1715. Blackwell, H. L. *Naval Combat Demolition Units (NCDUs] in Operation "Neptune" as Part of Task Force 122* (official report)
http://www.history.navy.mil/docs/wwii/norman1.htm

1716. Campbell, Kenneth L. *The Story of Motor Torpedo Squadron 35* (assigned to protect the flanks of the invasion armada)
http://members.home.net/squadron35/

1717. Campbell, Kenneth L. *The Story of PT518* (one of the PT boats protecting flanks of the invasion)
http://members.home.net/ptboat518/

1718. Copp, Terry. *D-Day at Sea and in the Air*
http://www.legionmagazine.com/features/canadianmilitaryhistory/98-03.asp

1719. Cragg, F. T. *CTF 122: Report of Sunk and Damaged Craft* (17 June 1944)
http://www.ibiblio.org/hyperwar/USN/rep/Normandy/CTF122-Damages.html

1720. Feduik, Frank R. *Oral History—Invasion of Normandy, June 1944* (at the time he was serving as Pharmacist Mate on the *USS LST 338*)
http://www.history.navy.mil/faqs/faq87-3d.htm

1721. Jones, Clifford L. *Neptune: Training, Mounting, the Artificial Ports* (1946; extensive extracts from a much longer manuscript work that treated other matters as well)
http://www.army.mil/cmh-pg/documents/wwii/beaches/bchs-fm.htm

1722. Morris, Robert. *Letter of a [Coast Guard] Veteran of Flotilla 4/10 to His Minister Describing Life before the Normandy Invasion*
http://www.uscg.mil/hq/g-cp/history/Morris_Ltr_2.html

1723. Naval Commander, Western Task Force. *D-Day: The Normandy Invasion, 6-25 June 1944: Sunk and Damaged Craft*
http://www.history.navy.mil/faqs/faq109-4.htm

1724. Naval Historical Center. *Naval Armed Guard Service: Merchant Ships at Normandy during the D-Day Invasion (Operation Neptune), June-July 1944*
http://www.history.navy.mil/faqs/faq104-7.htm

1725. Normandy Memorial Fund. *D-Day Naval Memorial*
http://www.eurosurf.com/ddaynavy/

1726. Price, Scott T. *The U.S. Coast Guard at Normandy*
http://www.uscg.mil/hq/g-cp/history/h_normandy.html

1727. Putnoky, Lou. *Interview.* (Coast Guardsman on *U.S.S. Bayfield* at Normandy and Southern France invasions and two additional ones in the Pacific)
http://www.tankbooks.com/intviews/putnoky/putnoky1.htm

1728. Rawlinson, Lee. *Memories from Navy Veterans aboard LCI(L) 489 during World War II*
http://www.jun6dday.com/

1729. Schools, Rodman S. *Project Mulberry: Building Safe Harbors at Normandy* (were the artificial ports essential or over-emphasized?)
http://www.military.com/Content/MoreContent?file=PRmulberryf

1730. Thompson, James W. *Oral History—Invasion of Normandy* (Thompson was serving as a Store Officer on *LST-505*, which was at Omaha Beach)
http://www.history.navy.mil/faqs/faq109-2a.htm

1731. [Unidentified.] *Mulberry B, SHAEF Report (1945)*
http://carlisle-www.army.mil/cgi-bin/usamhi/DL/showdoc.pl?doc-num=716

1732. Vyn, Jr., Arend. *Official Action Report LCI(L)-91 Concerning Operation Neptune* (this vessel was Coast Guard manned)
http://www.uscg.mil/hq/g-cp/history/LCIL91_Act_Rpt_10_June_1944.html

1733. Vyn, Jr., Arend. *Official Loss of Ship Report LCI(L)-91*
http://www.uscg.mil/hq/g-cp/history/LCIL91_Loss.html

1734. Wilson, George B. *CTF 122: Report of Naval Combat Demolition Units* (19 July 1944)
http://www.ibiblio.org/hyperwar/USN/rep/Normandy/CTF-122-NCDU.html

THE DIEPPE RAID

1735. Copp, Terry. *The Air over Dieppe*
http://www.legionmagazine.com/features/canadianmilitaryhistory/96-06.asp

1736. Sugarman, Martin. *Jack Nissenthall—The VC [Victoria Cross] Hero Who Never Was* (about the neglected role of a Jewish soldier, an expert on radar, involved in the raid)
http://www.harrypalmergallery.ab.ca/galwardieppe/nissenthal.html

1737. [Varied sources.] *The Dieppe Raid: The South Saskatchewan Regiment on Ford Island* (after action report and personal memoirs)
http://cap.estevan.sk.ca/ssr/documents/ford.html

SLAPTON SANDS (EXERCISE TIGER)

1738. Crapanzano, Angelo. *Interview* (survivor of the disaster)
http://www.tankbooks.com/intviews/angelo/angelo1.htm

1739. Eckstam, Eugene. *Oral History: Recollections of Lt. Eugene C. Eckstam, MC, USNR*
http://www.history.navy.mil/faqs/faq87-3g.htm

1740. Hoffman, Marion. *Slapton Sands: What Happened*
http://www.geocities.com/milbios/slaptonsands.html

1741. MacDonald, Charles B. *"Slapton Sands: The 'Cover Up' That Never Was"* (from *Army* magazine, June 1988 issue)
http://www.history.navy.mil/faqs/faq20-2.htm

1742. Naval Historical Center. *Operation Tiger*
http://www.history.navy.mil/faqs/faq20-1.htm

Southern France Invasion and Campaign

1743. Cerri, Alain. *The Battle of Glieres—A Fight for Honour*
http://worldatwar.net/article/glieres/index.html

1744. Cerri, Alain. *The Battle of Mount Froid—The Highest Battle in Europe*
http://worldatwar.net/article/mountfroid/index.html

1745. Clarke, Jeffrey J. *U.S. Army Campaigns of World War II: Southern France* (CMH Publication 72-31)
http://www.army.mil/cmh-pg/brochures/norfran/norfran.htm

1746. Edwards, Esther. *Nurses' Tales* (Army nurse)
http://www.pbs.org/wgbh/amex/guts/sfeature/nurses_esther.html

1747. Frank, Jr., Edward F. *Journal of Edward F. Frank, Jr.* (includes entries concerning crossing the Atlantic to Europe in LST-32 and the invasion of southern France)
http://users.erols.com/reds1/lst173htmfiles/LST32_Journal.htm

1748. Special Service Division, Army Service Forces. *Pocket Guide to the Cities of Southern France* (1944; requires Adobe Acrobat)
http://worldwar2.smu.edu/cgi-bin/Pwebrecon.cgi?v1=109&ti=101,109&CNT=50&Search_Arg=world+war&Search_Code=GKEY&x=30&y=5&y=5&PID=3725&SEQ=20020105195519&SID=1

1749. Tucker, Fielding. *Promise Made, Promise Kept*
http://www.memoriesofwar.com/veterans/promise.asp

Land Conflict in 1944 and 1945

BREAKOUT FROM NORMANDY

1750. Copp, Terry. *Opening Up the Channel Ports*
http://www.legionmagazine.com/features/canadianmilitaryhistory/00-03.asp

1751. Copp, Terrry. *Reassessing Operation Totalize*
http://www.legionmagazine.com/features/canadianmilitaryhistory/99-09.asp

1752. Copp, Terry. *The Approach to Verrieres Ridge*
http://www.legionmagazine.com/features/canadianmilitaryhistory/99-03.asp

1753. Copp, Terry. *The March to the Seine*
http://www.legionmagazine.com/features/canadianmilitaryhistory/00-03.asp

1754. Copp, Terry. *The Toll of Verieres Ridge*
http://www.legionmagazine.com/features/canadianmilitaryhistory/99-05.asp

1755. Dorsey, Mason H. *Link Up* (first hand account of the meeting of Third and Seventh U.S. Armies, closing the exit routes for the German forces)
http://members.aol.com/famjustin/Dorsey9.html

1756. Foye, Don. *Interview* (only survivor of a massacre)
http://www.tankbooks.com/intviews/foye/foye1.htm

1757. Hawk, John. *Interview* (winner of Congressional Medal of Honor)
http://www.tankbooks.com/intviews/hawk/hawk1.htm

1758. Reeder, Charles. *Memoirs* (served in Third Armored Division)
http://www.geocities.com/ResearchTriangle/Facility/3991/ww2reeder.htm

1759. [Unidentified.] *Then and Now: Caen*
http://home.talkcity.com/PassportPl/smeric/caen.html

1760. [Unidentified.] *World War II Photos* (mostly of France; some graphic)
http://www.geocities.com/Pentagon/Quarters/6171/

1761. [Unidentified; possibly a war casualty.] *See You in Hell: The Story of G Company, 357th Regiment, 90th Division* (surviving part of diary begins about a week after D-Day)
http://www.tankbooks.com/stories/gcompany/
g%20company%20diary%201.htm

1762. [Unidentified.] *Battle of France—1944*
http://history.sandiego.edu/gen/WW2Timeline/Europe07a.html

LIBERATION OF PARIS

1763. Barth, Norman. *Paris Libere* (photographs and variety of data)
http://www.paris.org/Expos/Liberation/

1764. Miles, Donna. *Liberation of Paris*
http://www.dtic.mil/soldiers/august94/p50.html

1765. [Unidentified.] *Chronology of the Liberation* (day by day listing, August 1944)
http://www.37.com/37w2.htm

BATTLE FOR NORTHERN FRANCE

1766. Copp, Terry. *2nd [Canadian] Division in September 1944*
http://www.legionmagazine.com/features/canadianmilitaryhistory/01-05.asp

1767. Delisle, Esther. *The Liberation of France: Image and Event* (a book review)
http://www2.h-net.msu.edu/reviews/showrev.cgi?path=12992913918595

1768. Eckhart, Phil. *My Army Life (1944-1946)* (a tank man who helped relieve Bastogne, among other battles)
http://www.tankbooks.com/stories/eckhart/eckhart1.htm

1769. Hogan, David W. *U.S. Army Campaigns of World War II: Northern France* (CMH Publication 72-30)
http://www.army.mil/cmh-pg/brochures/norfran/norfran.htm

1770. [Unidentified.] *Battle for France Ends—1944*
http://history.sandiego.edu/gen/WW2Timeline/Europe08.html

1771. [Unidentified.] *The Cigarette Camps: U.S. Army Camps in Le Havre Area* (camps were named after popular American cigarettes)
http://www.skylighters.org/special/cigcamps/cigmaps.html

1772. [Unidentified.] *The War of Attribution—1944*
http://history.sandiego.edu/gen/WW2Timeline/Europe07b.html

1773. Vannoy, Allyn. *Rainbow Division's Stand in Alsace* (against Hitler's desperate effort to retain the temporary offensive in France as his Ardennes offensive was faltering)
http://www.military.com/Content/MoreContent?file=PRrainbowf

1774. Wiechman, Florence H. *Nurses' Tales* (Army nurse)
http://www.pbs.org/wgbh/amex/guts/sfeature/nurses_florence.html

MARKET GARDEN AND THE LIBERATION OF COASTAL EUROPE (NETHERLANDS, BELGIUM, LUXEMBOURG, AND DENMARK

1775. Copp, Terry. *Canadian Participation in the World War II Battle to Win the Breskins Pocket* (the jumping off point for taking the Belgium port of Antwerp)
http://www.legionmagazine.com/features/canadianmilitaryhistory/01-03.asp

1776. Copp, Terry. *Crosing the Leopold* (to gain control of the access waters leading to the Beglium port of Antwerp)
http://www.legionmagazine.com/features/canadianmilitaryhistory/01-01.asp

1777. Copp, Terry. *Our [Canadian] Rescue Role at Arnhem*
http://www.legionmagazine.com/features/canadianmilitaryhistory/00-09.asp

1778. Copp, Terry. *Taking of Walcheren Island* (in Netherlands)
http://www.legionmagazine.com/features/canadianmilitaryhistory/01-11.asp

1779. Copp, Terry. *The Battle North of Antwerp*
http://www.legionmagazine.com/features/canadianmilitaryhistory/01-09.asp

1780. Copp, Terry. *The Liberation of Belgium*
http://www.legionmagazine.com/features/canadianmilitaryhistory/00-11.asp

1781. Delaveaux, Raymond. *A Canadian Officer in Belgium* (Belgium just after the war ended)
http://atschool.eduweb.co.uk/chatback/english/memories/~raymond.html

1782. Durflinger, Serge, and Bill McAndrew. *Fortress Europe: German Coastal Defences and the Canadian Role in Liberating the Channel Ports*
http://www.warmuseum.ca/cwm/disp/dis003_e.html

1783. Fowler, T. Robert. *Valor in the Victory Campaign: 3rd Canadian Infantry Division* (role in liberating Holland, smashing through Rhineland, and other successes)
http://www.ncf.ca/~em575/

1784. Horlings, Andreas. *Arnhem Spookstad* (Dutch language book on the

evacuation of Arnhem when the fighting started and what the people found when they returned)
http://www.geocities.com/capitolhill/1557/arnhem0.html

1785. Patrick, Bethanne K. *Sgt. Francis S. Currey* (Medal of Honor winner for role in halting a dangerous German breakthrough in Belgium)
http://www.military.com/Content/MoreContent?file=ML_currey_bkp

1786. Shrine, Dan R. *Frozen Hell* (January 1945 in Belgium)
http://www.tankbooks.com/stories/story97.htm

1787. [Unidentified.] *Arnhem Battle Research Group*
http://home.wxs.nl/~peter.vrolijk/ABRG.html

1788. [Unidentified.] *Flt. Lt. David S.A. Lord VC, DFC* (attempting to resupply assault troops)
http://freespace.virgin.net/f.cassidy/arnhemvc.htm

1789. [Unidentified.] *History of 4 Parachute Squadron Royal Engineers* (virtually destroyed at Arnhem)
http://www.28chatsworth.fsnet.co.uk/

1790. [Unidentified.] *Kriegsberichter* (discusses Battle of Arnhem from the standpoint of the German defenders)
http://home.wxs.nl/~peter.vrolijk/kriegsberichter.html

1791. [Unidentified.] *Operation Market Garden*
http://www.marketgarden.com/

1792. [Unidentified.] *Operation Market Garden*
http://home.planet.nl/~jan81951/marketgarden/

1793. [Unidentified.] *The Battles of Arnhem Archive*
http://www.extraplan.demon.co.uk/index.htm

1794. van der Heide, Albert. *Month-long Battle of the "Capelse Veer" Very Costly*
http://www.godutch.com/herald/ww2/950123.htm

1795. Versteegh, Marnix. *Nijmegen, 1944-1945* (photographs and data)
http://www.nijmegenweb.myweb.nl/

BATTLE OF THE BULGE

1796. Beaver, Johnie R. *"A Walk in My Shoes" during the Battle of the Bulge in World War II* (Beaver was part of the 106th Infantry Division)
http://www.eagnet.com/edipage/user/joanie/index.htm

1797. Cappellini, Matthew. *Butler's Battlin' Blue Bastards* (interview with Lt. Col. McClernand Butler)
http://www.military.com/Content/MoreContent?file=PRbutler

1798. Carmichael, Fred. *[Oral History]* (Sgt. Carmichael was part of the relief Patton's Third Army was moving to break the German thrust)
http://www.military.com/Content/MoreContent?file=vetstory_wwii_car michael

1799. Cirillo, Roger. *U. S. Army Campaigns of World War II: Ardennes-Alsace* (CMH Publication 72-26)
http://www.army.mil/cmh-pg/brochures/ardennes/aral.htm

1800. Cole, Hugh M. *U. S. Army in World War II (European Theater of Operations): The Ardennes: Battle of the Bulge*
http://www.army.mil/cmh-pg/books/wwii/7-8/7-8_CONT.HTM

1801. Druback, Bill, et al. *Mixed Nuts* (interview with Druback and four other members of the 101st Airborne Division about the Battle of Bastogne)
http://www.tankbooks.com/intviews/bastogne/bastogne1.htm

1802. Evans, Gary F. *The 501st Parachute Infantry Regiment at Bastogne, Belgium (December 1944)*
http://www.army.mil/cmh-pg/documents/wwii/501pirbulge.htm

1803. Hasenauer, Heike. *Battle of the Bulge*
http://www.37.com/37w2.htm

1804. Kissel, Robert P. *Death of a Division*
http://www.military.com/Content/MoreContent?file=PReifel

1805. Kline, John. *Battle of the Bulge: December 16, 1944 to January 25, 1945* (description)
http://www.mm.com/user/jpk/battle.htm

1806. Kline, John. *106th Infantry Division* (material from official accounts, diaries, and other sources)
http://www.mm.com/user/jpk/mindex.htm

1807. Patrick, Bethanne K. *1st Sergeant Leonard Funk, Jr.*
http://www.military.com/Content/MoreContent?file=ML_funk_bkp

1808. Patrick, Bethanne K. *General Anthony McAuliffe*
http://www.military.com/Content/MoreContent?file=ML_mcauliffe_bkp

1809. Peniche, Eduardo A. *Bastogne: December 1944—White Christmas, Red Snow!* (journal from one who served there)
http://www.nhmccd.edu/contracts/lrc/kc/peniche.html

1810. Sargent, David. *Battle of the Bulge; The Ardennes Offensive*
http://helios.acomp.usf.edu/~dsargent/bestbulge2.htm

1811. Spahr, Ed, et al. *Interview* (Spahr and three other crewmen describe the destruction of their tank at the Battle of the Bulge)
http://www.tankbooks.com/intviews/giffdarp/giffdarp1.htm

1812. Tours International. *Maps of Battle of the Bulge*
http://militarytours.com/Bulgemap.htm

1813. [Unidentified.] *Center for Research and Information on the Battle of the Bulge*
http://users.skynet.be/bulgecriba/

1814. [Unidentified.] *The Battle of the Bulge*
http://helios.acomp.usf.edu/~dsargent/bestbulge2.htm

1815. [Unidentified.] *The Last Roar* (the German reasoning behind the offensive)
http://www.geocities.com/iturks/html/worldwarii2.html

1816. [Unidentified London newspaper.] *Soldier's Battle* (arguing it was the everyday soldier and not leadership nor weapons that turned the tide)
http://www.geocities.com/ResearchTriangle/Facility/3991/ww2bas-togne.htm

HURTGEN FOREST

1817. Christensen, W. T. *Hurtgen Forest Battle: Costly, Unproductive, Ill-Advised* (Christensen was part of the 82nd Airborne)
http://www.memoriesofwar.com/veterans/christensen.asp

1818. Miele, Valentine. *Interview* (landed at Omaha; wounded at Hurtgen Forest)
http://www.tankbooks.com/intviews/miele/miele1.htm

1819. Miller, Edward G. *Desperate Hours at Kesternich*
http://www.military.com/Content/MoreContent?file=PRkesternich

1820. Miller, Edward G., and David T. Zabecki. *Tank Battle in Kommerscheidt*
http://www.military.com/Content/MoreContent?file=PRtankf

1821. Reading, Wesley. *A Medic's Journey across Europe* (was at the battles of St. Lo, Hurtgen Forest, and others)
http://www.memoriesofwar.com/veterans/reading/default.asp

BATTLE FOR GERMANY

1822. Austra, Kevin R. *Bloody Battle for Wurzburg*
http://www.military.com/Content/MoreContent?file=PRwurzburg

1823. Ballard, Ted. *U.S. Army Campaigns of World War II: Rhineland*
(CMH Publication 72-25)
http://www.army.mil/cmh-pg/brochures/rhineland/rhineland.htm

1824. Bedessem, Edward N. *U.S. Army Campaigns of World War II: Central Europe* (CMH Publication 72:36)
http://www.army.mil/cmh-pg/brochures/centeur/centeur.htm

1825. Caraccilo, Dominic J. *Capitulation of German Army Group South*
http://www.military.com/Content/MoreContent?file=PRcapitulation

1826. Clayton, Arthur J. *Mud and Guts: Personal Recollections of World War II*
http://mariposa.yosemite.net/mudnguts/index.htm

1827. Cleaver, Thomas M. *Donald J. M. Blakeslee and Battle of Germany, 1944*
http://www.elknet.pl/acestory/blake/blake.htm

1828. Curry, [? .] *Brothers-in-Arms* (tracing Company F, 331st Infantry, 83rd Division, from Normandy to Central Germany)
http://www.ncweb.com/~davecurry/brothers/

1829. Dupuy, Trevor N. *The Rhine Crossings*
http://www.geocities.com/Pentagon/Quarters/5433/rhine1.html

1830. Forster, Greg. *Biggest Wartime Airdrop* (interview with General Ridgley Gaither)
http://www.military.com/Content/MoreContent?file=PRgaither

1831. Fuller, Snuffy. *Interview*
http://www.tankbooks.com/intviews/fuller/fuller1.htm

1832. Haas, Kenneth. *Frightening Panorama along the Rhine*
http://www.memoriesofwar.com/veterans/haas.asp

1833. Heimaster, Carl. *Jump!* (shot down during a "milk run" gone bad on June 23, 1944)
http://members.aol.com/famjustin/Heimaster1.html

1834. Hoffman, Marion C. *A Memorable Christmas* (detailed description of a Christmas Eve 1944 bombing mission over Germany)
http://members.aol.com/famjustin/Hoffman1.html

1835. Irzyk, Albin F. (Brigadier General). *Daring Moselle Crossing* (first-hand account of penetrating from France into Germany)
http://www.military.com/Content/MoreContent?file=PRmoselle

1836. Karoly, Steve. *The 69th NCB's Long Haul* (American Seabees trans-ported by British to Bremen and Bremerhaven to engage in rehabilitat-ing the destroyed facilities)
http://www.seabeecook.com/history/69_ncb/overland.htm

1837. Reese, A. Willard. *Berlin* (description of February 3, 1945, bomb-ing of Berlin from perspective of 457th Bomber Group, 8th Air Force)
http://www.457thbombgroup.org/BERLIN.HTM

1838. Shrine, Dan R. *No Man's Land: March 19, 1945, Near Bensheim, Ger-many*
http://www.tankbooks.com/stories/story93.htm

1839. Swager, Brent. *Nazi Plunder of Europe's Treasures* (horde discovered by Third Army soldiers)
http://www.military.com/Content/MoreContent?file=PRspoils

1840. [Unidentified.] *Declassified Captured [German] Diary* (captured by 10th U.S. Infantry Division, 13 January 1945)
http://www.eagnet.com/edipage/user/joanie/diary.htm

1841. [Unidentified.] *150th Combat Engineers of World War II* (first assault force across the Rhine; site includes just under a 1,000 pictures)
http://www.150th.com/

1842. [Unidentified.] *Remagen* (personal reminiscences of taking of the bridge and the events preceding and after the capture)
http://thames.northnet.org/488thengineers/Remagen.html

1843. [Unidentified.] *617 Squadron: The "Dambusters"*
http://www.dambusters.org.uk/

1844. [Unidentified], Dave. *The Smoke Bomb* (reconaissance unit creates inadvertent panic)
http://members.aol.com/famjustin/Dave4.html

1845. [Unidentified.] *295th Combat Engineer Battalion* (from Normandy to the end of the war)
http://us295th.tripod.com/

1846. Walden, Geoff. *Third Reich in Ruins*
http://www.geocities.com/Pentagon/Barracks/1525/ruins/reichruins.htm

Battle for Berlin

1847. Heaton, Colin D. *[Russian] Assault at Seelow Heights*
http://www.military.com/Content/MoreContent?file=PRseelow

1848. McCaul, Ed. *Interview: The Bitter Battle for Berlin* (interview with Siegfried Knappe, who fought in the German defense of the city)
http://www.military.com/Content/MoreContent?file=PRinterview

1849. Uijl, Oscar. *The Location of Hitler's Bunker [in Contemporary] Berlin*
http://www.xs4all.nl/~odu/bunker.html

Austria

1850. Dorsey, Mason H. *Milky Way* (first hand account of the May 1945 surrender negotiations with General von Rendulic and the surrender of the 800,000 men under his command)
http://members.aol.com/famjustin/Dorsey9.html

1851. [Unidentified.] *First Encounter between Austrians and GIs* (includes brief interviews on attitudes toward U.S. during the war)
http://www.image-at.com/salzburg/15.htm

Propaganda

1852. Bytwerk, Randall. *German Propaganda Archive* (includes posters and war period materials)
http://www.calvin.edu/academic/cas/gpa/index.htm

1853. Cheveigne, Maurice de. *Radio Libre* (French language site)
http://lug.linguist.jussieu.fr/lug/garde.html

1854. Lewis, Rebecca. *World War II British Propaganda Posters*
http://www.wkac.ac.uk/hss/rlewi/docs/web/WW2Index.htm

1855. NSDAP Museum. *Nazi Propaganda*
http://www.nsdapmuseum.com/museum/propaganda.htm

1856. Smith, Robert B. *Personality: William Joyce* (a/k/a "Lord Haw Haw," who was ultimately executed for his propaganda broadcasts to Britain)
http://www.military.com/Content/MoreContent?file=PRpersonalityf

1857. [Unidentified.] *German Psyops—World War II* (samples of German propaganda for British soldiers, criticizing the behavior of the Americans)
http://carlisle-www.army.mil/usamhi/Sampler/britsold/index.htm

1858. [Unidentified.] *Old Eagle's Poster Archive* (emphasis on German, but includes U.S., British, Swedish, Greek, and Chinese)
http://www.oldeagle.nu/post/

1859. [Unidentified.] *Propaganda Leaflets of the Second World War* (primarily anti-Axis)
http://www.cobweb.nl/jmoonen/

1860. [Unidentified.] *The Collecting of Propaganda Leaflets* (left hand side has a variety of Japanese, Russian, and even a faked *Life* magazine dropped by the Germans)
http://www.cobweb.nl/jmoonen/main.htm

Resistance and Espionage Networks

1861. Aldrich, Richard J. *British and American Policy on Intelligence Archives*
http://www.cia.gov/csi/studies/95unclass/Aldrich.html

1862. Bentley, Stewart. *The Dutch Resistance and the OSS*
http://www.cia.gov/csi/studies/spring98/Dutch.html

1863. Colby, William E. *OSS Operations in Norway*
http://www.cia.gov/csi/studies/winter99-00/art5.html

1864. Glenn, John M. *Aaron Bank—Father of the Green Berets* (Bank served with the O.S.S. in France)
http://www.military.com/Content/MoreContent?file=PRabank

1865. Henderson, Diana M. *German Spies in Scotland*
http://www-saw.arts.ed.ac.uk/secret/spies.html

1866. Henderson, Diana M. *Scots and the [British] Secret Service*
http://www-saw.arts.ed.ac.uk/secret/secretservice.html

1867. Henderson, Diana M. *Special Operations Executive (SOE)*
http://www-saw.arts.ed.ac.uk/secret/soe.html

1868. Hodgson, Lynn. *Camp X [Canada]: Official Site* (espionage training school)
http://webhome.idirect.com/~lhodgson/campx.htm

1869. Kehoe, Robert R. *1944: An Allied Team with the French Resistance*
http://www.cia.gov/csi/studies/winter98-99/art03.html

1870. Koch, Scott A. *The Role Of U.S. Army Military Attaches between the World Wars*
http://www.cia.gov/csi/studies/95unclass/Koch.html

1871. Leary, William M. *Robert Fulton's Skyhook and Operation Cold Feet*
http://www.cia.gov/csi/studies/95unclass/Leary.html

1872. Mills, Anthony E. *Jedburg Teams, World War II* (behind enemy lines special forces teams normally consisting of one man each from Britain, America, and France)
http://www.jedburgh.demon.co.uk/

1873. Patrick, Bethanne K. *Captain John Morrison Birch* (China O.S.S.)
http://www.military.com/Content/MoreContent?file=ML_birch_bkp

1874. Patrick, Bethanne K. *Capt. Victor Baranski* (O.S.S. operative in Slovenia)
http://www.military.com/Content/MoreContent?file=ML_baranski_bkp

1875. Patrick, Bethanne K. *Lt. Col. Lucien E. Conein* (a "Jedburgh" with the French resistance)
http://www.military.com/Content/MoreContent?file=ML_conein_bkp

1876. Simon Wisenthal Center. *German Countermeasures [Against the French Resistance]*
http://motlc.wiesenthal.org/text/x18/xm1867.html

1877. Simon Wisenthal Center. *Role of Women in French Resistance*
http://motlc.wiesenthal.org/text/x18/xm1868.html

1878. Steury, Donald P. *Tracking Nazi "Gold:" The OSS and Project Safehaven*
http://www.cia.gov/csi/studies/summer00/art04.html

1879. Tompkins, Peter. *The OSS and Italian Partisans in World War II*
http://www.cia.gov/csi/studies/spring98/OSS.html

1880. [Unidentified.] *Jeburghs* (extensive French language site)
http://jedburghs.ifrance.com/jedburghs/

1881. [Unidentified.] *Special Operations Executive, SOE—1940-1946* (history of the organization)
http://www.nlc.net.au/~bernie/

1882. [Unidentified.] *Special Operations Executive: To Set Europe Ablaze*
http://www.btinternet.com/~m.a.christie/index.htm

1883. [Unidentified.] *The French Resistance (1940-1945)* (French language site)
http://www.polyinter.com/resistance/

1884. van der Heide, Albert. *Firebrand Pastor Criss-Crossed Country to Coordinate Resistance* (in Holland)
http://www.godutch.com/herald/ww2/950223.htm

1885. [Various Sources.] *Marines and the O.S.S.—World War II: Colonel Peter J. Ortiz, USMC*
http://www.angelfire.com/ca/dickg/MarinesAndTheOSS.html

1886. Woolsey, R. James, Doyle Anderson, and Linda Zall. *Honoring Two World War II Heroes*
http://www.cia.gov/csi/studies/95unclass/Woolsey.html

5

The Mediterranean War: Italy, Near East, North Africa, and the Mediterranean Islands, 1939–1945

North Africa

REGIONAL STUDIES

1887. Barthorpe, Alec J. *Memoirs* (served in North Africa and Italy)
http://www.memoriesofwar.com/veterans/barthorpe.asp

1888. Copp, Terry. *The Mediterranean Theatre*
http://www.legionmagazine.com/features/canadianmilitaryhistory/97-01.asp

1889. Lippman, David H. *Desert Dawn: North Africa before Rommel*
http://www.magweb.com/sample/seuropa/seu55daw.htm

1890. Lonsdale, Stuart. *"Just a So-So Day:" The Diaries of a Royal Medical Corps Dental Mechanic in the Western Desert, 1940-1945* (at top of screen click on "H-L;" pick this person's name from list on left screen; text appears to right)
http://www.warlinks.com/memories/index.html

1891. Martindale, Sid. *Sid's War: From El Alamein to Cassino* (includes personal photographs and memoirs)
http://www.geocities.com/Heartland/Pointe/8180/sid.html

1892. Ratuszynski, Wilhelm. *Hans-Joachim Marseille—[German] Desert Eagle*
http://www.elknet.pl/acestory/marse/marse.htm

1893. Tee, Ronald A. *A British Soldier Remembers* (served with British 8th Army in Africa, Sicily, Italy, and Austria)
http://www.britishsoldier.com/

1894. Tyminski, Dariusz. *Sanislaw Skalski and His [Polish Airmen's] "African Circus"*
http://www.elknet.pl/acestory/skalski/skalski.htm

1895. [Unidentified.] *Chronology: 1940-1943*
http://www.topedge.com/panels/ww2/na/chron.html

1896. [Unidentified.] *Colonel Vladimir Peniakoff (Popski) and the Men Who Followed Him, "Popski's Private Army"*
http://www.geocities.com/Pentagon/2477/

1897. [Unidentified.] *Das Deutsche Afrika-Corps* (German language site)
http://www.afrika-korps.de/

1898. [Unidentified.] *High Command Disputes and Interference*
http://www.topedge.com/panels/ww2/na/leaders.html

1899. [Unidentified.] *North African Campaign (1942)*
http://www.topedge.com/panels/ww2/na/index.html

1900. [Unidentified.] *North African Landings—1942*
http://history.acusd.edu/gen/WW2Timeline/Europe01c.html

1901. [Unidentified.] *Popski's Private Army (P.P.A.) Preservation Society*
http://users.online.be/ppa_preservation_society/

1902. [Unidentified.] *The Desert War: North Africa, 1940-1943*
http://www.bphprint.co.nz/desert/

1903. [Unidentified.] *World War II Study: North Africa*
http://www.topedge.com/panels/ww2/na/index.html

1904. Zabecki, David T. *Rommel's Rise and Fall*
http://www.military.com/Content/MoreContent?file=PRnafrica

EGYPT AND LIBYA

1905. Huntley, Ernest. *Alam Halfa* (at top of screen click on "H-L;" pick this person's name from list on left screen; text appears to right)
http://www.warlinks.com/memories/index.html

1906. Newell, Clayton R. *The U.S. Army Campaigns of World War II: Egypt-Libya* (CMH Publication 72-13)
http://www.army.mil/cmh-pg/brochures/egypt/egypt.htm

1907. Royal Australian Navy/The Gun Plot. *The Siege of Tobruk and the "Spud Run"* (how the Australians held the city for eight months against a German-Italian siege in 1941; click on this title way down left hand list; text appears on right hand side)
http://www.gunplot.net/

1908. Special Service Division, Army Service Forces. *Pocket Guide to Egypt* (1943)
http://worldwar2.smu.edu/cgi-bin/Pwebrecon.cgi?v1
=101&ti=101,101&CNT=50&Search_Arg=world+war&Search_Code
=GKEY&x=30&y=5&y=5&PID=3725&SEQ=20020105195519&SID=1

1909. [Unidentified.] *Daring Voyage of "S.S. Seatrain Texas," Code Name: Treasure Ship* (emergency American equipment being provided General Montgomery)
http://www.usmm.org/seatraintexas.html

1910. [Unidentified.] *Egypt in the Second World War*
http://www.spartacus.schoolnet.co.uk/2WWegypt.htm

1911. [Unidentified.] *El Alamein, 1942: Sands of Death and Valor*
http://www.geocities.com/Pentagon/6813/

1912. [Unidentified.] *"Lady Be Good"* (plane disappeared in 1943; redis-covered November 1958)
http://www.wpafb.af.mil/museum/history/wwii/lbg.htm

ALGERIA AND FRENCH MOROCCO

1913. Anderson, Charles R. *The U.S. Army Campaigns of World War II: Algeria-French Morocco* (CMH Publication 72-11)
http://www.army.mil/cmh-pg/brochures/algeria/algeria.htm

1914. Brown, Robert J. *Britain's Bold Strike on the French Fleet* (at Oran, Algeria)
http://www.military.com/Content/MoreContent?file=PRchurchill

1915. Caden, A. G. *U.S.S. Augusta (CA-31): War Diary, November 7-11, 1942*
http://www.internet-esq.com/ussaugusta/diary/1142.htm

1916. Headquarters, 3rd Battalion. *Journal for the 3rd Battalion, 26th Infantry, 1st Infantry Division, Commencing November 1, 1942*
http://historicaltextarchive.com/ww2/3bnlog.html

1917. Ross, Morey ("Rothholtz"). *My Eyewitness Account of the Battle for Fedala and Casablanca, French Morrocco, November 7, 1942-November 12, 1942, on board U.S.S. Augusta*
http://www.internet-esq.com/ussaugusta/torch/eyewitness.htm

1918. [Unidentified/] *Naval Order of Battle for Operation Torch: American Forces and French Forces*
http://www.internet-esq.com/ussaugusta/torch/orderofbattle.htm

1919. [Unidentified.] *Operation Torch* (description begins below initial links section)
http://www.internet-esq.com/ussaugusta/torch/index.htm

1920. [Unidentified.] *Operation Torch: The Anglo-American landings in North Africa—8th November 1942*
http://www.topedge.com/panels/ww2/na/torch.html

1921. [Unidentified.] *Parachute Troops in Operation Torch, Planning File, October 1942*
http://carlisle-www.army.mil/cgi-bin/usamhi/DL/showdoc.pl?doc-num=597

TUNISIA

1922. Anderson, Charles R. *The U.S. Army Campaigns of World War II: Tunisia* (CMH Publication 72-12)
http://www.army.mil/cmh-pg/brochures/tunisia/tunisia.htm

1923. Roberts, II, Douglas J. *Raid on Rommel's Railroad* (effort to destroy pivotal railroad bridge)
http://www.military.com/Content/MoreContent?file=PR2rommelf

1924. [Unidentified.] *34th Infantry Division Fondouk Commendation* (and the circumstances laying behind it)
http://www.milhist.net/34/34fondouk.shtml

1925. [Unidentified.] *To Bizerte with the II Corps: 23 April-13 May 1943* (1943; 1990 edition—CMH Publication 100-6)
http://www.army.mil/cmh-pg/books/wwii/bizerte/bizerte-intro.htm

1926. [Unidentified.] *Victory in Tunisia*
http://history.acusd.edu/gen/WW2Timeline/Europe02.html

War in Other Parts of Africa

OVERVIEW AND REGIONAL TREATMENTS

1927. Humphreys, Arthur. *Memories of Arthur Humphreys* (describes a Christmas in West Africa; at top of screen click on "H-L;" pick this person's name from list on left screen; text appears to right)
http://www.warlinks.com/memories/index.html

1928. Special Service Division, Army Service Forces. *Pocket Guide to West Africa* (1943; needs Adobe Acrobat)
http://worldwar2.smu.edu/cgi-bin/Pwebrecon.cgi?v1=111&ti
=101,111&CNT=50&Search_Arg=world+war&Search_Code=GKEY&x
=30&y=5&y=5&PID=3725&SEQ=20020105195519&SID=1

ETHIOPIA

1929. Garvey, Marcus. *Italy's Conquest* (a 1936 editorial blaming Mussolini's success on the ruler of Ethiopia's overreliance "on white Governments, including the white League of Nations")
http://www.commonlink.com/~olsen/RASTAFARI/
GARVEY/blackman3607.html

1930. Library of Congress. *Ethiopia: A Country Study*
http://lcweb2.loc.gov/frd/cs/ettoc.html

1931. Marcus, Harold J. *Haile Selassie vs Mussolini*
http://www.oneworldmagazine.org/focus/etiopia/musso.html

1932. Pankhurst, Richard. *A History of Early Twentieth Century Ethiopia: The Liberation Campaign, 1941 Mussolini's Entry into the European War*
http://archives.geez.org/AddisTribune/Archives/1997/
04/10-04-97/20cent-14.html

1933. [Selassie, Haile.] *Hail Selasssie's Appeal to the League of Nations (June 1936)*
http://www.mtholyoke.edu/acad/intrel/selassie.htm

1934. [Unidentified.] *Italian Rule and World War II*
http://lcweb2.loc.gov/cgi-bin/query/r?frd/cstdy:@field(DOCID+et0028.

1935. Yelvington, Kevin A. *Dislocating Diaspora: Caribbean Blacks and the Italo-Ethiopian War, 1935-1941*
http://www.cofc.edu/atlanticworld/newpage3.htm

Near East

REGIONAL STUDIES

1936. [Unidentified.] *Armed Forces of World War II: Near East* (concise history)
http://members.tripod.com/~marcin_w/index-2.html

TURKEY

1937. [Germany and Turkey.] *Turkish-German Friendship Treaty, Signed in Ankara (June 18, 1941)*
http://www.ibiblio.org/pha/policy/1941/410618a.html

1938. [Unidentified.] *Turkey and the Second World War*
http://www.spartacus.schoolnet.co.uk/2WWturkey.htm

SYRIA

1939. Library of Congress. *Syria: A Country Study* (select chapter on World War II)
http://memory.loc.gov/frd/cs/sytoc.html

1940. Special Service Division, Army Service Forces. *Pocket Guide to Syria* (1943; Adobe Acrobat required)
http://worldwar2.smu.edu/cgi-bin/Pwebrecon.cgi?v1=106&ti=101,106&CNT=50&Search_Arg=world+war&Search_Code=GKEY&x=30&y=5&y=5&PID=3725&SEQ=20020105195519&SID=1

1941. [Unidentified.] *Syria in the Second World War*
http://www.spartacus.schoolnet.co.uk/2WWsyria.htm

1942. [Unidentified,] Garth. *Australian Ski Troops—An Unusual Combination*
http://worldatwar.net/article/australianski/index.html

LEBANON

1943. Library of Congress. *Lebanon: A Country Study* (see the chapter on World War II)
http://memory.loc.gov/frd/cs/lbtoc.html

PALESTINE

1944. Ahlin, Marilynn. *Stockade and Tower Settlements: Reclaiming the Land*
http://www.bridgesforpeace.com/publications/dispatch/
lifeinisrael/Article-10.html

1945. Barker, Tom. *Memories of Pte Tom Barker 2982252, 1st Bn Argyll &
Sutherland Highlanders* (served in Palestine and Desert Long Range
Group before capture)
http://www.warlinks.com/cgi-bin/links/jump.cgi?ID=76

1946. Oren, Michael B. *Orde Wingate: A Friend under Fire* (a discussion of
the diametrically opposed evaluations of his career and abilities as a soldier, with an emphasis upon his late 1930s work in what became Israel)
http://www.shalem.org.il/azure/10-oren.htm

1947. Roosevelt, Franklin D. *Attitude of American Government toward
Palestine: Letter to King Ibn Saud (April 5, 1945)*
http://www.yale.edu/lawweb/avalon/decade/decad161.htm

1948. [Unidentified.] *Christian Zionism* (on General Wingate's encour-
agement of Zionism while serving in the region in the late 1930s)
http://www.icej.org/pages/events/zionist/what_is_CZ.html

TRANSJORDAN

1949. Luscombe, Stephan. *Transjordan* (importance of territory in the war
mentioned but not developed)
http://www.btinternet.com/~britishempire/empire/maproom/transjor-
dan.htm

1950. [Unidentified.] *The Making of Transjordan* (primarily stresses inter-
war years)
http://www.kinghussein.gov.jo/his_transjordan.html

Sicily

1951. Baumer, Robert W. *Lieutenant Colonel Bill Darby's Rangers in the
Invasion of Sicily*
http://www.grunts.net/army/darbysrangers.html

1952. Birttle, Andrew J. *The U.S. Army Campaigns of World War II: Sicily*
(CMH Publication 72-16)
http://www.army.mil/cmh-pg/Brochures/72-16/72-16.htm

1953. Copp, Terry. *The [Canadian] Invasion of Sicily*
http://www.legionmagazine.com/features/canadianmilitaryhistory/97-03.asp

1954. Morris, Robert. *A Letter Home: A Coast Guard Veteran describes Flotilla 4/10's Operations Prior to D-Day* (emphasis on north Africa and Sicily)
http://www.uscg.mil/hq/g-cp/history/Morris_Ltr.html

1955. Olinger, Mark A. *Quartermaster NCO Heroism during Sicily Invasion*
http://www.quartermaster.army.mil/oqmg/
Professional_Bulletin/1996/Winter/sicily.html

1956. Sharon, Richard O. *The Sharon Chronicles* (diary)
http://www.concentric.net/~drake725/june28.htm

1957. Straczek, J. H. *The Invasion of Sicily—Operation Husky*
http://www.navy.gov.au/history/ran_sicily.htm

1958. Texas Military Forces Museum. *443rd Antiaircraft Artillery Battalion in World War II: Sicilian Campaign* (map and other data)
http://www.kwanah.com/txmilmus/36division/archives/443/44348.htm

1959. [Unidentified.] *Road to Messina—Europe 1943*
http://history.acusd.edu/gen/WW2Timeline/Europe03.html

1960. [Unidentified.] *Sicily*
http://www.acusd.edu/~askora/sicily.html

1961. USAF Museum. *The Aerial Capture of Pantellera and Lampedusa*
http://www.wpafb.af.mil/museum/history/wwii/ce7.htm

Italy

1962. Bereznicki, Ron. *Battle of Monte Cassino*
http://www.accessweb.com/users/rbereznicki/over.html-ssi

1963. Berlin, Alvin. *Oral History* (emphasis on the non-combat portions of a soldier's life, especially in Italy)
http://www-personal.umich.edu/~amnornes/Josh.html

1964. Copp, Terry. *Battle Exhaustion in World War II* (in Italy and North Africa)
http://www.legionmagazine.com/features/canadianmilitaryhistory/98-01.asp

1965. Copp, Terry. *Looking Beyond the Casualties* (Canadian soldiers' attitudes in Italy)
http://www.legionmagazine.com/features/canadianmilitaryhistory/97-09.asp

1966. Copp, Terry. *The Battle for Ortona*
http://www.legionmagazine.com/features/canadianmilitaryhistory/97-11.asp

1967. Donogue, Michael J. *Michael John Donoghue Royal Ulster Rifles #7020301* (extracts from his diary, including poetry)
http://www3.ns.sympatico.ca/ppdono/pat/mjd/mjd.htm

1968. Fifteenth Army Group. *A Military Encyclopedia based on Operations in the Italian Campaigns, 1943-1945* (partly downloadable)
http://www.milhist.net/deep/milencyc.shtml

1969. Fleisher, Bob. *It's Another Night at the Front* (Christmas Eve, 1944; from *Stars and Stripes* [Mediterranean edition], 26 December 1944)
http://www.milhist.net/34/medics.shtml

1970. Green, John R. *My Life* (served in North Africa and Italy)
http://www.warlinks.com/cgi-bin/links/jump.cgi?ID=68

1971. Haskew, Michael E. *San Pietro: Capturing the Face of War*
http://www.military.com/Content/MoreContent?file=PRsanpietrof

1972. Iacono, Giuseppe. *Navida Battaglia Italiane* (Italian language site discussing Italian Navy during the war)
http://www.mediwork.com/navi/

1973. Laurie, Clayton D. *Rapido River Disaster* (bitterly controversial campaign that resulted in post-war Congressional hearings)
http://www.military.com/Content/MoreContent?file=PRrapido

1974. Laurie, Clayton D. *The U.S. Army Campaigns of World War II: Anzio* (CMH Publication 72-19)
http://www.army.mil/cmh-pg/brochures/anzio/72-19.htm

1975. Laurie, Clayton D. *The U.S. Army Campaigns of World War II: Rome-Arno* (CMH Publication 72-20)
http://www.army.mil/cmh-pg/brochures/romar/72-20.htm

1976. Lihou, Maurice. *The Wimpys [Wellington Bombers] of 205 Group* (Italian campaign)
http://www.guernsey.net/~mlihou/

1977. Mambem, Claudio C. *The Italian Navy: Unofficial Homepage* (covers entire history of Italian navy)
http://www.geocities.com/CapitolHill/9226/navy.html

1978. McCarthy, Joe. *Iron-Man Battalion* (from *Yank Magazine*, 22 December 1944)
http://www.milhist.net/deep/ironman.shtml

1979. [Newspaper Article.] *GI Joes Receive Rations from "Sullivan's Grocery"* (on feeding a massive army in wartime; from *The Stars and Stripes* [Mediterranean edition], 5 December 1944)
http://www.milhist.net/mto/sullivan.shtml

1980. [*New York Times* article.] *Forgotten Fronts* (November 23, 1944)
http://www.milhist.net/global/forgotten.shtml

1981. Oland, Dwight D. *The U.S. Army Campaigns of World War II: North Apennines: 10 September 1944-April 1945* (CMH Publication 72-34)
http://www.army.mil/cmh-pg/brochures/nap/72-34.htm

1982. Patrick, Bethanne K. *Army Captain Bob Dole* (future Presidential candidate; description of how he was wounded in Italy)
http://www.military.com/Content/MoreContent?file=ML_dole_bkp

1983. Patrick, Bethanne K. *Sgt. James Marion Logan* (and the Salerno beachhead)
http://www.military.com/Content/MoreContent?file=ML_logan_bkp

1984. Popa, Thomas A. *The U.S. Army Campaigns of World War II: Po Valley, 5 April-8 May 1945* (CMH Publication 72-33)
http://www.army.mil/cmh-pg/brochures/po/72-33.htm

1985. Panebianco, Albert R. *World War II Experiences* (Anzio to Dachau)
http://home.nc.rr.com/alpanebianco

1986. Silvestri, Flavio. *Franco Lucchini—the Top Italian Ace* (credited with "ace" status [five or more kills] in World War One, the Spanish Civil War, and World War Two)
http://www.elknet.pl/acestory/lucchini/lucchini.htm

1987. Smith, Kenneth V. *The U.S. Army Campaigns of World War II: Naples-Foggia* (CMH Publication 72-17)
http://www.army.mil/cmh-pg/brochures/naples/72-17.htm

1988. Special Service Division, Army Service Forces. *Pocket Guide to Italian Cities* (1944; Adobe Acrobat necessary)
http://worldwar2.smu.edu/cgi-bin/Pwebrecon.cgi?v1=103&ti

=101,103&CNT=50&Search_Arg=world+war&Search_Code=GKEY&x
=30&y=5&y=5&PID=3725&SEQ=20020105195519&SID=1

1989. Tice, Jr., Paul F. *How I Fought the War with a Typewriter* (pulled headquarters duty in both Italy and North Africa)
http://www.unclebud.f2s.com/

1990. [Unidentified.] *Battle of Monte Cassino* (map and study materials)
http://www.accessweb.com/users/rbereznicki/over.html-ssi

1991. [Unidentified.] *Commando Supremo: Italy at War, 1940-1943* (aims to rehabilitate the reputation of the Italian Army as a fighting force)
http://www.comandosupremo.com/

1992. [Unidentified.] *Custermen: Italian Campaign of World War II: 85th "Custer" Division, 328th Field Artillery Battalion*
http://hometown.aol.com/stevec01e/HOME/Home.html

1993. [Unidentified.] *88th Infantry Division, Summer 1945: Outline of POW Command Activities*
http://www.milhist.net/88/88powcmnd.shtml

1994. [Unidentified.] *Fifth Army at the Winter Line: 15 November 1943-15 January 1944* (1945; 1990 edition—CMH Publication 100-9)
http://www.army.mil/cmh-pg/books/wwii/winterline/winter-fm.htm

1995. [Unidentified.] *German Operations at Anzio* (Report, 1944)
http://carlisle-www.army.mil/cgi-bin/usamhi/DL/showdoc.pl?doc-num=422

1996. [Unidentified.] *History of Task Force 45 (29 July 1944 to 25 January 45)* (a polyglot American, British, Brazilian, partisan unit with a large number of civilian Italian construction personnel thrown in for good measure)
http://www.milhist.net/mto/taskforce45.shtml

1997. [Unidentified.] *Italian Campaign: Major Allied Units*
http://www.milhist.net/ord/mtounits.shtml

1998. [Unidentified.] *Italy and the Pacific: The "Forgotten" Campaigns of World War II*
http://www.geocities.com/techbloke/

1999. [Unidentified.] *La Regia Marina—the Italian Navy in World War II* (bilingual: Italian and English)
http://www.regiamarina.it/

2000. [Unidentified.] *Operation Shingle (Anzio), Fifth Army Outline Plane, January 1944*
http://carlisle-www.army.mil/cgi-bin/usamhi/DL/showdoc.pl?doc-num=23

2001. [Unidentified.] *Orders of Battle, World War II: Mediterranean Ground Forces, U.S. Divisions and Comparable Units, 1944-1945*
http://www.milhist.net/ord/ordbatusd.shtml

2002. [Unidentified.] *Regina Marina Italiana* (Italian Navy, 1940-1943; in English and Italian)
http://www.regiamarina.net/

2003. [Unidentified.] *Salerno: American Operations from the Beaches to the Voltunro, 9 September-6 October 1943* (1944; 1990 edition—CMH Publication 100-7)
http://www.army.mil/cmh-pg/books/wwii/salerno/sal-fm.htm

2004. [Unidentified.] *Secret World War II Italian Planes* (prototypes in development at end of war)
http://sfstation.members.easyspace.com/fstpxp.htm

2005. [Unidentified.] *Stalemate in Italy—Europe 1943*
http://history.acusd.edu/gen/WW2Timeline/Europe04.html

2006. [Unidentified.] *"The D-Day Dodgers" (Sung to the Tune "Lili Marlene")* (satirical look by Allied soldiers about how they were "dodging" the dangers of D-Day by fighting in Italy)
http://www.milhist.net/mto/ddaydodg.shtml

2007. [Unidentified.] *The Italian Navy during World War II*
http://www.geocities.com/CapitolHill/9226/ww2.html

2008. [Unidentified.] *War Diary* (German 14th Army, covering January 22 to May 31, 1944; downloadable in Office 2001 format—far down page; most everything else are links rather than downloads)
http://members.tripod.com/~Sturmvogel/Panzerkeil.html

2009. [Unidentified.] *Taranto* (British use of torpedoes to sink Italian warcraft; often viewed as prototype of what Japanese imitated at Pearl Harbor)
http://www.geocities.com/Broadway/Alley/5443/tar.htm

2010. [Unidentified.] *U.S. 4th Naval Beach Battalion* (includes accounts of the invasion at Salerno, Italy)
http://www.4thbeachbattalion.com/

2011. Vasta, Salvatore. *Italian World War II History and Reenacting* (seeks to rebuild reputation of Italian military of the period)
http://members.tripod.com/~nembo/welcome.html
http://www.italianfront.com (scheduled new site)

2012. Waldrop, J. D. *World War II Memories* (primarily of Italy)
http://www.geocities.com/Pentagon/Quarters/5173/mapindex.html

2013. Whitlock, Flint. *Allied Agony at Anzio*
http://www.military.com/Content/MoreContent?file=PRanzio

Cyprus

2014. Library of Congress. *Cyprus: A Country Study*
http://lcweb2.loc.gov/frd/cs/cytoc.html

2015. Turkish Republic of Northern Cyprus. *World War II and Postwar Nationalism* (a Turkish Cypriot interpretation of both periods)
http://lcweb2.loc.gov/cgi-bin/query/r?frd/cstdy:@field(DOCID+cy0020.

Malta

2016. Calleja, Ray. *Cottonera in World War 2*
http://www.geocities.com/Heartland/Fields/9419/w_w2.html

2017. Henwood, Louis. *Senglea [in Malta] during World War II*
http://www.geocities.com/louishenwood/page2.html

2018. Ratuszynski, Wilhelm. *George "Buzz" Beurling—the Top Scoring Canadian [Fighter Pilot]* (he built his reputation during the defense of Malta)
http://www.elknet.pl/acestory/beurling/beurling.htm

2019. [Unidentified.] *A History of Malta*
http://www.geocities.com/TheTropics/Palms/3401/

2020. [Unidentified.] *Before Malta Became an Island* (a history from the most ancient to the modern)
http://www.angelfire.com/80s/senglea/history/history.html

2021. [Unidentified.] *British Military in Malta*
http://www.targetwords.com/pop/front_page.html?a_id=1337

2022. Williams, Jack. *Minesweeping at Malta*
http://www.cronab.demon.co.uk/malta.htm

6

The Pacific Islands War: 1941-1945

Japan's Military and Navy

2023. Ballendorf, Dirk. *The Japanese Amphibious Blitzrieg of World War II*
http://www.uog.edu/faculty/ballendo/japblitz.htm

2024. Bauer, Jim. *Japanese Battle Fleet of World War II* (battleships, heavy
cruisers, light cruisers)
http://www.ww2pacific.com/japbb.html

2025. Bauer, Jim. *Japanese Carriers of World War II*
http://www.ww2pacific.com/japcv.html

2026. Brown, Bryan. *Markings on Japanese Arisaka Rifles of World War II*
http://www.radix.net/~bbrown/japanese_markings.html

2027. Duncan, Basil. *Unit 731—Japan's Secret Laboratory of Death and
Other Atrocities You Won't Read about in Your History Books*
http://www.geocities.com/Heartland/Plains/5850/deathcamp.html

2028. Dyer, III, Edwin M. *Hikoyi: 1946—Experimental Jet, Rocket & Pro-
peller Aircraft of the IJN [Imperial Japanese Navy] and IJA [Imperial Japanese Army]*
http://www.pelzigplatz.f2s.com/index.html

2029. Ford, Dan. *Japan at War, 1931-1945* (internal links to different events
and issues of these war years)
http://www.danford.net/japan.htm

2030. Hall, Tom, Editor. *Ashai Journal: Web Edition* (studies Japanese military aviation from 1900-1945)
http://www.marksindex.com/japaneseaviation/asahi.html

2031. Hansen, Michael. *The Building of the "Yamato" and "Musashi"*
http://www.ibiblio.org/pub/academic/history/marshall/
military/wwii/Japanese.navy/jap_yamoto_bat.txt

2032. Hoffman, Scott. Japanese Military History (emphasis on the "Kate" and "Val" aircrafts)
http://www.qni.com/~hoffman/

2033. [Japanese Military.] *Japanese Field Service Code (January 8, 1941)*
http://www.sunsite.unc.edu/pha/policy/1941/410108a.html

2034. Kato, K. *Internet Museum of Imperial Japanese Airplanes*
http://home.interlink.or.jp/~katoh00/

2035. Krivosheyev, Vadim ("Watson"). *Watson's Imperial James Navy Page*
http://canopus.lpi.msk.su/~watson/ijn.html

2036. Lewis, Peter. *Zero-Sen*
http://mitsubishi_zero.tripod.com/index.htm

2037. Mabry, Don. *Comparative Fleet Strengths: December 1, 1941, U.S. and Japan*
http://historicaltextarchive.com/sections.php?op=viewarticle&artid=194

2038. Maisov, [?]. *Organizations of Imperial Japanese Army and Navy*
http://www.interq.or.jp/japan/maisov/e/index.htm

2039. Maloney, Mike. *The Restoration of Shinhoto Chi-Ha* (an insight into the construction of Japanese tanks by the effort to restore one on display at Admiral Nimitz State Historical Park, Fredricksburg, Texas)
http://member.nifty.ne.jp/takixxx/chi-ha/chi-ha.htm

2040. McDonald, Jason. *The Imperial Japanese Navy*
http://www.worldwar2database.com/html/kaigun.htm

2041. Nevitt, Allyn D. *Long Lancers* (Japanese destroyers in the war)
http://www.combinedfleet.com/lancers.htm

2042. Pluth, Dave. *J-Aircraft: Japanese Aircraft and Ship Modeling*
http://www.j-aircraft.com/

2043. Quan, Robert. *Japanese Military Reference* (uniforms, samurai traditions, etc.)
http://quanonline.com/military/military_reference/japanese/japanese.html

2044. Ross, Kelley L. *Advanced Japanese Destroyers of World War II*
http://www.friesian.com/destroy.htm

2045. Sasaki, Mako. *Who Became Kamikaze Pilots and How Did They Feel Towards Their Suicide Mission?* (essay from the *Concord Review*)
http://www.tcr.org/kamikaze.html

2046. Taki, [?]. *Imperial Japanese Army* (organization, rank system, etc.)
http://member.nifty.ne.jp/takixxx/

2047. Toppan, Andrew. *Japanese Aircraft Carriers* (concise history and description)
http://www.hazegray.org/navhist/carriers/ijn_cv.htm

2048. Toppan, Andrew. *Japanese Dreadnoughts* (= Battleships; key design characteristics)
http://www.hazegray.org/navhist/battleships/ijn_dr.htm

2049. [Unidentified.] *Bamboo Shoots: A New Digest of Comment on Japanese War Crimes and their Consequences*
http://www.baronage.co.uk/bambshoo.html

2050. [Unidentified.] *Imperial Japanese Army Airplanes* (organized by type of plane)
http://home.interlink.or.jp/~katoh00/rikgun/r-frame.html

2051. [Unidentified.] *Imperial Japanese Aviation Resource Centers* (describing varied types of Japanese craft utilized during the war years)
http://www.warbirdsresourcegroup.org/IJARG/index.html

2052. [Unidentified.] *Japanese Naval Officers* (photographs and concise biographies; evaluation of talents of various commanders; site still under construction)
http://www.combinedfleet.com/officer.htm

2053. [Unidentified.] *Japanese Orders & Medals* (site under construction)
http://www.militarygamer.net/CloseCombatRealred/OMB/index.html

2054. [Unidentified.] *JGSDF Ordnance School Museum* (photos of combat equipment)
http://www.geocities.co.jp/MotorCity-Rally/7109/Tsuchiura.htm

2055. [Unidentified.] *Mitsubishi A6M Zero*
http://www.compass.dircon.co.uk/zeke.htm

2056. [Unidentified.] *Takeo Tanimizu: Japanese Fighter Pilot* (biography)
http://www.rjgeib.com/heroes/tanimizu/tanimizu.html

2057. [Unidentified.] *Yushukan* (Tokyo war museum; photos of war equipment)
http://www.geocities.co.jp/MotorCity-Rally/7109/Yushukan.htm

2058. Wlodarczyk, Mark T. *Japanese Aircraft*
http://www.marksindex.com/japaneseaviation/

2059. Wlodarczyk, Mark T. *Unit Structure of Imperial Japanese Army Air Force* (extract [English translation] from a Polish language study)
http://www.marksindex.com/japaneseaviation/jaafstructure.html

2060. Womack, Tom. *Sword of the Rising Sun*
http://www.military.com/Content/MoreContent?file=PRsword

Pearl Harbor

2061. Abe, Zeni, *A Japanese Pilot Remembers*
http://history1900s.about.com/library/prm/blpilotremembers1.htm

2062. Arizona Memorial. *1941 Map of Pearl Harbor*
http://www.execpc.com/~dschaaf/bshipro2.html

2063. Ballendorf, Dirk. *Preface to Pearl Harbor*
http://www.uog.edu/faculty/ballendo/perharbor.html

2064. Blonskey, Madelyn. *Survivor, Army Nurse Corps* (interview with)
http://www.military.com/Content/MoreContent?file=blonskey01

2065. Borgquist, Daryl S. *Advance Warning? The Red Cross Connection*
http://www.usni.org/navalhistory/Articles99/NHborgquist.htm

2066. Byong-kuk, Kim. *Remember Pearl Harbor* (a Korean journalist recalls hearing first news of the attack)
http://www.hankooki.com/kt_op/200106/t2001061417295148110.htm

2067. Carson, Carl. *Survivor, "U.S.S. Arizona"* (interview with)
http://www.military.com/Content/MoreContent?file=carson01

2068. Chief of Naval Operations. *CNO War Warning Message of November 24 and November 27, 1941*
http://www.ibiblio.org/hyperwar/PTO/EastWind/CNO-411127.html

2069. Cressman, Robert J., and J. Michael Wenger. *Infamous Day: Marines at Pearl Harbor, 7 December 1941* (1992; in the "Marines in World War II Commemorative Series")
http://www.ibiblio.org/hyperwar/USMC/USMC-C-Pearl.html

2070. Deac, Will. *Takeo Yoshikawa: The Pearl Harbor Spy Provided Valuable Intelligence to Japanese War Planners Prior to the Surprise Attack*
http://www.worldwarii.com/WorldWarII/articles/1997/05973_text.htm

2071. Dewa, Kichiji. *Japanese Mother Sub I-16* (interview with Kichi)
http://www.military.com/Content/MoreContent?file=dewa01

2072. Dorn, Edwin. *Advancement of Rear Admiral Kimmel and Major General Short on the Retired List* (December 1, 1995 report from the Office of the Under Secretary of Defense for Personnel and Readiness on the treatment of Kimmel and Short)
http://www.ibiblio.org/pha/pha/dorn/dorn_0.html

2073. Erickson, Ruth. *Naval Hospital Pearl Harbor, 7 December 1941* (account of her experiences)
http://www.history.navy.mil/faqs/faq66-3b.htm
http://www.military.com/Content/MoreContent?file=erickson01

2074. Fritz, Mark. *Inside the Empire*
http://www.boston.com/globe/nation/packages/secret_history/index2.shtml

2075. Fuchida, Mitsuo. *Attack at Pearl Harbor, 1941—the Japanese View* (Fuchida led the first wave of planes)
http://www.ibiscom.com/pearl2.htm

2076. Givens, Jr. Benjamin M. *Map of Pearl Harbor* (positions of each naval craft noted)
http://www.geocities.com/Pentagon/Quarters/7858/mapofpearl.html

2077. Guttman, Jon. *Taking Charge under Fire* (interview with Burdick H. Brittin, who saw combat on a destroyer at Pearl, Coral Sea, and Midway, among others)
http://www.military.com/Content/MoreContent?file=PRbrittin

2078. Historical Section, Fourteenth Naval District. *Administrative History of the Fourteenth Naval District and the Hawaiian Sea Frontier* (Volume 1; Hawaii, 1945)
http://www.ibiblio.org/hyperwar/USN/fac/PH/USN-Hawaii.html

2079. Historical Section, Submarine Command. *History of the Pearl Harbor Submarine Base, 1918-1945* (manuscript dated 1946)
http://www.ibiblio.org/hyperwar/USN/fac/PH/USN-PH-January 1, 1990.html

2080. Hughes, William. *U.S.S. Utah Association Official Web Site*
http://www.ussutah.org/

2081. Ibis Communications. *Attack on Pearl Harbor, 1941*
http://www.ibiscom.com/pearl.htm

2082. Jewell, Larry W. *The Myths of Pearl Harbor* (anti "revisionist" site)
http://www.ibiblio.org/pha/myths/myths.html

2083. Jewell, Larry W. *The Pearl Harbor Attack Hearings: Additional Documents* (selection of documents cited in the Pearl Harbor Congressional investigations as well as certain documents not included there)
http://www.ibiblio.org/pha/pha/extra.html

2084. Kubek, Anthony. *Communism and Pearl Harbor* (argues that the Communists lobbied for policies that guaranteed confrontation between Japan and the United States)
http://www.geocities.com/Pentagon/6315/fdr.html

2085. Lacouture, John E. *Pearl Harbor Attack* (Lacouture was serving as Assistant Engineer aboard the *USS Blue* the day of the attack)
http://www.history.navy.mil/faqs/faq66-3d.htm

2086. Military History Section, Headquarters, Army Forces Fast East. *Pearl Harbor Operations: General Outline of Orders and Plans* (Japanese Monograph 97)
http://ibiblio.org/pha/monos/097/index.html
http://www.ibiblio.org/pha/monos/097/index.html
http://www.ibiblio.org/pha/myths/jm-097.html

2087. Nagumo, Chuichi. *Japanese Battle Order* (describing to the units of the attack fleet, the goals and methodology)
http://www.execpc.com/~dschaaf/battle.html

2088. National Geographic. *Beyond The Movie "Pearl Harbor"* (pictures and concise biographies of key participants in the battle; list on left hand side of screen)
http://plasma.nationalgeographic.com/pearlharbor/
ngbeyond/people/people10.html

2089. Naval Historical Center. *Pearl Harbor Navy Medical Activities*
http://www.history.navy.mil/faqs/faq66-5.htm

2090. Naval Historical Center. *Pearl Harbor Raid, 7 December 1941* (photographs)
http://www.history.navy.mil/photos/events/wwii-pac/pearlhbr/pearl-hbr.htm

2091. Naval Historical Center. *The U.S. Navy in Hawaii, 1826-1945: An Administrative History*
http://www.history.navy.mil/docs/wwii/pearl/hawaii.htm

2092. Navy Department. *Statement on the Attack at Pearl Harbor on December 7, 1941 (December 5, 1942)* (progress report on repairing damage)
http://www.sunsite.unc.edu/pha/policy/1942/421205a.html

2093. Nightingale, E. C. *Attack at Pearl Harbor, 1941* (eyewitness aboard the *Arizona*)
http://www.ibiscom.com/pearl.htm

2094. O'Brien, Thomas. *Pearl Harbor's Forgotten Ship* (the *Utah*)
http://www.usni.org/NavalHistory/articles01/NHobrien8.htm

2095. Osprey Publishing. *Essential Pearl Harbor: Real-Time Interactive Military History* (animated maps and planes, memoirs of survivors, day by day calendar of what happened on the current date in 1941)
http://www.essentialpearlharbor.com/

2096. Patrick, Bethanne K. *Rear Adm. Isaac C. Kidd, Sr.* (perished on the *Arizona*)
http://www.military.com/Content/MoreContent?file=ML_kidd_bkp

2097. Perry, Mark J. *Nevada's Heroic Run* (to escape Pearl Harbor)
http://www.military.com/Content/MoreContent?file=PRnevada

2098. Portillo, Michael. *Remembering Pearl Harbor*
http://web.tampabay.rr.com/mspusf/pearlharbor.html

2099. Roberts, Chalmers M. *A Day that Will Live*—(a reporter's memories of bringing out a Sunday "extra" edition after the story broke)
http://www.washingtonpost.com/wp-dyn/articles/A5955-2001Dec6.html

2100. Rodgaard, John. *Pearl Harbor: Attack from Below* (argues that the Japanese midget submarines enjoyed more success than previously believed)
http://www.usni.org/navalhistory/Articles99/Nhrodgaard.htm

2101. Sallet, George J. *The Six Long Years* (Sallet was serving on the destroyer *Bagley* both before and after the attack)
http://www.cronab.demon.co.uk/sallet.htm

2102. Schuessler, Nick. *Pearl Harbor* (concise review of theories concerning the assault and also movie treatments of the subject)
http://battlefieldvacations.com/asia/pearl.asp

2103. Schultz, Fred L. *Resurrecting the Kimmel Case*
http://www.usni.org/NavalHistory/Articles95/NHschultz8.htm

2104. Simmons, Clark. *Survivor, "U.S.S. Utah"* (interview with African-American sailor)
http://www.military.com/Content/MoreContent?file=clark_simmons01

2105. Soucy, Lee. *Pearl Harbor Attack* (Soucy was serving as Pharmacist's Mate on the *USS Utah* the day of the assault)
http://www.history.navy.mil/faqs/faq66-3a.htm
http://www.military.com/Content/MoreContent?file=soucy01

2106. Twetan, Stone. *Road To Pearl Harbor* (chronology)
http://history.acusd.edu/gen/WW2Timeline/RD-PEARL.html

2107. [Unidentified.] *Battleship Row* (includes selected survivor accounts)
http://www.ibiblio.org/phha/Main.html

2108. [Unidentified.] *Coast Guard Units in Hawaii on December 7, 1941* (photographs of vessels)
http://www.uscg.mil/hq/g-cp/history/PearlHarbor.html

2109. [Unidentified.] *Ginger's Diary 1941* (she was a seventeen year old living at Hickham Field at the time the war began)
http://www.gingersdiary.com/

2110. [Unidentified.] *History of the Battleship U.S.S. Pennsylvania (BB-38)*
http://www.usspennsylvania.com/

2111. [Unidentified.] *Japan and Pearl Harbor* (stresses that many who were anti-intervention in regard to Europe were far more receptive to action in the Pacific)
http://www.blinncol.edu/brazos/socialscience/jgorman/hist1302/Japan%20and%20Pearl%20harbor.htm

2112. [Unidentified.] *Japanese Strike Force: The Ships that Attacked Pearl Harbor and Their Fate*
http://www.navsource.org/Naval/japan.htm

2113. [Unidentified.] *Pearl Harbor Remembered* (links to survivor remembrances and other materials)
http://www.execpc.com/~dschaaf/mainmenu.html

2114. [Unidentified.] *Pearl Harbor Revisionism* (types of)
http://www.geocities.com/Athens/3682/phrevisionism.html

2115. [Unidentified.] *The Amazing George Welch (Part One:) The Tiger of Pearl Harbor* (one of the few pilots to get aloft during the attack)
http://home.att.net/~historyzone/Welch1.html

2116. [Unidentified.] *The Coast Guard's Role in Hawaii during the Japanese Attack on Pearl Harbor, 7 December 1941*
http://www.uscg.mil/hq/g-cp/history/PearlHarborNarrative.html

2117. [Unidentified.] *The Pacific Fleet NOT at Pearl Harbor* (on December 7th and where they were at the time)
http://www.ww2pacific.com/notpearl.html

2118. [Unidentified.] *U.S.S. St. Louis (CL-49)* (a light cruiser; largest craft to get up steam and exit Pearl Harbor the day of the attack)
(existing:) http://sites.netscape.net/swede51/homepage
(future:) http://sites.netscape.net.swede51/homepage

2119. United States Congress. *Pearl Harbor Attack Hearings Report* (the joint Senate-House committee's final report and selected other materials from earlier investigations)
http://www.ibiblio.org/pha/pha/index.html

2120. University of Hawaii. *An Era of Change: Oral Histories of Civilians in World War II Hawaii* (brief extracts from several about the war years)
http://www2.soc.hawaii.edu/css/oral_hist/war.html

2121. University of Hawaii. *Hawaii War Records Depository* (1,325 newspaper photos from the war years in Hawaii; selection available on line)
http://libweb.hawaii.edu/hwrd/HWRD_html/HWRD.html

2122. [Various Individuals.] *Reports by Survivors of Pearl Harbor Attack: "Arizona"*
http://www.history.navy.mil/docs/wwii/pearl/survivors2.htm

2123. [Various Individuals.] *Reports by Survivors of Pearl Harbor Attack: "California"*
http://www.history.navy.mil/docs/wwii/pearl/survivors1.htm

2124. [Various Individuals.] *Reports of Survivors of Pearl Harbor Attack: "Maryland"*
http://www.history.navy.mil/docs/wwii/pearl/survivors3.htm

2125. [Various Individuals.] *Reports of Survivors of Pearl Harbor Attack: "Tennessee"*
http://www.history.navy.mil/docs/wwii/pearl/survivors4.htm

2126. [Various Individuals.] *Reports by Survivors of Pearl Harbor Attack: "West Virginia" and "Oklahoma"*
http://www.history.navy.mil/docs/wwii/pearl/survivors.htm

2127. [Various Officers.] *Pearl Harbor Action Reports, 7 December 1941* (links to the reports filed by the officer in charge of each vessel)
http://www.history.navy.mil/faqs/faq66-4.htm
http://www.ibiblio.org/hyperwar/USN/rep/Pearl/index.html

2128. [Various individuals and committees.] *The Investigations of Pearl Harbor* (can download the text of each of the pre-Congressional investigations)
http://www.ibiblio.org/pha/pha/invest.html

2129. Warden, Horace C. *Pearl Harbor Attack* (Ward was Medical Officer on the *USS Breese* the day of the assault)
http://www.history.navy.mil/faqs/faq66-3c.htm
http://www.military.com/Content/MoreContent?file=warden01

2130. Wells, Arthur W. *A Marine's War: from Pearl Harbor to Okinawa* (site provides an extract from the Pearl Harbor chapter of the book)
http://hometown.aol.com/dolart/dolart.htm

2131. Wels, Susan. *Pearl Harbor: America's Darkest Day* (excerpts from the book)
http://www.coffeetablebooks.com/PearlHarbor/start.html?id=ctb

Other Early Battles

ALEUTIANS AND ALASKA

2132. Blum, Samuel E. *Oral History Interview* (served with Navy in Alaska during the war)
http://fas-history.rutgers.edu/oralhistory/blum.htm

2133. Dailey, Jr., Franklyn E. *Socked In! Instrument Flying in Northern Latitudes* (book length analysis)
http://www.daileyint.com/flying/flying2.htm

2134. Hunter, Matthew. *Sitka, Alaska* (harbor defenses)
http://mchunter1.tripod.com/

2135. 11thAirForce.Com. *11th Air Force: World War II Fighters and Bomber Units*
http://www.warlinks.com/cgi-bin/links/jump.cgi?ID=439

2136. Jameson, Colin G., with the assistance of L. C. Smith (originally published without attribution). *The Aleutians Campaign, June 1942-*

August 1943 (in the "Office of Naval Intelligence Combat Narratives" series)
http://www.ibiblio.org/hyperwar/USN/USN-CN-Aleutians.html

2137. MacGarrigle, George L. *The U.S. Army Campaigns of World War II: Aleutian Islands* (1992; CMH Publication 72-6)
http://www.ibiblio.org/hyperwar/USA/C-Aleutians/USA-C-Aleutians.html
http://www.army.mil/cmh-pg/brochures/aleut/aleut.htm

2138. National Park Service. *Aleutians in World War II* (historic site administered by Park Service)
http://www.nps.gov/aleu

2139. [Unidentified.] *Battle of the Aleutian Islands*
http://www.uss-nashville.com/aleautions.htm

2140. [Unidentified.] *Casco Field: Naval Air Station Attu, Alaska* (collection of photographs)
http://www.ibiblio.org/hyperwar/USN/fac/Attu/index.html

2141. [Unidentified.] *Kodiak Alaska Military History* (photographs, maps, data on military installations)
http://www.kadiak.org/

2142. [Unidentified.] *Sitka Military History*
http://www.mehs.educ.state.ak.us/sitka/ww2.html

WAKE ISLAND

2143. Cressman, Robert J. *A Magnificent Fight: Marines in the Battle for Wake Island* (1992; in the "Marines in World War II Commemorative Series")
http://www.ibiblio.org/hyperwar/USMC/USMC-C-Wake.html
http://metalab.unc.edu/hyperwar/USMC/USMC-C-Wake.html

2144. Heinl, Jr., R. D. *Defense of Wake* (in the "U.S. Marine Corps Historical Monographs" series; 1947)
http://www.ibiblio.org/hyperwar/USMC/USMC-M-Wake.html
http://www.ibiblio.org/hyperwar/USMC/Wake/USMC-M-Wake-1.html

2145. Pierce, M. R. *The Race for Wake Island*
http://www-cgsc.army.mil/milrev/English/MayJun00/alma.htm

EAST INDIES

2146. Anderson, Charles R. *The U.S. Army Campaigns of World War II: East Indies* (CMH Publication 72-22)
http://www.army.mil/cmh-pg/brochures/eindies/eindies.htm

2147. Beckett, Anthea. *Special Mission 43*
http://www.beckett73.freeserve.co.uk/baker/sm43.htm

2148. Biemond, Arie. *A Guest of the Japanese in the Dutch East Indies* (family were civilian internees during the war)
http://www.danford.net/biemond.htm

2149. Clarke, Philip. *43 Special Mission—Synopsis*
http://www.icon.co.za/~pjclarke/miss00.html

2150. DePalma, Arthur R. *Japanese Naval Nightmare*
http://www.military.com/Content/MoreContent?file=PRjapanesef

2151. Dunn, Peter. *Netherlands East Indies Air Force in Australia during World War 2*
http://home.st.net.au/~dunn/nei-af.htm

2152. Golesworthy, Anna. *Personal Experience* (a civilian detainee of the Japanese)
http://www.war-experience.org/archives/personal/golesworthy.htm

2153. Imperial History Group. *Netherlands East Indies, 1941-1942*
http://www.geocities.com/dutcheastindies/

2154. Royal Australian Navy/The Gun Plot. *HMAS Kuru: Small Ship—Big Heart* (the rescue of a contingent of Australians and Dutch who had refused to surrender to the Japanese; click on this title way down left hand list; text appears on right hand side)
http://www.gunplot.net/

2155. [Unidentified.] *Biographies: The Dutch East Indies Campaign, 1941-1942*
http://www.geocities.com/dutcheastindies/biographies.html

2156. [Unidentified.] *Pakan Baroe Death Railway* (on Sumatra)
http://au.geocities.com/frans_taminiau/

2157. van der Heide, Albert. *Chinese Civil War Helps Consolidate Japanese Claims on Mainland, 1926-1963* (in spite of the title, a major secondary theme in the year by year chronology is the Dutch East Indies)
http://www.godutch.com/herald/ww2/950823.htm

HONG KONG

2158. Copp, Terry. *Hong Kong: There Was a Reason*
http://www.legionmagazine.com/features/canadianmilitaryhistory/96-03.asp

2159. Parker, [?]. *The Royal Rifles of Canada in the Battle of Hong Kong*
http://www.geocities.com/rcwpca/

2160. [Unidentified.] *A Savage Christmas: The Fall of Hong Kong* (Canadian participation in battle)
http://www.valourandhorror.com/HK/HKsyn.htm

2161. [Unidentified.] *Hong Kong War Diary: December 1941* (bringing together accounts related to the fall of the city)
http://www.hongkongwardiary.com/

SINGAPORE AND MALAYA

2162. Department of the Army. *Fall of Singapore* (from *Army Area Handbook* on Singapore)
gopher://gopher.umsl.edu/00/library/govdocs/armyahbs/aahb5/aah50011

2163. Ford, Daniel. *Colonel Tsuji of Malaya*
http://www.danford.net/tsuji.htm

2164. Glendinning, Alex. *Civilian Internees of the Japanese in Singapore during WWII*
http://user.itl.net/~glen/CivilianInternees.html

2165. Glendinning, Alex. *The British in Singapore and Malaya*
http://user.itl.net/~glen/BritishinSingapore%26Malaya.html

2166. Royal Australian Navy/The Gun Plot. *Z Force: Operation Jaywick* (attack on Japanese shipping in the harbor in 1943; click on this title way down left hand list; text appears on right hand side)
http://www.gunplot.net/

2167. Taylor, Ron. *Royal Norfolks in Far East*
http://www.britain-at-war.org.uk/royal_norfolks_in_far_east/index.htm

SINKING OF HMS *REPULSE* AND *PRINCE OF WALES*

2168. Historical Division, GHQ, AFPAC. *Interrogation of Captain Sonokawa Kamero* (November 14, 1945; he commanded the aircraft that sank the two British warships)
http://www.j-aircraft.com/research/interrogation_of_captain_sonokaw.htm

2169. Matthews, Alan. *As a Bit of an Introduction* (interview with a Japanese pilot involved in the sinkings)
http://www.j-aircraft.com/research/iki.htm

2170. Matthews, Alan (compiler). *The Sinking of the "Prince of Wales" and*

the "Repulse:" A Series of Personal Accounts Compiled from Crew Members
http://www.microworks.net/pacific/personal/pow_repulse.htm

2171. Matthews, Alan. *The War Ships: The Sinking of the "Repulse" and the "Prince of Wales"* (link button at end to continuation of discussion)
http://www.btinternet.com/~m.a.christie/warship1.htm

Doolittle Raid

2172. Clancey, Patrick. *Thirty Seconds over Tokyo: The Halsey-Doolittle Raid* (three source documents including Doolittle's after-action report and two post-war accounts)
http://www.ibiblio.org/hyperwar/AAF/rep/Doolittle/index.html

2173. Glines, C. V. *Strike Against Japan*
http://www.military.com/Content/MoreContent?file=PRstrike

2174. Lanzendorfer, Tim. *The Doolittle Raid: April 1942*
http://www.microworks.net/pacific/battles/doolittle_raid.htm

2175. Naval Historical Center. *Doolittle Raid on Japan, 18 April 1942* (with photographs)
http://www.history.navy.mil/photos/events/wwii-pac/misc-42/dooltl.htm

2176. Oxford, Edward. *Against All Odds*
http://www.military.com/Content/MoreContent?file=PRodds

2177. Patrick, Bethanne K. *Gen. James H. Doolittle* (biography of pre-war and post-war career)
http://www.military.com/Content/MoreContent?file=ML_doolittle_bkp

2178. Stork, Royden. *Doolittle Raid* (interview with a participant)
http://www.military.com/Content/MoreContent?file=stork01

2179. Todd, Joyce. *Doolittle Tokyo Raiders*
http://members.home.net/doolittleraider/

2180. [Unidentified.] *The Doolittle Raid and Its Aftermath* (second part requires use of link button on page)
http://www.grunts.net/wars/20thcentury/wwii/doolittle/doolittle.html

Philippines:
Conquest and Occupation

2181. Bailey, Jennifer L. *The U.S. Army Campaigns of World War II: Philippine Islands* (1992; CMH Publication 72-3; fall of islands)
http://www.ibiblio.org/hyperwar/USA/USA-C-Philippines.html
http://www.army.mil/cmh-pg/brochures/pi/PI.htm

2182. Barber, Laurie. *Yamashita War Crimes Trial Re-visited*
http://www.waikato.ac.nz/wfass/subjects/history/
waimilhist/1998/yamashita.html

2183. Bauer, Jim. *Admiral Thomas C. Hart—Commander of the U.S. Asiatic Fleet* (based in the Philippines; discussion of Hart's career and what happened to the fleet)
http://www.ww2pacific.com/admhart.html

2184. Beaber, Herman K. *Deliverance! It Has Come!* (diary of American preacher interned in the Philippines 1942-1945)
http://www.geocities.com/ithascome/

2185. Corregidor Historic Society. *Corregidor: Then and Now*
http://www.witman.jatoga.net.au/index1.html

2186. Derks, Tracy L. *MacArthur's Return*
http://www.military.com/Content/MoreContent?file=PRmacarthurf

2187. Elliott-Hogg, Natasha. *The War within a War: The Philippine Resistance, 1941-1945*
http://www.waikato.ac.nz/wfass/subjects/history/
waimilhist/1997/neh-folder/neh-p1.html

2188. Feuer, A. B. *Convoy's Route to Disaster*
http://www.military.com/Content/MoreContent?file=PRpensacola

2189. Feuer, A. B. *Heroic "Pigeon" in the Philippines* (the story of a salvage vessel)
http://www.military.com/Content/MoreContent?file=PRpigeon

2190. Gordon, Richard M. *The Battling Bastards of Bataan*
http://home.pacbell.net/fbaldie/Battling_Bastards_of_Bataan.html

2191. Himchak, Elizabeth M. *Bataan Project* (cast in the broader scope of why the defense of the Philippines failed)
http://www.acusd.edu/~ehimchak/WWII.project.html

2192. Leonie, Aling. *"Amerikanitos:" Life during the Japanese Occupation of the Philippines*
http://www.culturalbridge.com/phwwii.htm

2193. Morton, James. *U.S. Army in World War II (The War in the Pacific): The Fall of the Philippines* (1953)
http://www.ibiblio.org/hyperwar/USA/USA-P-PI.html

2194. National Archives and Records Administration. *Philippine Army and Guerrilla Records*
http://www.nara.gov/regional/mprnote2.html

2195. Organizational Web Site. *Battling Bastards of Bataan* (run for and on behalf of survivors of the Bataan death march)
http://home.pacbell.net/fbaldie/Battling_Bastards_of_Bataan.html

2196. Romero, Joseph. *Childhood Memories of the Pacific War*
http://www.culturalbridge.com/phwwii6.htm

2197. Rosal, Brian. *Manila under World War II* (invasion and conquest by Japanese)
http://www.geocities.com/Pentagon/Bunker/6613/

2198. Stoveberg, Irving. *The Fall of Corregidor: Radio Broadcasts* (last broadcasts before surrender)
http://earthstation1.simplenet.com/stroebng.html

2199. SWPA Intelligence. *Guerrilla Resistance Movement in the Philippines: SWPA Intelligence History (1946)*
http://carlisle-www.army.mil/cgi-bin/usamhi/DL/showdoc.pl?doc-num=577

2200. [Unidentified.] *American Defenders of Bataan and Corregidor*
http://harrisonheritage.com/adbc/

2201. [Unidentified.] *Guerrilla Resistance Movement in the Philippines—SWPA Intelligence History* (1946)
http://carlisle-www.army.mil/cgi-bin/usamhi/DL/showdoc.pl?doc-num=577

2202. [Unidentified.] *Japanese Landings at Zamboanga, 1942*
http://www.army.mil/cmh-pg/documents/zambo.htm

2203. [Unidentified.] *Philippine Division (1940-1945)* (organizational structure and leadership)
http://www.ibiblio.org/hyperwar/USA/OOB/Philippine-Division.html-January 1, 1990

2204. [Unidentified.] *The Official Corregidor Page*
http://members.tripod.com/~Corregidor/index.html

2205. Weaver, George. *Mike Weaver: Bataan Death March Survivor*
http://www.nemisys.com/memorial/mike261.html

2206. Whitman, John W. *Air Raid on Cavite*
http://www.military.com/Content/MoreContent?file=PRcavite

2207 Whitman, John W. *Delaying Action in the Philippines*
http://www.military.com/Content/MoreContent?file=PRaction

2208. Whitman, John W. *Last U.S. Horse Cavalry Charge*
http://www.military.com/Content/MoreContent?file=PRcavalry

2209. Whitman, John W. *Manila: How Open Was This Open City?*
http://www.military.com/Content/MoreContent?file=PRmanila

2210. Willey, Mark. *Sacrifice at Bataan* (argues that the forward strategy of attacking Japanese on the beaches and not moving all resources into Bataan guaranteed the defeat)
http://www.geocities.com/Pentagon/6315/bataan.html

Midway

2211. Allmon, William B. *Midway Islands' Undaunted Defenders* (article from *World War II* magazine)
http://www.thehistorynet.com/WorldWarII/articles/0596_cover.htm
http://www.military.com/Content/MoreContent?file=PRmidway01

2212. Bernice Pauahi Bishop Museum. *Battle of Midway* (on multiple web pages)
http://explorers.bishopmuseum.org/nwhi/batmid.shtml

2213. Best, Richard H. *In His Own Words* (only pilot to successfully drop bombs on two different Japanese carriers)
http://www.immf-midway.org/narrative.html

2214. Buckmaster, E. *Action Report of the Battle of Midway: Commanding Officer, USS Yorktown* (18 June 1942)
http://www.history.navy.mil/docs/wwii/mid7.htm
http://www.ibiblio.org/hyperwar/USN/ships/logs/CV/cv5-Midway.html

2215. Capra, Frank. *Battle of Midway* (in technicolor, 18 minutes; viewable online in two parts)
http://www.liketelevision.com/web1/movies/midway/

2216. Craven, Wesley F., and James L. Cate. *Battle of Midway: Army Air Forces* (extract concerning the battle from their work, *Plans and early Operations, June 1939 to August 1942;* volume 1 of *The Army Air Forces in World War II* [Chicago: University of Chicago Press, 1948])
http://www.history.navy.mil/faqs/faq81-9.htm

2217. Crossen, John. *Midway* (internal links on left hand side)
http://history.acusd.edu/gen/WW2Timeline/midway/index.html

2218. Ford, John (Commander, USNR). *Recollections.* (Ford was an Oscar winner and his footage of the battle of Midway was edited into a popular war era film)
http://www.history.navy.mil/faqs/faq81-8b.htm

2219. Frisbee, John L. *Marauders at Midway*
http://www.afa.org/magazine/valor/0486valor.html

2220. Fuchida, Mitsuo. *The Battle of Midway, 1942* (Fuchida witnessed the battle from the flight deck of the *Akagi*)
http://www.ibiscom.com/midway.htm

2221. Gay, George (Lieutenant, USNR). *Recollections* (he was the only survivor from Torpedo Squadron Eight, of the USS *Hornet*)
http://www.history.navy.mil/faqs/faq81-8c.htm
http://www.ibiblio.org/hyperwar/USN/ships/logs/CV/cv8-EnsGay.html
http://www.history.navy.mil/photos/pers-us/uspers-g/g-gay.htm (collection of photographs)

2222. Hartigan, Jr., C. C. *Action Report of the Battle of Midway: Commander Destroyer Squadron Six* (Serial 094 of 12 June 1942)
http://www.history.navy.mil/docs/wwii/mid9.htm

2223. Hawkinson, Chris. *Battle of Midway, June 3–6, 1942* (web site of a post-war individual with an on-going interest in the Battle)
http://www.centuryinter.net/midway/midway.html

2224. Heinl, Jr., R. D. *Marines at Midway* (in the "U.S. Marine Corps Historical Monographs" series; 1948)
http://www.ibiblio.org/hyperwar/USMC/USMC-M-Midway.html
http://www.au.af.mil/au/awc/awcgate/usmchist/midway.txt

2225. Hough, Frank O., Verle E. Ludwig, and Henry J. Shaw. *Battle of Midway: U.S. Marine Corps* (extract on the battle from their work, *From Pearl Harbor to Guadalcanal;* volume 1 of *History of U.S. Marine Corps Operations in World War II*)
http://www.history.navy.mil/faqs/faq81-10.htm
http://www.ibiblio.org/hyperwar/USMC/USMC-I.html (entire book)

2226. Hull, Michael D. *Midway*
http://www.military.com/Content/MoreContent?file=PRmidway

2227. Huygen, Michaele L. *The Battle of Midway: A Bibliography* (Naval Postgraduate School)
http://web.nps.navy.mil/~library/bibs/midwaytoc.htm

2228. International Midway Memorial Foundation. *Learn about Midway*
http://www.immf-midway.org/learn.html

2229. Fletcher, Jack. *Action Report of the Battle of Midway: Commander Cruisers, Pacific Fleet* (14 June 1942)
http://www.history.navy.mil/docs/wwii/mid3.htm

2230. Lanzendorfer, Tim. *Stopping the Tide: The Battle of Midway, 4-6 June 1942: Prelude, Battle, Epilogue* (detailed study)
http://www.microworks.net/pacific/battles/midway.htm

2231. Midway Atoll National Wildlife Refuge. *Midway Atoll in World War II*
http://www.r1.fws.gov/midway/past/ww2.html

2232. Mitscher, M. A. *Action Report of the Battle of Midway: Commanding Officer, USS Hornet* (Serial 0018 of 13 June 1942)
http://www.history.navy.mil/docs/wwii/mid5.htm
http://www.ibiblio.org/hyperwar/USN/ships/logs/CV/cv8-Midway.html

2233. Mozun, Rafael. *Battle of Midway, 1942: The Fight for the Pacific* (site in English and Spanish)
http://www.geocities.com/Colosseum/Arena/2951/english.html

2234. Murray, G. D. *Action Report of the Battle of Midway: Commanding Officer, USS Enterprise* (Serial 0033 of 8 June 1942)
http://www.history.navy.mil/docs/wwii/mid6.htm
http://www.ibiblio.org/hyperwar/USN/ships/logs/CV/cv6-Midway.html

2235. National Geographic. *Return to Midway* (site on post-war explorations at site of the battle)
http://www.nationalgeographic.com/features/98/midway/

2236. Naval Historical Center. *Battle of Midway: 4-7 June 1942—Composition of Japanese Forces*
http://www.history.navy.mil/faqs/faq81-6.htm

2237. Naval Historical Center. *Battle of Midway: 4-7 June 1942—Composition of U.S. Forces*
http://www.history.navy.mil/faqs/faq81-5.htm

2238. Naval Historical Center. *Battle of Midway: 4-7 June 1942—Online Action Reports Relating to the Battle* (with links; includes Admiral Nimitz's official account)
http://www.history.navy.mil/faqs/faq81-4.htm

2239. Naval Historical Center. *Battle of Midway: 4-7 June 1942—Online Art Exhibit* (paintings)
http://www.history.navy.mil/ac/midway/midway1.htm

2240. Naval Historical Center. *Battle of Midway: 4-7 June 1942—Overview and Special Image [Picture] Selection*
http://www.history.navy.mil/photos/events/wwii-pac/midway/midway.htm

2241. Naval Historical Center. *Battle of Midway: 4-7 June 1942—Select Bibliography*
http://www.history.navy.mil/faqs/faq81-2.htm

2242. Nimitz, Chester W. *Action Report of the Battle of Midway: Commander in Chief, U.S. Pacific Fleet* (Serial 01753 of 21 June 1942)
http://www.history.navy.mil/docs/wwii/mid2.htm

2243. Nimitz, Chester W. *Action Report of the Battle of Midway: Commander in Chief, U.S. Pacific Fleet* (Serial 01849 of 28 June 1942)
http://www.history.navy.mil/docs/wwii/mid1.htm

2244. Penland, J. R. *Action Report of the Battle of Midway: Bombing Squadron Six ACA Report* (4 June 1942)
http://www.history.navy.mil/docs/wwii/mid10.htm

2245. Pollard, Joseph P. (Lieutenant). *Recollections of the Battle of Midway* (graphic; Pollard was Medical Officer on the carrier *Yorktown*)
http://www.history.navy.mil/faqs/faq81-8a.htm

2246. Ponce, Paul, interview of Robert Ballard. *Under the Sea* (discovery of site where *Yorktown* sank)
http://www.pbs.org/newshour/bb/science/jan-june98/ballard_6-4.html

2247. Sauer, E. P. *Action Report of the Battle of Midway: Commanding Officer, USS Hammann* (Serial 2 of 16 June 1942)
http://www.history.navy.mil/docs/wwii/mid8.htm

2248. Schorreck, Henry F. *The Role of COMINT [Combat Intelligence] in the Battle of Midway* (SRH-230)
http://www.history.navy.mil/faqs/faq81-3.htm

2249. Spruance, R. A. *Action Report of the Battle of Midway: Commander Task Force Sixteen* (Serial 0144-A of 16 June 1942)
http://www.history.navy.mil/docs/wwii/mid4.htm

2250. Stekovic, Srdjan. *Midway* (click on this title on left hand of screen; text and illustrations will appear on the right side)
http://www.everblue.net/1942

2251. [Unidentified.] *Battle of Midway* (many pictures and a lengthy, detailed description of the battle)
http://www.geocities.com/Athens/Rhodes/8384/midway.html

2252. [Unidentified.] *Captain Marion E. Carl (VMF-223)* (first Marine ace; 18 plane kills)
http://www.westnet.com/~ssherman/usmc_carl.html#top

2253. [Unidentified.] *Japanese Order of Battle at Midway*
http://www.microworks.net/pacific/orders_of_battle/midway_japan.htm

2254. [Unidentified.] *Master of the Game: Nimitz at Midway* (in Adobe Acrobat)
http://www.rand.org/publications/MR/MR775.chap3.pdf

2255. [Unidentified.] *The Principle of the Objective: Nagumo vs Spruance at Midway*
http://www.centurytel.net/midway/objective.html

2256. [Unidentified] to Admiral Chester A. Nimitz. *Action Report: USSS Hammann (DD-412)* (the vessel was sunk during the battle and the report compiled from memory)
http://www.ibiblio.org/hyperwar/USN/ships/logs/DD/dd412-Midway.html

2257. USS Wiseman DE 67 website. *The Battle of Midway* (divided between two sites, with historical and other data)
http://www.sunwest-emb.com/wiseman/bmidway.htm
http://www.sunwest-emb.com/wiseman/bmidway2.htm

2258. Vickrey, B. K. *Spruance or Halsey: Who was the Better Man for the Job [at Midway]?*
http://www.centurytel.net/midway/veterans/spruance.html

Guadalcanal and Associated Sea Battles (Eastern Solomons, Cape Esperance, Savo, and Tassaffaronga)

2259. Allen, Robert J., and Otis Carney. *The Story of SCAT*
(part 1:) http://www.centercomp.com/cgi-bin/dc3/stories?1910
(part 2:) http://www.centercomp.com/cgi-bin/dc3/stories?1909

2260. Anderson, Norman J., and William K. Snyder. *SCAT* (= South Pacific Combat Air Transport; introduction of resupply of Guadalcanal by air; published in the *Marine Corps Gazette*, September 1992)
http://www.centercomp.com/cgi-bin/dc3/stories?1908

2261. Anderson, Charles R. *The U.S. Army Campaigns of World War II: Guadalcanal* (1993; CMH Publication 72-8)
http://www.ibiblio.org/hyperwar/USA/USA-C-Guadalcanal.html
http://www.army.mil/cmh-pg/brochures/72-8/72-8.htm
http://metalab.unc.edu/hyperwar/USA/USA-C-Guadalcanal.html

2262. Bauer, Jim. *Battle of Cape Esperance—October 11, 1942*
http://www.ww2pacific.com/capesper.html

2263. Bauer, Jim. *Battle of Santa Cruz—October 25, 1942*
http://www.ww2pacific.com/santacrz.html

2264. Bauer, Jim. *Battle of Tassafaronga—November 30, 1942*
http://www.ww2pacific.com/tassafaronga.html

2265. Bauer, Jim. *The Battle off Savo Island—August 9, 1942 (off Guadalcanal, Solomon Islands)*
http://www.ww2pacific.com/savo.html

2266. Bauer, Jim, and Gregory Mackenzie. *Updates and Corrections on the Battle of Savo Island: Correspondence with LCDR Mackenzie J. Gregory, RAN*
http://www.ww2pacific.com/savoupdt.html

2267. Browning, Jr., Robert M. *Douglas Munro, the Coast Guard and the Guadalcanal Campaign*
http://www.uscg.mil/hq/g-cp/history/Munro.html

2268. Davis, Scott. *Naval Battle of Guadalcanal (November 13-15, 1942)* (units and participants on both sides)
http://www.geocities.com/Pentagon/5133/guadb.htm

2269. Donahue, James. *Guadalcanal Journal* (first-hand account)
http://users.erols.com/jd55/guadalcanal.html

2270. Flahavin, Peter. *Guadalcanal Battle Sites Today* (photographs from the 1990s)
http://www.guadalcanal.homestead.com/

2271. Garrett, Joe. *Official USMC Photos* (previously unpublished)
http://www.gnt.net/~jrube/guadpics/guadalb.htm
http://www.gnt.net/~jrube/indx2.html

2272. Garrett, J. R. *A Marine Diary: My Experiences on Guadalcanal*
http://www.gnt.net/~jrube/intro.html

2273. Gregory, Mackenzie J. *HMAS Canberra Lost off Savo Island* (personal account)
http://members.tripod.com/Tenika/savo.htm

2274. Guttman, Jon. *Three-War Marine Hero* (in an interview with Raymond G. Davis, Davis describes service at Guadalcanal, in detail, and at Peleliu, in passing)
http://www.military.com/Content/MoreContent?file=PRmarine

2275. Headquarters, Army Air Forces. *Pacific Counterblow: The 11th Bombardment Group and the 67th Fighter Squadron in the Battle for Guadalcanal: An Interim Report* (In the "Wings of War" series, number 3; 1992 reissue)
http://www.ibiblio.org/hyperwar/AAF/WW-3.html

2276. Hollway, Don. *The Cactus Air Force*
http://www.military.com/Content/MoreContent?file=PRcactus

2277. Inui, Genjirou. *The Diary of Genjirou Innui* (Innui was a platoon leader in an anti-tank company)
http://www.gnt.net/~jrube/Genjirou/cover.htm

2278. Lippman, David H. *First Naval Battle of Guadalcanal*
http://www.military.com/Content/MoreContent?file=PRguadalcanal

2279. Miller, Robert C. *Guadalcanal Fast Freight*
http://www.centercomp.com/cgi-bin/dc3/stories?1913

2280. Miller, Jr., John. *Guadalcanal: The First Offensive.* (1949; 1991 edition; in the series: *U.S. Army in World War II: The War in the Pacific*)
http://www.army.mil/cmh-pg/books/wwii/GuadC/GC-fm.htm
http://metalab.unc.edu/hyperwar/USA/USA-C-Guadalcanal.html

2281. Moens, John. *Marine Raider in the Pacific* (John Apergis' combat before formally becoming part of Carlson's Raiders)
http://www.military.com/Content/MoreContent?file=PRpacraider

2282. Naval Historical Center. *The Sullivan Brothers: The Loss of USS "Juneau," (CL-52)*
http://www.history.navy.mil/faqs/faq72-2.htm

2283. Nicholas, John. *Guadalcanal Online* (links to varied materials to the battle)
http://www.geocities.com/Heartland/Plains/6672/canal_index.html

2284. O'Neil, Roger. *Sinking of USS "Juneau"* (O'Neill was the highest ranked known survivor; covers actions of vessel, November 11-13, 1942)
http://www.history.navy.mil/faqs/faq72-2a.htm

2285. Ortega, Louis. *Oral History: Battle of Guadalcanal, 1942-1943* (Ortega was Pharmacist Mate First Class with the Marines)
http://www.history.navy.mil/faqs/faq87-3c.htm

2286. Patrick, Bethanne K. *Gunnery Sgt. John Basilone*
http://www.military.com/Content/MoreContent?file=ML_basilone_bkp

2287. Patrick, Bethanne K. *Lt. Gen. Lewis "Chesty" Puller* (Marine commander at Guadalcanal)
http://www.military.com/Content/MoreContent?file=ML_puller_bkp

2288. Patrick, Bethanne K. *Sgt. Albert A. Schmid* (though blinded, kept up covering fire for his men)
http://www.military.com/Content/MoreContent?file=ML_schmid_bkp

2289. Patrick, Bethanne K. *Signalman 1st Class Douglas Munro* (only Coast Guardsman to win the Medal of Honor)
http://www.military.com/Content/MoreContent?file=ML_munro_bkp_htm

2290. Patrick, Bethane K. *The Sullivan Brothers*
http://www.military.com/Content/MoreContent?file=ML_sullivans_bkp

2291. Richter, John F. *A Navy Corpsman on Guadalcanal (1942)*
http://www.tankbooks.com/stories/story102.htm

2292. Richter, John F. *Farewell to Arms* (medics at Guadalcanal)
http://members.aol.com/famjustin/Richter1.html

2293. Roberts, Misty. *Sullivan Brothers* (five brothers who died in the sinking of the same ship)
http://www.utexas.edu/projects/latinoarchives/narratives/
vol1no2/SULLIVAN_BROTHERS/SULLIVAN_BROTHERS.HTML

2294. Ross, Kelly L. *A Guadalcanal Chronology: 7 August 1942-6 March 1943*
http://www.friesian.com/history/guadal.htm

2295. Royal Australian Navy/The Gun Plot. *Guadalcanal Campaign: The Battle of Savo Island* (click on this title way down left hand list; text appears on right hand side)
http://www.gunplot.net/

2296. Shaw, Jr., Henry I. *First Offensive: The Marine Campaign for Guadalcanal* (1992; in the "Marines in World War II Commemorative Series")
http://www.ibiblio.org/hyperwar/USMC/USMC-C-Guadalcanal.html
http://metalab.unc.edu/hyperwar/USMC/USMC-C-Guadalcanal.html

2297. Snead, W. J. *The Great Commission* (religion at Guadalcanal and other battle sites)
http://www.fortunecity.com/millenium/redwood/372/part8.htm

2298. Stekovic, Srdjan. *Cape Esperance* (click on this title on left hand of screen; text and illustrations will appear on the right side)
http://www.everblue.net/1942

2299. Stekovic, Srdjan. *Eastern Solomons* (click on this title on left hand of screen; text and illustrations will appear on the right side)
http://www.everblue.net/1942

2300. Stekovic, Srdjan. *Santa Cruz* (click on this title on left hand of screen; text and illustrations will appear on the right side)
http://www.everblue.net/1942

2301. Stekovic, Srdjan. *Second Savo* (click on this title on left hand of screen; text and illustrations will appear on the right side)
http://www.everblue.net/1942

2302. Stekovic, Srdjan. *Third Savo* (click on this title on left hand of screen; text and illustrations will appear on the right side)
http://www.everblue.net/1942

2303. Stekovic, Srdjan. *Tasaffaronga* (click on this title on left hand of screen; text and illustrations will appear on the right side)
http://www.everblue.net/1942

2304. Straczek, J. H. *Battle of Savo Island—Loss of HMAS Canberra*
http://www.navy.gov.au/history/ran_savo.htm

2305. [Unidentified.] *Cactus Airforce* (nickname given to the ground based planes on Guadalcanal)
http://www.ixpres.com/ag1caf/cactus/

2306. [Unidentified.] *Guadalcanal Online* (accounts of the battle and other material)
http://www.geocities.com/Heartland/Plains/6672/canal_index.html

2307. [Unidentified.] *Japanese Account Third Battle of Savo Island*
http://www.flash.net/~hfwright/jap_acct.htm

2308. [Unidentified.] *Narrative History of Task Force 6814, Americal Division—January 23, 1942 to June 30, 1943*
http://www.ibiblio.org/hyperwar/USA/OOB/Americal-history.html

2309. [Unidentified.] *Pacific Counterblow: The 11th Bombardment Group and the 67th* 2310. *Fighter Squadron in the Battle for Guadalcanal* ("Wings at War Series No. 3;" 1992, new edition)
http://www.ibiblio.org/hyperwar/AAF/WW-3.html

2310. [Unidentified.] *The Carriers Meet Again: The Battle of the Eastern Solomons, 23rd August-24th August, 1942*
http://www.microworks.net/pacific/battles/eastern_solomons.htm

2311. [Unidentified.] *The Unsung Heroes of SCAT*
http://www.centercomp.com/cgi-bin/dc3/stories?1903

2312. [Unidentified.] *U.S.S. O'Bannon* (story of Guadalcanal told in detail from the standpoint of this destroyer; links to next parts of story on left hand of screen)
http://www.domeisland.com/ussobannon/prelude.html

2313. Valenzi, Kathleen D. *Scouting Guadalcanal* (interview with Michael C. Capraro)
http://www.military.com/Content/MoreContent?file=PRguadal

2314. White, David. *A Comparison of U.S. and Japanese Forces at Guadalcanal*
http://www.waikato.ac.nz/wfass/subjects/history/waimilhist/1997/dw-folder/dw-p1.html

2315. Young, Peter L. *Henderson Field: Aftermath of a Bloody Holocaust*
http://www.centercomp.com/cgi-bin/dc3/stories?1912

2316. Zimmerman, John L. *The Guadalcanal Campaign* (in the "U.S. Marine Corps Historical Monographs" series; 1949)
http://www.ibiblio.org/hyperwar/USMC/USMC-M-Guadalcanal.html

2317. Zucker, Kevin. *Japanese Navy at Guadalcanal 1942: Japanese Navy Order of Battle* (page has links to several additional intra-site articles on the Japanese side of the battle)
http://www.magweb.com/sample/ww2/co01guao.htm

Other Island Battles

OVERVIEW

2318. Anderson, Charles R. *The U.S. Army Campaigns of World War II: Western Pacific* (CMH Publication 72-29)
http://www.army.mil/cmh-pg/brochures/westpac/westpac.htm

2319. Edgecombe, Helen. *The Coastwatchers*
http://www.waikato.ac.nz/wfass/subjects/history/waimilhist/1997/he-folder/he-p1.html

BISMARCK ARCHIPELAGO

2320. Hirrel, Leo. *The U.S. Army Campaigns of World War II: Bismarck Archipelago* (CMH Publication 72-24)
http://www.army.mil/cmh-pg/brochures/bismarck/bismarck.htm

2321. Historic Wings. *Battle of the Bismarck Sea*
http://www.historicwings.com/features99/bismarcksea/

2322. [Unidentified.] *Battle of the Bismarck Sea*
http://www.combinedfleet.com/bismksea.htm

BOUGAINVILLE

2323. Frankel, Stanley W. *Battle for Bounganville: Hell on Hill 700*
http://www.thehistorynet.com/WorldWarII/articles/1997/09972_text.htm

2324. Goita, Sabino L. *Journal of Pfc Sabino L. Goita, MC (37th Division), 1943-1945*
http://www.ibiblio.org/hyperwar/USA/pers/sal/Goitia-Jnl.html

2325. Ramsdell, Lorraine. *Battle of Bougainville* (in the "World War II Fact Sheet, USMC" series)
http://www.usmc.mil/history.nsf/Table+of+Contents/77f992b2acb682eb852564d70059c642?OpenDocument&ExpandSection=10
http://www.navy.mil/navpalib/wwii/facts/bougbttl.txt

GUAM

2326. Moulton, [? .] *1st Lt. Irving Moulton* (stationed at Corps of Engineering Supply Depot on island)
http://srd.yahoo.com/drst/47907782/http://www.ultranet.com/~kmoulton/

2327. Patrick, Bethanne K. *Lt. Gen. Henry Larsen*
http://www.military.com/Content/MoreContent?file=ML_larsen_bkp

2328. [Unidentified.] *Guam: Operations of the 77th Division, 21 July–10 August 1944* (1946; 1990 edition—CMH Publication 100-5)
http://www.army.mil/cmh-pg/books/wwii/guam/guam77div-fm.htm

2329. [Unidentified.] *Objective: Guam* (analysis of how the known and suspected facts affected planning of the invasion)
http://www.army.mil/cmh-pg/books/wwii/guam/guam77-objective.htm

Iwo Jima

2330. Backstrom, Raymond C. *Iwo Jima: A Look Back* (a variety of resources on the battle)
http://www.geocities.com/rbackstr2000/

2331. Bradley, John. *Oral History: Iwo Jima Flag Raising* (Pharmacist Mate Bradley was the only navy man involved in the raising of the flag on Mt. Suribachi)
http://www.history.navy.mil/faqs/faq87-31.htm

2332. Clancey, Patrick. *Japanese Order of Battle at Iwo Jima*
http://www.ibiblio.org/hyperwar/PTO/Iwo/IJcmd.html

2333. Clancey, Patrick. *United States and Japanese Casualties at Iwo Jima*
http://www.ibiblio.org/hyperwar/PTO/Iwo/Casualties.html

2334. Clancey, Patrick. *US Order of Battle at Iwo Jima*
http://www.ibiblio.org/hyperwar/PTO/Iwo/UScmd.html

2335. Eiler, Dorothea M. *Flags on Iwo: A True Story* (interview with one of the men who raised the flag)
http://www.military.com/Content/MoreContent?file=PReiler

2336. Gibson, Arvin S. *My Time on Iwo Jima*
http://members.aol.com/famjustin/Gibsonbio.html

2337. Kyle, Jim. *W. C. Reeves Recalls Iwo Jima* (newspaper article)
http://www.geocities.com/Heartland/Plains/5850/reeves.html

2338. Miller, Kimberley J. *Battle for Iwo Jima* (in the "World War II Fact Sheet, USMC" series)
http://www.usmc.mil/history.nsf/Table+of+Contents/77f992b2acb682eb852564d70059c642?OpenDocument&ExpandSection=2

2339. Nowell, M. K. *Iwo Jima: "Eight Square Miles of Hell"* (a poem)
http://www.geocities.com/Heartland/Plains/5850/iwo.html

2340. Patrick, Bethanne K. *Pvt. Rene Gagnon* (one of the flag raisers at Iwo)
http://www.military.com/Content/MoreContent?file=ML_gagnon_bkp

2341. Patrick, Bethanne K. *Sgt. Darrell S. Cole*
http://www.military.com/Content/MoreContent?file=ML_dscole_bkp

2342. [Unidentified.] *Iwo Jima* (includes photographs and film clips)
http://www.iwojima.com/index.cfm

2343. Wiley, H. V. *USS West Virginia Action Report: Bombardment of and Fire Support for Landings, Iwo Jima Island, 19 February 1945 to 1 March 1945 Inclusive* (Serial Report 0120, 10 March 1945)
http://www.ibiblio.org/hyperwar/USN/ships/logs/BB/bb48-IwoJima.html

MARIANA ISLANDS

2344. Kukral, Lyn. *Marines in the Mariana Islands* (in the "World War II Fact Sheet, USMC" series)
http://www.usmc.mil/history.nsf/Table+of+Contents/
77f992b2acb682eb852564d70059c642?OpenDocument&ExpandSection=6

2345. Wukovits, John W. *Greatest Aircraft Carrier Duel*
http://www.military.com/Content/MoreContent?file=PRduel

MARSHALL ISLANDS

2346. Knight, Rex A. *Commander's Calculated Risk*
http://www.military.com/Content/MoreContent?file=PRkwaj

2347. Kukral, L. C. *Marines in the Marshall Islands* (in the "World War II Fact Sheet, USMC" series)
http://www.usmc.mil/history.nsf/Table+of+Contents/77f992b2acb6
82eb852564d70059c642?OpenDocument&ExpandSection=7
http://www.chinfo.navy.mil/navpalib/wwii/facts/marshlls.txt

2348. Seedorf, Robert. *Experiences in World War II* (major section on Marshall Islands)
http://flag.blackened.net/daver/1sthand/seedorf/seedorf.html

2349. Wright, III, Burton. *The U.S. Army Campaigns of World War II: Eastern Mandates* (CMH Publication 72-23)
http://www.army.mil/cmh-pg/brochures/eastman/eastman.htm

NEW GUINEA

2350. Crary, Charles W. *My Life as a Soldier, 1939-1945* (detailed account, including service in New Guinea)
http://www.memoriesofwar.com/veterans/crary.asp

2351. Drea, Edward J. *U.S. Army Campaigns of World War II: New Guinea.* (CMH Publication 72-9)
http://www.army.mil/cmh-pg/brochures/new-guinea/ng.htm

2352. Forman, Mark. *Air Apache Home Page* (with emphasis on New Guinea)
http://screeningroom.com/pacificwar.html

2353. Leach, Amanda. *The Atfield Accounts of the Pacific War* (four accounts dealing with the fighting in New Guinea)
http://www.geocities.com/Pentagon/Quarters/9715/index.html

2354. Sheftall, Bucky. *Saburo Sakai's Mercy over Java Jungle*
http://www.elknet.pl/acestory/sakai/sakai.htm

2355. [Unidentified.] *New Guinea Was My Introduction to War* (bomber pilot flying out of New Guinea)
http://www.danford.net/newguine.htm

NORTHERN SOLOMONS

2356. Clifton, Francis H. *[Auto]Biography of Francis H. Clifton* (PBY experiences, especially in the Solomons)
http://members.aol.com/famjustin/Clifton1.html

2357. Lofgren, Stephen J. *The U.S. Army Campaigns of World War II: Northern Solomons* (CMH Publication 72-10)
http://www.army.mil/cmh-pg/brochures/northsol/northsol.htm

2358. Sabel, Bill. *Bringing New Knowledge to the South Pacific* (Sabel introduced watermelons [!] to the Solomons in order to provide a different type food for the American hospital)
http://www.memoriesofwar.com/veterans/sabel.asp

OKINAWA AND THE RYUKUS

2359. Alison, Carolyn. *Campaign for Okinawa* (in the "World War II Fact Sheet, USMC" series)
http://www.usmc.mil/history.nsf/Table+of+Contents/
77f992b2acb682eb852564d70059c642?OpenDocument&ExpandSection=3

2360. Becton, Frederick J. *Oral History—Battle for Okinawa, 24 March-30 June 1945* (Becton served as Commanding Officer of the *USS Laffey* when it survived hits by eight kamikazes)
http://www.history.navy.mil/faqs/faq87-3r.htm

2361. Fisch, Arnold G. *The U.S. Army Campaigns of World War II: Ryukus* (CMH Publication 72-35)
http://www.army.mil/cmh-pg/brochures/ryukyus/ryukyus.htm

2362. Gebhardt, Jack. *War in the Pacific: Actions in the Philippines including Leyte Gulf, as Well as the Battles of Iwo Jima and Okinawa, 1943-1945* (his vessel was sunk by a kamikaze attack at Okinawa)
http://www.history.navy.mil/faqs/faq87-3m.htm

2363. Harper, Dale P. *The "U.S.S. Laffey"* (horrendously damaged by kamikazes)
http://www.military.com/Content/MoreContent?file=PRlaffey

2364. Hurley, William J. *Better Late than Never*
http://www20.brinkster.com/bettybomber/default.htm

2365. Imwalle, Kristin. *James Jameson: A Survivor of Okinawa*
http://www.itp.berkeley.edu/~hzaid/kristin/wwii.html

2366. Naval Historical Center. *Typhoons and Hurricanes: Pacific Typhoon, June 1945* (hit hard U.S. naval vessels operating near Okinawa)
http://www.history.navy.mil/faqs/faq102-5.htm

2367. Naval Historical Center. *Typhoons and Hurricanes: Pacific Typhoon, October 1945* (hit hard U.S. Naval vessels at Okinawa and temporarily devastated shore facilities)
http://www.history.navy.mil/faqs/faq102-6.htm

2368. [Unidentified.] *Kamikaze: Japan's Last Offensive in Okinawa*
http://ac.acusd.edu/History/WW2Timeline/LUTZ/okin.html

2369. [Unidentified.] *Okinawa: The American Years, 1945-1972* (detailed year by year account from the time of the conquest; includes brief biographies of key participants involved in the island's affairs throughout the period)
http://faculty.tamu-commerce.edu/sarantakes/Okinawa.html

2370. [Unidentified.] *U.S.S. Inaugural AM242—World War II "Admirable" Class Minesweeper* (saw duty at Okinawa)
http://www.angelfire.com/journal2/ussinaugural/

PAPUA

2371. Anderson, Charles R. *The U.S. Army Campaigns of World War II: Papua, 23 July 1942-January 1943* (CMH Publication 72-7)
http://www.army.mil/cmh-pg/brochures/papua/papua.htm

2372. Rubitsky, David. *David Rubitsky's Story* (career soldier who served at Papua)
http://www.rubitsky.com/

2373. [Unidentified.] *Papuan Campaign: Introduction*
http://www.army.mil/cmh-pg/books/wwii/papuancamp/papcpn-intro.htm

2374. [Unidentified.] *Papuan Campaign: The Buna-Sanananda Operation: 16 November 1942-23 January 1943* (1945; 1990 edition—CMH Publication 100-1)
http://www.army.mil/cmh-pg/books/wwii/papuancamp/papcpn-fm.htm

2375. [Unidentified.] *U.S.S. Aaron War (D-31)* (hit by six kamikazes but avoided sinking; photos and excerpts from ship's records)
http://ussaaronward.com/

2376. Warmenhoven, Simon. *Medical Department—32nd Infantry Division, Papuan Campaign*
http://www.armymedicine.army.mil/history/booksdocs/
wwii/PapuanReport/32IDSurgPapua.html

PELELIU

2377. Crappie, A. M. *The Army Gets the Glory, the Navy Gets Its AAte Out: Eating 1* (emphasis on Peleliu and Yap)
http://www.fortunecity.com/millenium/redwood/372/part10.htm

2378. Owen, Charles H. *Capture of Peleliu*
http://www.military.com/Content/MoreContent?file=PRpeleliu

2379. Prizeman, Sean. *Battle for Peleliu* (web site with links to information on various aspects of the battle)
http://www.peleliu.net/
(map page:) http://www.peleliu.net/Maps/Maps.htm

2380. [Unidentified.] *Battle of Peleliu* (in the "World War II Fact Sheet, USMC" series)
http://www.usmc.mil/history.nsf/Table+of+Contents/
77f992b2acb682eb852564d70059c642?OpenDocument&ExpandSection=11

2381. Watkins, R. Bruce. *Peleliu: Brothers in Battle* (Bruce was a Marine platoon leader)
http://vm.uconn.edu/~don4762/brothers.htm

ROI-NAMUR

2382. Lapahie, Harrison. *Restricted U.S. Marine Map*
http://www.lapahie.com/Navajo_Code_Talker_
Burlesque-Camouflage_Map.cfm

2383. [Unidentified.] *Roi-Namur* (remaining remnants of the battle)
http://www.pacificwrecks.com/provinces/marshall_roi.html

2384. [Various Individuals.] *Roi-Namur Anchorage Journal Entries* (a return to the island in 2000)
http://www.oceanicresearch.org/kwajhtmls/journentryroi.html

SAIPAN AND TINIAN

2385. American Battle Monuments Commission. *Saipan American Memorial*
http://www.usabmc.com/si.htm

2386. Blodgett, Brian. *The Invasion of Saipan*
http://members.tripod.com/~Brian_Blodgett/Saipan.html

2387. Duncan, Basil. *War Stories: My Personal Account*
http://www.geocities.com/Heartland/Plains/5850/warstories.html

2388. Gugeler, Russell A. *Army Amphibian Tractor and Tank Battalion in the Battle of Saipan, 15 June-9 July 1944* (1945; originally classified "secret")
http://www.army.mil/cmh-pg/documents/wwii/amsai/amsai.htm

2389. Hall, Lloyd C. *Recollections* (click on this entry under "links")
http://members.tripod.com/~Brian_Blodgett/Saipan.html

2390. Ide, Douglas. *Stepping Stones to Tokyo*
http://www.dtic.mil/soldiers/july94/p52.html

2391. Kawaguchi, Taro. *Diary* (hospital unit service; diary discovered during combat in July 1944; click on this entry under "links")
http://members.tripod.com/~Brian_Blodgett/Saipan.html

2392. [Military Intelligence.]. *Interrogation of Major Kiyoski Yoshida* (11 July 1944; Yoshida was intelligence officer of the 43rd Division; click on this entry under "links")
http://members.tripod.com/~Brian_Blodgett/Saipan.html

2393. Saito, [General]. *Lieutenant General Saito's Last Order* (text)
http://web.nmsu.edu/~pauberve/Saito.htm

2394. Sanders, Frank. *Tinian Airfield* (used to launch the atomic strikes against Japan)
http://www.oz.net/~chrisp/tinian.htm

2395. Swigart, Soren. *Operation Forager: The Invasion of Saipan, Tinan and Guam* (Saipan receives nearly all the attention)
http://worldatwar.net/article/forager/index.html

2396. Winter, Joseph W. *Recollections* (click on this entry under "links")
http://members.tripod.com/~Brian_Blodgett/Saipan.html

TARAWA

2397. Ballendorf, Dirk. *The Battle for Tarawa: A Validation of the U.S. Marines* (thesis: the amphibious doctrine utilized was weak but the Marines made up for it)
http://www.uog.edu/faculty/ballendo/tarawa.htm

2398. Kukral, L. C. *The Battle of Tarawa*
http://www.chinfo.navy.mil/navpalib/wwii/facts/tarawa.txt

2399. Moise, Norman S. *Terror and Survival at Tarawa* (first person account)
http://www.military.com/Content/MoreContent?file=PRtarawa

2400. Molnar, Alexander. *Battle for Tarawa* ("in the "World War II Fact Sheet, USMC" series)
http://www.usmc.mil/history.nsf/Table+of+Contents/
77f992b2acb682eb852564d70059c642?OpenDocument&ExpandSection=9

2401. Nelson, Donald R. *[Tarawa]* (Lt. Com. in the medical corps; describes the invasion to his parents)
http://www.military.com/Content/MoreContent?file=nelson_01

2402. [Unidentified.] *Betio: Assault of an Island Fortress*
http://history.acusd.edu/gen/WW2Timeline/Betio.html

2403. [Unidentified.] *The Battle for Tarawa*
http://history.acusd.edu/gen/WW2Timeline/CRAIGE/tarawa.html
http://history.sandiego.edu/gen/WW2Timeline/CRAIGE/tarawa.html

Philippines: Liberation and Associated Sea Battles (Philippine Sea and Leyte Gulf)

2404. Anderson, Charles R. *The U.S. Army Campaigns of World War II: Leyte* (CMH Publication 72-27)
http://www.army.mil/cmh-pg/brochures/leyte/leyte.htm

2405. Azzole, Peter. *Afterthoughts: Rochefort on the Battle of Leyte Gulf* (interview with one of U.S.'s best war-time cryptanalysts)
http://www.cl.cam.ac.uk/Research/Security/Historical/azzole5.html
http://www.usncva.org/clog/leyte.html

2406. Brooks, Henry. *Henry's Answers about His Time in World War II* (answers to varied e-mail queries about his time in the service)
http://www.angelfire.com/hi/RedArrowDivision/ww2.html

2407. Brown, J. F. *Oral History—Luzon Operation, Lingayen Gulf Landing, 4-18 January 1945* (Brown was commanding officer of *USS LCI(M) 974* during the invasion)
http://www.history.navy.mil/faqs/faq87-3q.htm

2408. Burwell, Walter B. *Oral Histories—Battle of Leyte Gulf, 23-25 October 1945* (Burwell was a medical officer on the *USS Suwannee* when it was hit by two kamikaze aircraft)
http://www.history.navy.mil/faqs/faq87-3h.htm

2409. Cox, Robert J. *The Battle off Samar: Taffy III at Leyte Gulf*
http://www.bosamar.com/home.html

2410. Crappie, A. M. *The Army Gets the Glory, the Navy Gets Its AAte Out: Eating 2* (Leyte and Philippines)
http://www.fortunecity.com/millenium/redwood/372/eating2

2411. Furgol, Edward. *Battle of Leyte Gulf*
http://www.stat.virginia.edu/leyte.html

2412. Guttman, Jon. *Battleships: The Last Duel*
http://www.military.com/Content/MoreContent?file=PRleyte

2413. Harper, Dale P. *Flash of Darkness*
http://www.military.com/Content/MoreContent?file=PRhood

2414. Hasenaeur, Heike. *Back to the Philippines*
http://www.stat.virginia.edu/philippines.txt
http://www.dtic.mil/soldiers/oct94/p50.html

2415. Keasler, Carlos A. *Lest We Forget: A Memoir of the Philippine Liberation Campaign*
http://www.webcom.com/wak/lestweforget/

2416. Lofgren, Stephen J. *U.S. Army Campaigns in World War II: Southern Philippines* (CMH Publication 72-40)
http://www.army.mil/cmh-pg/brochures/southphil/southphils.htm

2417. Lutze, A. J. *End of the Japanese Navy: The Battle of Leyte Gulf* (chronology of events leading up to the confrontation)
http://history.acusd.edu/gen/WW2Timeline/LUTZ/leyte.html

2418. MacArthur, Douglas. *Address on the Re-establishment of the Philippine Government (February 27, 1945)*
http://www.sunsite.unc.edu/pha/policy/1945/450227b.html

2419. Margolis, Erick. *Taffy-3: A Study in Heroism* (Battle of Leyte Gulf, October 1944)
http://www.foreigncorrespondent.com/archive/taffy-3.html

2420. McGown, Sam. *Liberating Los Banos* (a camp for civilian internees)
http://www.military.com/Content/MoreContent?file=PRlosbanos

2421. Moore, Jr., E. Ray. *"Who is Guarding the San Bernardino Strait?"*
http://www.christianity.com/partner/Article_Display_Page/
0,,PTID21938%7CCHID122759%7CCIID364225,00.html

2422. Naval Historical Center. *Typhoons and Hurricanes: Pacific Typhoon, 18 December 1944* (did great damage to American vessels near the Philippines)
http://www.history.navy.mil/faqs/faq102-4.htm

2423. Patrick, Bethanne K. *Capt. David McCampbell* (navy pilot; nine kills in one day over Leyte Gulf)
http://www.military.com/Content/MoreContent?file=ML_mccampbell_bkp

2424. Popham, Harry. *Death of "U.S.S. Princeton"*
http://www.military.com/Content/MoreContent?file=PRprinceton

2425. Royal Australian Navy/The Gun Plot. *HMAS Australia—Against the "Divine Wind"* (combat with kamikazes in the Philippines; click on this title way down left hand list; text appears on right hand side)
http://www.gunplot.net/

2426. Stekovic, Srdjan. *Leyte Gulf* (click on this title on left hand of screen; text and illustrations will appear on the right side)
http://www.everblue.net/1942

2427. Stekovic, Srdjan. *Philippine Sea* (click on this title on left hand of screen; text and illustrations will appear on the right side)
http://www.everblue.net/1942

2428. Stuckenschneider, Placid L. *The Last Campaign: Mindanao*
http://www.military.com/Content/MoreContent?file=PRmindanao

2429. [Unidentified.] *Battle of the Philippine Sea, 19-20 June 1944*
http://www.angelfire.com/fm/odyssey/philippinesea.htm

2430. [Unidentified.] *Battle for Leyte Gulf, 23-26 October 1944*
http://www.djjp.demon.co.uk/leytegulf.htm

2431. [Unidentified.] *Halsey's Decision in the Battle for Leyte Gulf to leave San Bernandino Unguarded*
http://www.angelfire.com/fm/odyssey/Halsey_decision.htm

2432. [Unidentified Pilot.] *November 1944* (narration of being shot down over sea in the battle for the Philippines and of the recuperation afterwards)
http://www.geocities.com/hsemerson/story2.html

2433. [Unidentified.] *Takao* (discussion of a Japanese vessel that fought at Leyte Gulf)
http://www.mckennas.demon.co.uk/takao.htm

2434. [Unidentified.] *The U.S. Army Campaigns of World War II: Luzon, 1944-1945*
http://www.army.mil/cmh-pg/brochures/luzon/72-28.htm

2435. Winter, Roland. *Oral History Interview* (served in Army in Philippines and Okinawa)
http://fas-history.rutgers.edu/oralhistory/winter.htm

Other Sea Battles of the Pacific

JAVA SEA

2436. O'Hara, Vincent P. *Battle of the Java Sea: 27 February 1942*
http://www.microworks.net/pacific/battles/java_sea.htm

2437. Stekovic, Srdjan. *Java Sea* (click on this title on left hand of screen; text and illustrations will appear on the right side)
http://www.everblue.net/1942

2438. [Unidentified.] *Battle of the Java Sea: 27th February 1942*
http://members.ozemail.com.au/~spruso/vasea.htm

2439. [Unidentified.] *The Java Sea Battle*
http://www.geocities.com/dutcheastindies/java_sea.html

2440. [Unidentified.] *The Java Sea Campaign*
http://www.geocities.com/Athens/Crete/7962/battles/javasea.html

CORAL SEA

2441. Campbell, Kristen. *Battle of the Coral Sea*
http://history.acusd.edu/gen/WW2Timeline/coral.html

2442. Casey, Gavan. *Admirals of the Nihon Kaigun (Imperial Japanese Navy)*
(as of the Battle of the Coral Sea)
http://home.vicnet.net.au/~gcasey/JNavy.html

2443. Casey, Gavan. *Battle of the Coral Sea, May 4-10, 1942*
http://home.vicnet.net.au/~gcasey/battle.html

2444. Dunn, Peter. *Battle of the Coral Sea Fought off Townsville*
http://home.st.net.au/~dunn/coralsea.htm

2445. Hassell, Walter. *One Last Look at Lady Lex* (by an eyewitness)
http://www.military.com/Content/MoreContent?file=PRlex

2446. Naval Historical Center. *Battle of the Coral Sea, 7-8 May 1942—
Overview and Special Image Selection*
http://history.navy.mil/photos/events/wwii-pac/coralsea/coralsea.htm

2447. Royal Australian Navy/The Gun Plot. *Saving Australia: USN/RAN,
Battle of Coral Sea—May 1942* (click on this title way down left hand
list; text appears on right hand side)
http://www.gunplot.net/

2448. Stekovic, Srdjan. *Coral Sea* (click on this title on left hand of screen;
text and illustrations will appear on the right side)
http://www.everblue.net/1942

2449. [Unidentified.] *Battle of the Coral Sea*
http://www.gunplot.net/coralsea/coralsea.html

2450. [Unidentified.] *Battle of the Coral Sea*
http://www.navy.gov.au/history/ran_coral.htm

2451. [Unidentified.] *Stemming the Tide: Battle of the Coral Sea, 7th-8th
May 1942—and Prologue, Early April-7th May 1942*
http://www.microworks.net/pacific/battles/coral_sea.htm

2452. [Unidentified.] *The Battle for the Coral Sea*
http://www.tachna.com/In%20Memorium/Coral%20Sea.htm

2453. [Unidentified.] *The Met Advancing* (meteorological conditions and the battle)
http://www.austehc.unimelb.edu.au/fam/0282.html

Submarine Warfare in the Pacific

2454. Anderson, Matthew. *U.S. Submarine History* (emphasis on the Pacific)
http://users.neca.com/anderson/

2455. Bauer, Jim. *Dud Torpedoes* (a major American problem)
http://www.ww2pacific.com/torpedo.html

2456. Bauer, Jim. *Submarine Attacks, August–September 1942* (important as factor in holding onto Guadalcanal)
http://www.ww2pacific.com/subattack.html

2457. Clark, Harold L. *Sunk by Submarine, 1944* (first hand account; the American *S.S. John A. Johnson* was sunk between San Francisco and Honolulu)
http://www.ibiscom.com/sunk.htm

2458. Dale, John. *U.S.S. Parche (SS-384)*
http://www.ipa.net/~klaatu/384/

2459. Feuer, A. B. *U.S.S. Growler's War* (in order to save vessel and crew, skipper had sub descend though still on deck himself)
http://www.military.com/Content/MoreContent?file=PRgrowler

2460. Historic Naval Ships Association. *U.S.S. Drum (SS-228)*
http://www.maritime.org/hnsa-drum.htm

2461. Lipes, Wheeler B. *Appendectomy Performed on Fourth War Patrol of USS "Seadragon," 1942* (Lipes was Pharmacist's Mate)
http://www.history.navy.mil/faqs/faq87-3a.htm
(official report on:) http://www.history.navy.mil/faqs/faq87-3a1.htm

2462. McFayden, Ian. *The Success and Failure of Submarine Warfare in the Pacific*
http://www.waikato.ac.nz/wfass/subjects/history/
waimilhist/1997/im-folder/im-p1.html

2463. Merrigan, Don. *World War II "Silent Service"*
http://www.subnet.com/causs/wwii.htm

2464. Milford, Frederick J. *U.S. Navy Torpedoes: The Great Torpedo Scandal, 1941-1943*
http://www.geocities.com/Pentagon/1592/ustorp2.htm

2465. Naval Historical Center. *History of S-33 (SS-138)*
http://www.history.navy.mil/danfs/s/s-33.htm

2466. Nevitt, Allyn D. *Who Sank the [U.S.S.] Triton?*
http://www.combinedfleet.com/triton.htm

2467. Pacific Fleet Submarine Memorial Association. *U.S.S. Bowfin Submarine Museum and Park (Honolulu, Hawaii)* (one of fifteen surviving WWII era submarines left; offers a "virtual reality tour" of the vessel)
http://www.bowfin.org/

2468. Parks, James. *The Silver Dolphins of the Submarine Service* (Asiatic Fleet)
http://www.geocities.com/Baja/Dunes/4791/subs1.html

2469. Patrick, Bethanne K. *Capt. George L. Street* (captain of the *U.S.S. Tirante*)
http://www.military.com/Content/MoreContent?file=ML_street_bkp

2470. Shireman, Douglas A. *U.S. Torpedo Troubles*
http://www.military.com/Content/MoreContent?file=PRtorpedo

2471. Smith, Ron. *U.S.S. Seal (SS-183)*
http://www.geocities.com/Athens/Acropolis/7612/seal1.html

2472. Toon, Frank. *U.S.S. Blenny, SS-324* (war-time service)
http://www.webenet.net/~ftoon/memory/f_memory.html

2473. [Unidentified.] *Full Fathom Five: The U.S. Submarine War against Japan* (includes text of patrol reports filed by submarines)
http://www.geocities.com/Pentagon/1592/

2474. [Unidentified.] *Ships and Tonnage Sunk or Damaged in World War II by US Submarines* (arranged alphabetically)
http://www.rddesigns.com/ww2/ww2sinkings.html

2475. [Unidentified.] *Submarines in the Pacific War* (United States)
http://history.acusd.edu/gen/WW2Timeline/subpac.html

2476. [Unidentified.] *The Story of the U.S.S. Darter I, U.S.S. Dace I, and U.S.S. Menhaden II*
http://members.aol.com/Emblume/index5.html

2477. [Unidentified.] *U.S.S. Batfish (SS-310)* (seven war-time patrols, each described)
http://www.ussbatfish.com/batfish-main.html

2478. [Unidentified.] *U.S.S. Cod: SS-224, World War II Fleet Submarine*
http://www.usscod.org/

2479. [Unidentified.] *U.S.S. Croaker (SSK-246)*
http://www.geocities.com/CapeCanaveral/1056/croaker.htm

2480. [Unidentified.] *U.S.S. Drum (SS-228)*
http://www.geocities.com/CapeCanaveral/1056/drum.htm

2481. [Unidentified.] *U.S.S. Gunnel (SS-53)* (details on each war patrol; patrols in both Mediterranean and Pacific)
http://members.aol.com/jmlavelle2/newintro.htm

2482. [Unidentified.] *U.S.S. Springer (SS-414)*
http://www.subnet.com/fleet/ss414.htm

Japan During the War: Homefront and Target

2483. Aoki, Maho. *An Interview about World War II* (with both grandparents)
http://www.intnl.doshisha.ac.jp/projects/sarah/maho3/interview%20.html

2484. Goto, Yumi (Mrs.) *Those Days in Muramatsu* (diary stressing September-December 1945)
http://falcon.cc.ukans.edu/~ceas/EPP/Muramatsu/Muramatsu.html

2485. Halsema, James J. *1940 Japanese-American Student Conference: Diary of James J. Halsema* (includes observations on Japan itself as well as Japanese occupied Manchuria, China, and Korea)
http://falcon.cc.ukans.edu/~ceas/Halsema%20Diary/jasc1.html

2486. Hoshi, Saeko. *An Interview about World War II* (with grandfather)
http://www.intnl.doshisha.ac.jp/projects/sarah/
hoshi3/friend%27s%20story%20p3.html

2487. Ishikawa, Yuka. *An Interview about World War II* (with grandmother)
http://www.intnl.doshisha.ac.jp/projects/sarah/yuka3/yuka.html

2488. Kawasaki, Ayako. *An Interview about World War II* (with grandmother)
http://www.intnl.doshisha.ac.jp/projects/sarah/yuka3/ayako.html

2489. Koiso, Kuniashi. *Premier Kuniashi Koiso's New Year's Address (January 1, 1945)*
http://www.sunsite.unc.edu/pha/policy/1945/450101a.html

2490. Paulsen, John. *The Firebombing of Kobe and Osaka during World War II*
http://www.folds.net/Haney/firebombing.html

2491. Pulu-Toro, Teena. *The [Re]invention of Tradition within Japanese Society* (covers1931-1945)
http://www.waikato.ac.nz/wfass/subjects/history/
waimilhist/1997/tpt-folder/tpt-p1.html

2492. Sherman, Samuel R. *Oral Histories—Attacks on Japan, 1945* (Sherman was a Flight Surgeon on the *USS Franklin* when it survived heavy damage on March 19, 1945)
http://www.history.navy.mil/faqs/faq87-3i.htm

2493. Soga, Michitoshi. *Oral History* (description of culture and attitudes in Japan during the war years)
http://www-personal.umich.edu/~amnornes/Jason.html

2494. Taliaferro, Jeffrey W. *Imperial Family of Japan* (emphasis on current ruler)
http://www.geocities.com/Tokyo/Temple/3953/

2495. [Unidentified.] *A Long Way Home: Growing up Nisei in Japan during the Pacific War* (their parents were stateside when war broke out)
http://www.culturalbridge.com/jpyam.htm

2496. [Unidentified.] *Koreans Resident in Japan* (translated study, March 1945)
http://carlisle-www.army.mil/cgi-bin/usamhi/DL/showdoc.pl?doc-num=722

Japanese Efforts in and Against the Americas

2497. Covington, John. *Fugos: Japanese Balloon Bombs of WWII*
http://www.seanet.com/~johnco/fugo.htm

2498. Mikesh, Robert H. *Balloon Bombs: What Are They?*
http://www.af.mil/news/airman/0298/bombsb.htm

2499. [Unidentified.] *Balloon Bomber* (story of a young boy who helped make them at the end of the war)
http://www.af.mil/news/airman/0298/bomb2.htm

2500. [Unidentified.] *Pieces of Paper: Japanese Air Balloon Bombing against North America*
http://collections.ic.gc.ca/balloons/

2501. [Unidentified.] *Some News Clippings of Fugos from 1945-1946* (provided by Tacoma Public Library)
http://www.seanet.com/~johnco/somenew.htm

Australia and New Zealand

2502. Brodie, Ian J. *New Zealand Fighter Pilots Museum* (data on both pilots and their equipment)
http://www.nzfpm.co.nz/welcome/welcome.htm

2503. Charles Stuart University. *Military Archeology in Australasia and the Pacific*
http://life.csu.edu.au/~dspennem/MILARCH/MILARCH.HTM

2504. Curtin, John [Prime Minister]. *Australia Declares War on Japan (December 9, 1941)*
http://www.ibiblio.org/pha/policy/1941/411209a.html

2505. Donaldson, Graham. *Royal Australian Naval Volunteer Reserve* (role in the war)
http://worldatwar.net/article/australiannavyreserve/index.html

2506. Dragicevic, George. *Clive Caldwell—Stuka Party* (Australia ace; most kills in North Africa with only a minority in Pacific)
http://www.elknet.pl/acestory/caldw/caldw.htm

2507. Dunn, Peter. *Australia Cities Shelled by Japanese Submarines during World War 2*
http://home.st.net.au/~dunn/japsubs/japsshell.htm

2508. Dunn, Peter. *German U-Boat Attacks off the Australian Coast during World War 2*
http://home.st.net.au/~dunn/subsoz.htm

2509. Dunn, Peter. *Japanese Air Raids in Australia*
http://home.st.net.au/~dunn/bomboz.htm

2510. Dunn, Peter. *Military Camps/Locations in Australia during World War 2*
http://home.st.net.au/~dunn/ozatwar/militarycamps.htm

2511. Dunn, Peter. *Military Units in Australia during World War 2*
http://home.st.net.au/~dunn/muoz.htm

2512. Dunn, Peter. *Prisoner of War and Internment Camps in Australia during World War 2*
http://home.st.net.au/~dunn/ozatwar/pow.htm

2513. Dunn, Peter. *Reconnaissance Flights over Australia from Japanese Submarines during World War 2*
http://home.st.net.au/~dunn/japrecce/japrecce.htm

2514. Dunn, Peter. *Royal Navy Fleet Air Arm in Australia during WW2* (includes material on carriers and units not necessarily exclusive to Australia)
http://home.st.net.au/~dunn/navy/rnfaa.htm

2515. Dunn, Peter. *The "Brisbane Line:" Was It Fact or Was It Myth?*
http://home.st.net.au/~dunn/ozatwar/brisbaneline.htm

2516. Dunn, Peter. *U.S. Army Units in Australia during World War 2*
http://home.st.net.au/~dunn/usarmy/usarmy.htm

2517. Ferguson, Bali. *Diggers: Lords of Battle* (Australia)
http://www.geocities.com/Pentagon/8839/index2.html

2518. Firkins, Peter. *460 Squadron, Royal Australian Air Force, Bomber Command*
http://www.netlink.com.au/~gstooke/460squadron.htm

2519. Ip, Manying. *Dinkun Aliens: Chinese New Zealanders in World War II*
http://www.stevenyoung.co.nz/chinesevoice/misc/dinkum.htm

2520. Johnson, Peter. *467 463 RAAF RAF Lancaster Squadrons World War Two*
http://www.467463raafsquadrons.com/

2521. Langtry, Paul. *Australia's War* (tensions between Australia and Britain as to the use of Australian troops)
http://worldatwar.net/article/australiaswar/index.html

2522. New Zealand Embasy. *NZ/US History* (with section of World War II)
http://www.nzemb.org/embassy/history.htm

2523. Pevin, R. H., and J. H. Straczek. *RAN [Royal Australian Navy] in the Pacific War*
http://www.navy.gov.au/history/pacwar.htm

2524. Royal Australian Navy/The Gun Plot. *HMAS Sydney 2: History, Loss and Controversy* (click on this title way down left hand list; text appears on right hand side)
http://www.gunplot.net/

2525. Royal Australian Navy/The Gun Plot. *Services Reconnaissance Department (SRD)* (performed surveillance and commando operations into islands north of Australia; click on this title way down left hand list; text appears on right hand side)
http://www.gunplot.net/

2526. Simes, Cheryl. *Not Your Average Trial: The Statutory Unfairness of Courts-Martial in New Zealand* (a survey of contemporary practice and how the rules have changed during New Zealand's history)
http://www.waikato.ac.nz/wfass/subjects/history/
waimilhist/1998/notyouraveragecourt.html

2527. Special Service Division, Army Service Forces. *Pocket Guide to New Zealand* (1943; must use Adobe Acrobat)
http://worldwar2.smu.edu/cgi-bin/Pwebrecon.cgi?v1=105&ti
=101,105&CNT=50&Search_Arg=world+war&Search_Code=GKEY&x
=30&y=5&y=5&PID=3725&SEQ=20020105195519&SID=1

2528. Straczek, J. H. *RAN [Royal Australian Navy] in the Second World War*
http://www.navy.gov.au/history/ranww2.htm

2529. [Unidentified.] *Aussie's at War* (a developing site tracing Australian participation in a variety of conflicts)
http://www.geocities.com/shae2000_au/

2530. [Unidentified.] *Corvettes of the Australian Navy in World War 2*
http://vader.nw.com.au/~stella/

2531. [Unidentified.] *The Australian Merchant Navy, 1939-1946*
http://www.merchant-navy-ships.com/

2532. [Unidentified.] *The Second World War* (emphasis on New Zealand's participation)
http://www.nzhistory.net.nz/New/oxcomp/wwtwo.htm

2533. Waters, Darcy. *Capital Defence [of New Zealand]: Wellington's Built Military Defences*
http://capitaldefence.orcon.net.nz/

2534. Whitford, Lance. *Kiwis in Armor* (armoured fighting vehicles used by New Zealanders)
http://www.kithobbyist.com/AMPSNewZealand/KiwisInArmour/

The Atomic Bomb and the End of the War

2535. A.J. Software and Multimedia. *Atomic Archive* (first hand accounts of development of bomb, maps of amount of Hiroshima and Nagasaki damaged, etc.)
http://www.atomicarchive.com/main.shtml

2536. Alperovitz, Gar. *Gar Alperovitz and the H-Net Debate* (Alperovitz defends his views concerning the use of nuclear weapons in response to various critics)
http://www.doug-long.com/debate.htm

2537. Arens, Mark P. *V (Marine) Amphibious Corps Planning for Operation "Olympic" and the Role of Intelligence in Support of Planning* (plans for invasion of Kyushu)
http://www.fas.org/irp/eprint/arens/

2538. Bauer, Jim. *Japan's Surrender: Important Facts about the Closing Days of World War 2*
http://www.ww2pacific.com/surrender.html

2539. Bauer, K. Jack. *Olympia versus Ketsu-go* (the Japanese plan to defend Kyushu; from the *Marine Corps Gazette*, August 1965)
http://www.ibiblio.org/pha/war.term/olympic.html

2540. Brookings Institute. *The Costs of the Manhattan Project*
http://www.brook.edu/FP/PROJECTS/NUCWCOST/MANHATTN.HTM

2541. Compton, Karl T. *If the Atomic Bomb Had Not Been Dropped* (from the December 1946 issue of *Atlantic Monthly*)
http://www.whistlestop.org/study_collections/bomb/large/background/bmb4-2.htm

2542. Dannen, Gene. *Web Links to Hiroshima* (all located in Hiroshima; all have at least some English text)
http://www.dannen.com/hiroshima_links.html

2543. Dannen, Gene. *Web Links to Nagasaki* (with text in both English and Japanese)
http://www.dannen.com/nagasaki_links.html

2544. Dannen, Gene. *Atomic Bomb Decision: Documents on the Decision to Use Atomic Bombs on the Cities of Hiroshima and Nagasaki* (the documents are overwhelmingly from 1945)
http://www.dannen.com/decision/index.html

2545. Einstein, Albert. *Einstein's Letter to Roosevelt concerning the Atomic Bomb* (August 1939)
http://www.danshistory.com/ww2/docs/einstein_letter.txt

2546. Ford, Daniel. *The Last Raid: How World War II Ended* (post Hiroshima conventional bombing)
http://www.airspacemag.com/ASM/Mag/Index/1995/AS/tlrd.html

2547. Ford, Daniel. *The Third Bomb* (evidence that the U.S. held off on the dropping of a third nuclear weapon and speculation as to why)
http://www.danford.net/third.htm

2548. Giangreco, D. M. *Operation Downfall [American invasion of Japan]: U.S. Plans and Japanese Counter-Measures* (lecture at the U.S. Army Command and General Staff College, 16 February 1998)
http://www.mtholyoke.edu/acad/intrel/giangrec.htm

2549. Hachiya, Michihiko. *Surviving the Atomic Attack on Hiroshima, 1945* (Hachiya was a medical doctor and hospital administrator)
http://www.ibiscom.com/hiroshima.htm

2550. Haynes, Lewis L. *Oral History—The Sinking of "USS Indianapolis"* (Haynes was senior medical officer on board; the *Indianapolis*, which delivered the atomic bomb to the Pacific)
http://www.history.navy.mil/faqs/faq30-5.htm

2551. Hicks, George E. *Tibbets, Enola Gay, and the Bomb* (interview with Tibbets)
http://www.military.com/Content/MoreContent?file=PRtibbets

2552. Holloway, David. *How the Bomb Saved Soviet Physics* (from the *Bulletin of the Atomic Scientists*)
http://www.thebulletin.org/issues/1994/nd94/nd94Holloway.html

2553. Leahy, William D. (Fleet Admiral). *The Leahy Diary: Prospect of a Negotiated Surrender*
http://www.historians.org/archive/hiroshima/180645.html

2554. Lee, Bruce. *Why Truman Bombed Hiroshima*
http://www-users.cs.umn.edu/~dyue/wiihist/hiroshima/ytruman.htm

2555. Lee, Bruce. *Why Truman Dropped the Atomic Bomb on Hiroshima*
(different text than other Lee article on the subject)
http://www.geocities.com/Heartland/Plains/5850/hiroshimabomb.html

2556. Long, Doug. *Hiroshima: Was It Necessary?* (extracts from contemporary materials plus bibliography of later analyses)
http://www.doug-long.com/

2557. MacEakin, Douglas J. *The Final Months of the War with Japan: Signals Intelligence, U.S. Invasion Planning, and the A-Bomb Decision* (1998 CIA sponsored historical study)
http://www.odci.gov/csi/monograph/4253605299/csi9810001.html
http://www.cia.gov/csi/monograph/4253605299/csi9810001.html

2558. McVay, III, Charles B. *Oral history—The Sinking of "USS Indianapolis"* (he was Commanding Officer when the vessel was sunk on July 30, 1945)
http://www.history.navy.mil/faqs/faq30-7.htm

2559. National Atomic Museum. *The Manhattan Project*
http://www.nhmccd.edu/contracts/lrc/kc/decade40.html

2560. Nuclear Age Peace Foundation. *Manhattan Project* (collection of source documents about development and decision to use the bomb)
http://www.nuclearfiles.org/docs/manhattan.html

2561. Ohba, Mitsauru. *A Bomb WWW Museum* (available in Japanese or English)
http://www.csi.ad.jp/ABOMB/index.html

2562. Patrick, Bethanne K. *Gen. Paul W. Tibbets* (pilot of the plane that dropped the first atomic bomb)
http://www.military.com/Content/MoreContent?file=ML_tibbets_bkp

2563. Project Whistlestop. *The Decision to Drop the Bomb* (links to various aspects of the evidence and controversy)
http://www.whistlestop.org/study_collections/bomb/large/bomb.htm

2564. Race, Chandler E. *The Decision to Drop the Atomic Bomb*
http://www.utexas.edu/projects/latinoarchives/narratives/
vol1no2/ATOMIC_BOMB/ATOMIC_BOMB.HTML

2565. Seattle Tribune. *Fifty Years from Trinity: On July 6, 1945, Everything Changed Forever*
http://seattletimes.nwsource.com/trinity/index.html

2566. Siomes, P. (Father). *Atomic Bombing of Hiroshima* (account by a German Jesuit, written soon after the event)
http://www.wtj.com/archives/hiroshima.htm

2567. Smith, J. B. *The Last Mission of World War II* (post Hiroshima conventional bombing)
http://pweb.netcom.com/~jb29miss/

2568. Takeharu, Terao. *Personal Record of Hiroshima A-Bomb Survival*
http://www.coara.or.jp/~ryoji/abomb/e-index.html

2569. Truman, Harry. *Truman A-Bomb Speech* (audio recording)
http://www.geocities.com/wmaxwell/truman.au

2570. [Unidentified.] *Enola Gay and the Bombing of Hiroshima: The Official Website of Brigadier General Paul W. Tibbits*
http://www.theenolagay.com/

2571. [Unidentified.] *Japanese Plan for September Defense of Kyushu* (Report, December 1945)
http://carlisle-www.army.mil/cgi-bin/usamhi/DL/showdoc.pl?docnum=27

2572. [Unidentified.] *Operation Downfall (Invasion of Japan): Strategic Plan (May 1945)*
http://carlisle-www.army.mil/cgi-bin/usamhi/DL/showdoc.pl?docnum=20

2573. [Unidentified.] *Remembering Nagaski*
http://www.exploratorium.edu/nagasaki/

2574. [Unidentified.] *Survey of Japanese Seacoast Artillery* (1946)
http://carlisle-www.army.mil/cgi-bin/usamhi/DL/showdoc.pl?docnum=726

2575. [Unidentified.] *Uranium Correspondence* (includes images of actual documents involved in urging bomb development and defending the possibility of nuclear fission)
http://gantner.webhouse.cc/einstein.htm

2576. U.S. Strategic Bombing Survey. *Japan's Struggle to End the War* (issued July 1, 1946)
http://www.whistlestop.org/study_collections/bomb/large/strategic_bombing/text/bmc6-1tx.htm

2577. [Various Individuals.] Voice of Hibakusha: Eye-Witness Accounts of the Bombing of Hiroshima (fifteen accounts)
http://www.inicom.com/hibakusha/

2578. Vischer, Ross. *The Atom Bomb* (why dropped; Truman's reasoning; etc)
http://www.atombomb.f2s.com/

2579. Walker, Ansil L. *Greatest Battle Never Fought* (Operation Downfall; scheduled invasion of Japan)
http://www.military.com/Content/MoreContent?file=PRinvasion

7

The Mainland Asian War, 1941–1945

China

2580. Abbey, Phil. *The Yangtze Patrol: U.S. Gunboats in China, 1854-1942* (survey of history, selected pictures, and other data)
http://www.geocities.com/Vienna/5047/YANGTZE.html

2581. APTSJW. *Alliance for Preserving the Truth of Sino-Japanese War*
http://www.cnd.org/njmassacre/aptsjw.html

2582. Arndt, C. O., Severin K. Turosienski, and Tung Yuen Fong. *Education in China Today* (1944; requires Adobe Acrobat for viewing)
http://worldwar2.smu.edu/cgi-bin/Pwebrecon.cgi?v1=42&ti
=1,42&CNT=50&Search_Arg=world+war&Search_Code
=GKEY&x=30&y=5&y=5&PID=3725&SEQ=20020105193815&SID=1

2583. Cook, Theodore F. *The China War: A Bibliographical Exploration of Major Works in English on the China-Japan Conflict and Sino-Japanese Relations in the Second World War* (in Adobe Acrobat)
http://www.fas.harvard.edu/~asiactr/sino-japanese/ChinaWarEssay.pdf

2584. Gaines, Richard W. *China Marines* (Marine experiences in China from 1920s through late 1940s)
http://www.expage.com/page/chinamarines

2585. Hanson, Mike. *Yangtze Patrol: American Naval Forces in China: A Selected Partially-Annotated Bibliography*
http://web.nps.navy.mil/~library/bibs/yangtzetoc.htm

2586. Hooker, Richard. *Nationalist China*
http://www.wsu.edu:8001/~dee/MODCHINA/NATIONAL.HTM

2587. Kai-shek, Chiang. *Message to Friendly Nations (July 7, 1941)*
http://www.sunsite.unc.edu/pha/policy/1941/410707b.html

2588. Kai-shek, Chiang. *Message to Nation on the Tenth Anniversary of the Moukden Incident (September 18, 1941)*
http://www.sunsite.unc.edu/pha/policy/1941/410918a.html

2589. Kelly, Christopher N. *World War II in Hunan Province* (including photographs by an American assigned to help upgrade the Chinese Army's fighting capacity)
http://home.att.net/~christopher.kelly/index.htm

2590. Kraus, Theresa L. *The U.S. Army Campaigns of World War II: China Offensive* (CMH Publication 72-39)
http://www.army.mil/cmh-pg/brochures/chinoff/chinoff.htm

2591. Murphy, Rhoads. *Oral History* (served 1942-46 in China with the "Friends Ambulance Unit")
http://www-personal.umich.edu/~amnornes/murphey.html

2592. Phillips, Steven. *English-Language Sources on China at War, 1937-1945* (requires Adobe Acrobat)
http://www.fas.harvard.edu/~asiactr/sino-japanese/sinojpaper.pdf

2593. Poon, Leon. *History of China* (based upon a U.S. Army study)
http://www-chaos.umd.edu/history/

2594. Royer, Mark, with Arthur E. Goodwin. *War of Resistance: Sino-Japanese (1937-1941) Wargame Rules—Japanese and Chinese Equipment* (although for "gamers," it provides detailed data on the type of arms used by the two sides)
http://www.magweb.com/sample/ww2/japequip.htm

2595. Sherry, Mark D. *The U.S. Army Campaigns of World War II: China Defensive* (CMH Publication 72-38)
http://www.army.mil/cmh-pg/brochures/72-38/72-38.htm

2596. Special Service Division, Army Special Forces. *Pocket Guide to China* (1943; Adobe Acrobat required)
http://worldwar2.smu.edu/cgi-bin/Pwebrecon.cgi?v1=100&ti
=51,100&CNT=50&Search_Arg=world+war&Search_Code=GKEY&x
=30&y=5&y=5&PID=3725&SEQ=20020105194602&SID=1

2597. Thomas, George W. *Oral History Interview* (served in U.S. Army and assigned to a Chinese Army unit)
http://fas-history.rutgers.edu/oralhistory/thomasgw.html

2598. Tse-Tung (= Zedong), Mao (1893-1976). *On Tactics against Japanese Imperialism [in China]* (December 27, 1935)
http://csf.colorado.edu/psn/marx/Other/Mao/351227.htm

2599. Tse-Tung (= Zedong), Mao (1893-1976). *The Task of Chinese Community Party in the Period of Resistance to Japan* (May 3, 1937)
http://csf.colorado.edu/psn/marx/Other/Mao/370503.htm

2600. Tyminski, Dariusz. *Witold Urbanowicz and "Flying Tigers"* (after doing duty with the Polish Air Force and the RAF, this skilled pilot landed up flying with the Americans in China)
http://www.elknet.pl/acestory/urbano/urbano.htm

2601. [Unidentified.] *China Incident, 1937* (chronology and foreign impact)
http://history.sandiego.edu/gen/WW2Timeline/step05.html

2602. [Unidentified.] *Chinese Alliance for Commemoration of the Sino-Japanese War Victims* (available in English, Japanese, or Chinese)
http://www.ww2.org.hk/

2603. [Unidentified.] *Chronology of the Chinese Revolution, 1800-1949*
http://www.unc.edu/courses/hist083/chronology.htm

2604. [Unidentified.] *Chronology of U.S.-China Relations, 1844-1990s*
http://www.unc.edu/courses/hist083/uschina_chrono.htm

2605. [Unidentified.] *Handouts: Maps* (a variety of maps related to China in the 1930s and 1940s)
http://www.unc.edu/courses/hist083/handouts.htm#Maps

2606. [Unidentified.] *Mascots of the China Marines*
http://www.scuttlebuttsmallchow.com/maschina.html

2607. van der Heide, Albert. *Chinese Civil War Helps Consolidate Japanese Claims on Mainland, 1926-1963* (year by year chronology)
http://www.godutch.com/herald/ww2/950823.htm

2608. Wen, Pu Rung. *Oral History* (life in China during the Japanese expansionism)
http://www-personal.umich.edu/~amnornes/peter.html

2609. West Point. *Maps of the Chinese Civil War* (1925-1949)
http://www.dean.usma.edu/history/dhistorymaps/
ChineseCWPages/ChineseCWToC.htm

2610. Youngkirst, Gus. *The Magic Carpet and Shanghai China* (transporting U.S. troops homeward at end of the war)
http://members.aol.com/famjustin/Youngkrist1.html

India-Burma

OVERLAPPING STUDIES: CHINA-BURMA-INDIA AS A JOINT THEATER

2611. Bloom, Bernard J. *War on Their Minds* (interview; after being a drill instructor and going to OCS, he was assigned to CBI)
http://www.whshistoryproject.org/ww2/Interviews/mr_bloom.html

2612. CBI Info. *Remember These CBI Generals?*
http://www.cbiinfo.com/generals.htm

2613. CBI Info. *The Central Archive for all Material Related to the China Burma India Theater of World War II* (including historical and veteran information)
http://www.cbiinfo.com/index.htm

2614. Hacking, Ruth A. *Dad's CBI Page*
http://home.earthlink.net/~rhack/

2615. Hoover Library. *China-Burma-India (CBI) Theater during World War II*
http://hoover.nara.gov/gallery/China/Political%20Evolution/1932-49/CBI.htm

2616. Kitterman, Ernest R. *A Tribute to the 14th Air Force*
http://community-2.webtv.net/cbivet/ATRIBUTETOTHE14th/

2617. Pussanis, Sr., Robert E. *Merrill's Marauder's Association Web Site*
http://www.marauder.org/

2618. Strottman, Tony. *308th Bombardment Group: China-Burma-India, 1942-1945*
http://www.geocities.com/308thbombgroup/index.htm

2619. Stutzman, Ralph. *347th Airdrome Squadron* (1944-1945)
http://www.geocities.com/pentagon/barracks/3407/

2620. [Unidentified.] *Imphal, the Hump and Beyond: U.S.A.A.F. Combat Cargo Groups of the Second World War*
http://comcar.org/comcarhome.htm

2621. Unidentified. *341st Bombardment Group, CBI*
http://www.341stbombgroup.org/

OVERLAPPING STUDIES: INDIA-BURMA

2622. Armed Forces Retirement Home. *Home For Heroes* (short biographies of selected retired vets)
http://www.defenselink.mil/specials/heroes/profiles.html

2623. Dilatush, Carleton C. *Oral History Interview* (served in U.S. Army Quartermaster Corps in India)
http://fas-history.rutgers.edu/oralhistory/dilatush.html

2624. Hogan, David W. *U.S. Army Campaigns in World War II: India-Burma* (CMH Publication 72-25)
http://www.army.mil/cmh-pg/brochures/indiaburma/indiaburma.htm

2625. Kohi, Jagjit (Mrs.) *The Bombing of Mandalay* (a three month flight on foot from Burma brought her to safety in northern India)
http://atschool.eduweb.co.uk/chatback/english/memories/~kohli.html

2626. Maas, Tom. *1213th Military Polish of the 10th AAF, 1943-1946* (served at bases in India and Burma)
http://www.angelfire.com/mi2/1213mp/index.html

2627. Stone, James W (compiler and editor). *Crisis Fleeting: Original Reports on Military Medicine in India and Burma in the Second World War* (1969)
http://www.armymedicine.army.mil/history/
booksdocs/wwii/CrisisFleeting/default.htm

INDIA

2628. Backman, Melvin. *Oral History* (served in India during the war)
http://www-personal.umich.edu/~amnornes/marc.html

2629. Karpstein, Rudy. *7th Bombardment Group: 1941 to 1945*
http://www.7thbg.org/

2630. Nelsen, Myron J. *Highlights of My Army Career*
http://www.geocities.com/Pentagon/Quarters/4667/

BURMA

2631. Carpenter, Eric E. *Excerpts from Letters of Eric Carpenter, Gunner, Royal Artillery, England 1940-Burma [1945]-1946*
http://homepage.ntlworld.com/the.carpenters/earlyday.htm

2632. Cochrane, S. *Black Watch: Chindits*
http://www.geocities.com/cochrane_94403/

2633. Hazarika, Sanjoy, *Stilwell Road: Stillborn or Reborn?* (from the *Assam Tribune* of September 1999; discussing exact route the road took and proposals to rebuild it to help the local economy)
http://www.northeastvigil.com/00091999a.htm

2634. Hedges, Rolfe. *The Chindits*
http://www.magweb.com/sample/sfront/sfr11chi.htm

2635. Latimer, Billy P. *Memories of the CBI Theater* (living conditions at Burma airfields the most discussed single theme)
http://www.centercomp.com/cgi-bin/dc3/story?1250

2636. Latimer, Billy P. *Memories of the Ranger's Support Operations*
http://www.centercomp.com/cgi-bin/dc3/story?1254

2637. Loseby, Paul. *Burma Star Association* (Chindits' purposes; chronology of the conflict that centered in Burma but overlapped into surrounding nations)
http://www.burmastar.org.uk/warr2.htm

2638. MacGarrigle, George L. *U.S. Army Campaigns in World War II: Central Burma* (CMH Publication 72-37)
http://www.army.mil/cmh-pg/brochures/centburma/centburma.htm

2639. Newell, Clayton R. *Burma, 1942* (CMH Publication 72-21)
http://www.army.mil/cmh-pg/brochures/pi/PI.htm

2640. Pearce, Frederick James. "*Grandad's War Memoirs," 1940-1945* (Burma)
http://www.users.waitrose.com/~grandad/

2641. Robinson, J. Ian. *George V. Faulkner, MD* (Faulkner served as a doctor with the Chindits)
http://www.glanmore.org/gvf/jri1.html

2642. Rothwell, Steve. *Burma Campaign*
http://www.rothwell.force9.co.uk/burmaweb/

2643. Sparkes, Edward. *The Mumblings of Edward Sparkes*
http://www.users.zetnet.co.uk/sparkes/

2644. Taylor, Ron. *Death Railway* (from Bangkok through Burma; built by western POWs)
http://www.britain-at-war.org.uk/Death_Railway/index.htm

2645. [Unidentified.] *Merrill's Maruaders, February–May 1944* (1945; 1990 edition—CMH Publication 100-4)
http://www.army.mil/cmh-pg/books/wwii/marauders/marauders-fw.htm

2646. [Unidentified.] *14639680 Private David Bennett—Chindit*
http://www.lindahome.freeuk.com/David/David.htm

2647. [Unidentified.] *The Burma Front*
http://history.acusd.edu/gen/WW2Timeline/Pacific06b.html

2648. Wingate, O. C. *Report of Operations of 77th Indian Infantry Brigade in Burma, February to June 1943* (excerpts)
http://www.glanmore.org/gvf/reportcvr.html

Other Southeast Asian Countries

2649. Kindman, W. *South East Asia 1944-1947* (over 200 photographs)
http://uk.geocities.com/walking2uk/

2650. Noor, Farish A. *Remembering Siam's Forgotten Hero: The Legacy of Pridi-Banomyong*
http://alpha.tu.ac.th/events/2000/preedee.100y/news/farish.a.noor.htm

2651. O'Hara, Danny. *The Origins of the War in Indochina* (including World War II section)
http://members.tripod.co.uk/Indochine/hist/begin.html

2652. Roosevelt, Franklin D. *On French Rule in Indochina* (February 23, 1945 press conference remarks)
http://www.mtholyoke.edu/acad/intrel/fdrpc.htm

2653. [Unidentified.] *Chronology of Cambodian History, 1940-1949*
http://www.geocities.com/khmerchronology/1940.htm

2654. [Unidentified.] *Franco-Thai Conflict in WW2*
http://www.netcomuk.co.uk/~dpohara/thai.htm

2655. [Unidentified.] *World War II—Occupation and Liberation [of Vietnam]*
http://www.vwam.com/vets/early2.html

2656. [U.S. State Department.] *Document on Indochina Handed by the Secretary of State to the Japanese Ambassador [Nomura], 8 August 1941*
http://www.mtholyoke.edu/acad/intrel/WorldWar2/nomura4.htm

2657. [Vichy France and Japan.] *Agreement between Japan and France Pledging Military Co-operation in Defense of Indo-China (Tokyo, July 29, 1941)*
http://www.ibiblio.org/pha/policy/1941/410729a.html

2658. Welles, Sumner. *Acting Secretary of State Sumner Welles' Statement on Japanese-French Collaboration in Indochina (July 24, 1941)*
http://www.ibiblio.org/pha/policy/1941/410724a.html

2659. Welles, Sumner. *Memorandum by the Acting Secretary of State [Welles] on a Meeting between President Roosevelt and the Japanese Ambassador on the Japanese Occupation of Indochina, 24 July 1941*
http://www.mtholyoke.edu/acad/intrel/WorldWar2/welles7.htm

Section Three

Wartime Leaders

8

Major Civilian and Military Leaders of the War Years

Overview

2660. Amnentorp, Steen. *The Generals of World War II* (site hoping to ultimately list and provide biographies on all generals of the war)
http://www.generals.dk/

2661. Noomen, E. J. *Graves [Sites] of World War II Personalities*
http://www.lp-net.com/pow/

Arnold, Henry H. ("Hap")

2662. Daso, Dik. *Origins of Airpower: Hap Arnold's Early Career in Aviation Technology, 1903-1935*
http://www.airpower.maxwell.af.mil/airchronicles/apj/win96/daso.html

2663. Simpson, Diana. *Henry H. Arnold: A Bibliography*
http://www.au.af.mil/au/aul/bibs/great/arnold.htm

2664. [Unidentified.] *Henry H. Arnold*
http://www.airpower.maxwell.af.mil/airchronicles/cc/arnold.html

2665. [Unidentified.] *Henry H. "Hap" Arnold—Portrait of a Visionary*
http://www.arnold.af.mil/aedc/visionary.htm

Auchinleck, Claude

2666. [Unidentified.] *Claude Auchinleck*
http://www.spartacus.schoolnet.co.uk/2WWauchinleck.htm

Bradley, Omar N.

2667. Hollister, Jay. *General Omar Nelson Bradley*
http://history.sandiego.edu/gen/WW2Timeline/bradley3.html

2668. Jewell, Larry W. *Oscar Nelson Bradley*
http://www.army.mil/cmh-pg/faq/brad_bio.htm

2669. Kirkpatrick, Charles E. *Omar Nelson Bradley* (Center of Military History)
http://www.army.mil/cmh-pg/brochures/bradley/bradley.htm

2670. MacDonald, Charles B. *Omar Bradley*
http://gi.grolier.com/wwii/wwii_bradley.html

2671. Simpson, Diana. *Omar N. Bradley* (a bibliography)
http://www.au.af.mil/au/aul/bibs/great/brad.htm

2672. [Unidentified.] *General of the Army Omar Nelson Bradley* (emphasis on ancestry)
http://www.rootsweb.com/~morandol/brad.htm

2673. [Unidentified.] *Omar Nelson Bradley*
http://www.odedodea.edu/k-12/D-Day/GVPT_stuff/Omar/Omar1.html

Chennault, Claire

2674. Barnett, Mindie. *Common Names, Uncommon People*
http://www.region10.com/new/exc_news_body_1.html

2675. Ford, Daniel. *China Tiger: Claire Lee Chennault, 1893-1958*
http://www.danford.net/clc.htm

2676. [Unidentified.] *Checking in with Anna Chan Chennault* (his wife)
http://www.taiwanheadlines.gov.tw/20011213/20011211f3.html

2677. [Unidentified.] *Claire Lee Chennault*
http://www.famoustexans.com/claireleechennault.htm

Chiang Kai-shek

2778. Huang, Ray. *Facing up to History-s Judgment—How to Pay Tribute on the Anniversary of Chiang Kai-shek's Death* (his limitations as a military leader)
http://weekly.china-forum.org/CCF95/ccf9518-1.html

2779. Litten, Frederick S. *Did Chiang Kai-shek Trigger the Fujian Rebellion? A Look at Some Western Archival Documents*
http://litten.de/fulltext/fujian2.htm

2780. Reese, Lori. *China's Christian Warrior*
http://www.cnn.com/ASIANOW/time/asia/magazine/1999/990823/cks.html

2781. Whitman, Alden. *The Life of Chiang Kai-Shek: A Leader Who Was Thrust Aside by Revolution* (obituary)
http://www.nytimes.com/learning/general/onthisday/bday/1031.html

2782. Yeu, Hsiu-Hua. *Chiang Kai-shek*
http://www.york.cuny.edu/~clip/student/yeh_h/lifefile/lifefile.html

Churchill, Winston S.

2683. Berlin, Isaiah. *Churchill and Roosevelt* (extract from *Winston Churchill in 1940*)
http://www.rjgeib.com/heroes/berlin/churchill-roosevelt.html

2684. Chance, Sue. *Churchill's Black Dog* (Churchill's euphemism for his tendency toward depression)
http://www.mhsource.com/exclusive/chanceth0196.html

2685. Churchill Center. *Life and Times of Winston S. Churchill*
http://www.winstonchurchill.org/index.html

2686. Churchill, Winston. *"Blood, Toil, Tears and Sweat" Speech (May 13, 1940)*
http://www.fordham.edu/halsall/mod/churchill-blood.html

2687. Churchill, Winston S. *Complete Speeches of Winston Churchill* ("complete" apparently refers to completeness of the text rather than this containing all his speeches; primarily war-time orations)
http://www.winstonchurchill.org/speeches.htm

2688. Churchill, Winston. *Famous Quotes & Stories of Winston Churchill*
http://www.winstonchurchill.org/bonmots.htm

2689. Churchill, Winston S. *Speeches of Winston Churchill: Sound Page* (recordings of varied speeches)
http://www.earthstation1.com/churchil.html

2690. DeAngelo, Don. *The Rise to Power of Winston Churchill—May 10, 1940*
http://history.acusd.edu/gen/WW2Timeline/churchill.html

2691. Keegan, John. *Sir Winston Churchill*
http://www.rjgeib.com/thoughts/britain/winston-churchill.html

2692. Mieder, Wolfgang. *"Make Hell While the Sun Shines:" Proverbial Rhetoric in Winston Churchill's The Second World War*
http://babel.its.utas.edu.au/docs/flonta/DP,1,2,95/CHURCHILL.html

2693. National Library of Scotland and Churchill Archive Center. *Churchill: The Evidence*
http://www.churchill.nls.ac.uk/main.html

2694. [Unidentified.] *The Rise to Power of Winston Churchill—May 10, 1940* (with summary of his career throughout the 30s)
http://history.acusd.edu/gen/WW2Timeline/churchill.html

2695. [Unidentified.] *Winston Churchill*
http://www.spartacus.schoolnet.co.uk/PRchurchill.htm

Clark, Mark

2696. Molnar, Jr., Alexander. *Secret Mission to Algeria: Operation Torch, North Africa*
http://www.navo.navy.mil/Bulletin/Feb_Mar_Apr_2001/mission_algiers.html

2697. Sandler, Stanley (editor). *Mark Clark*
http://korea50.army.mil/history/biographies/clark.html

de Gaulle, Charles

2698. Leahy, [Admiral] to Franklin D. Roosevelt. *[De Gaulle's Intention of Visiting Washington]* (no title on original; dated November 27, 1942)
http://www.fdrlibrary.marist.edu/psf/box2/t23qq01.html

2699. Roosevelt, Franklin D., and Charles de Gaulle. *Exchange of Toasts*

between President Roosevelt and General De Gaulle (follow link for the second toast)
http://www.fruitfromwashington.com/Recipes/literary/roosevelt1.htm

2700. [Unidentified.] *Appointment with the History*
http://www.geocities.com/iturks/html/appointment_with_history.html

2701. [Unidentified.] *Charles de Gaulle*
http://www.chateauversailles.fr/en/290.asp

Eisenhower, Dwight D.

2702. Edeiken, Yale F. *Dwight D. Eisenhower* (on the fate of the German General Staff)
http://www.nizkor.org/hweb/people/e/eisenhower-dwight/eisenhower-003.html

2703. Libowitz, Steve. *Liberating Ike's Letters*
http://www.jhu.edu/~jhumag/694web/policy.html

2704. Patrick, Bethanne K. *General Dwight D. Eisenhower*
http://www.military.com/Content/MoreContent?file=ML_eisenhower_bkp

2705. Seymour, Janet L. *Dwight D. Eisenhower* (a bibliography)
http://www.au.af.mil/au/aul/bibs/great/eisen99.htm

2706. [Unidentified.] *Dwight David Eisenhower* (follow links)
http://www.infoplease.com/ce6/people/A0816900.html

2707. [Unidentified.] *Dwight David Eisenhower: The Centennial* (1990; in the "Fiftieth Anniversary Commemorative Histories" series)
http://www.army.mil/cmh-pg/brochures/ike/ike.htm

2708. [Unidentified.] *General Eisenhower: Ideology and Rhetoric* (only has part of the "Conclusion")
http://spot.colorado.edu/~chernus/Research/General%20E.html

2709. [Unidentified.] *Time Man of the Year 1944*
http://www.time.com/time/special/moy/1944.html

Fletcher, Frank Jack

2710. Bauer, Jim. *Admiral Frank Jack Fletcher—Task Force Commander* (note internal links to "the battles" and to "the aftermath")
http://www.ww2pacific.com/fletcher.html

2711. Dennis, Christopher L. *Admiral Frank Jack Fletcher* (note links at bottom to two more sections)
http://www.marshallnet.com/~manor/ww2/fletcher.html

2712. Naval Historical Center. *Admiral Frank Jack Fletcher, USN (1885-1973)* (photographic collection)
http://www.history.navy.mil/photos/pers-us/uspers-f/fj-fltr.htm

2713. [Unidentified.] *Vice Admiral Frank Jack Fletcher* (concise biography).
http://www.microworks.net/pacific/biographies/frank_fletcher.htm

Goebbels, Joseph

2714. Goebbels, Joseph. *Nazi Propaganda by Joseph Goebbels, 1933-1945* (a large selection of speeches and articles)
http://www.calvin.edu/academic/cas/gpa/goebmain.htm

2715. Wistrich, Robert S. *Joseph Goebbels (1897-1945)*
http://www.us-israel.org/jsource/Holocaust/goebbels.html

Göring, Herman

2716. Nikor Project. *[Accusations against Goering at Nuremberg]* (with links to texts of details)
http://www3.ca.nizkor.org/hweb/imt/nca/nca-02/nca-02-16-01-index.html

2717. [Unidentified.] *Herman Goering*
http://www.spartacus.schoolnet.co.uk/2WWgoring.htm

2718. [Unidentified.] *Herman Goring (January 12, 1893-October 15, 1946)* (detailed chronology of events of his life)
http://history1900s.about.com/library/holocaust/
blgoering.htm?iam=ask&terms=goering+karinhalle

2719. [Unidentified.] *Herman Goring: German Ace of WWI, CO of Richthofen Group*
http://www.acepilots.com/wwi/ger_goering.html

Halsey, William Frederick, Jr.

2720. Naval Historical Center. *Fleet Admiral William F. Halsey, Jr.* (biography)
http://www.history.navy.mil/faqs/faq36-5.htm

2721. Naval Historical Center. *Fleet Admiral William F. Halsey, Jr., USN (1882-1959)* (photograph collection)
http://www.history.navy.mil/photos/pers-us/uspers-h/w-halsy.htm

2722. Patrick, Bethanne K. *Fleet Adm. William F. Halsey*
http://www.military.com/Content/MoreContent?file=ML_halsey_bkp

2723. [Unidentified.] *Admiral William F. Halsey*
http://www.microworks.net/pacific/biographies/william_halsey.htm

2724. [Unidentified.] *Admiral William ("Bull") Frederick Halsey*
http://www.stat.virginia.edu/halsey.html

2725. [Unidentified.] *Fleet Admiral William F. ("Bull") Halsey*
http://www.angelfire.com/fm/odyssey/Halsey.htm

2726. [Unidentified.] *William F. Halsey, Jr., Admiral, 1882-1959*
http://www.wardocuments.com/Halsey.html

Hess, Rudolph

2727. Grose, Thomas K. *A Bumbled Flight: Hitler's Deputy Crashed in Scotland. Why?*
http://www.usnews.com/usnews/doubleissue/mysteries/rudolph.htm

2728. Henderson, Diana M. *Rudolph Hess*
http://www-saw.arts.ed.ac.uk/secret/hess.html

2729. History Place. *Rudolph Hess*
http://www.historyplace.com/worldwar2/biographies/hess.htm

2730. [Unidentified.] *Rudolph Hess* (argues that the imprisoned Hess was an Allied "double")
http://www.rudolphhess.com/

2731. [Unidentified.] *Rudolph Hess* (German language site)
http://www.hetillegaleparool.nl/summary.html

2732. [Unidentified.] *Rudolph Hess: Flight from Reality?*
http://news.bbc.co.uk/hi/english/uk/scotland/newsid_1326000/1326958.stm

Heydrich, Reinhard

2733. Colombus, Tina. *Reinhard Heydrich* (internal links to different parts of his life)
http://www.megspace.com/education/trp/heydrich.html

2734. History Place. *SS Leader Reinhard Heydrich*
http://www.historyplace.com/worldwar2/biographies/heydrich.htm

2735. Schoenberg, Shira. *Reinhard Heydrich (1904-1942)*
http://www.us-israel.org/jsource/Holocaust/Heydrich.html

2736. [Unidentified.] *Heydrich Becomes Leader of RSHA [Reich Main Security Office]* (with details of organizational setup of the RSHA)
http://www.historyplace.com/worldwar2/holocaust/h-rsha.htm

2737. [Unidentified.] *Obergruppenfuehrer Reinhard Heydrich (1904-1942)*
http://www.joric.com/Conspiracy/Heidrich.htm

2738. [Unidentified.] *Reinhard Heydrich*
http://www.spartacus.schoolnet.co.uk/GERheydrich.htm

2739. [Unidentified.] *Richard Heydrich, Hitler's Nazi Butcher*
http://auschwitz.dk/Heydrich.htm

Himmler, Heinrich

2740. Himmler, Heinrich. *Heinrich Himmler* (quotations on proper treatment of "inferior" peoples)
http://fcit.coedu.usf.edu/holocaust/resource/document/DocHimml

2741. IB Holocaust Project. *Himmler Timeline*
http://www.historyplace.com/worldwar2/holocaust/h-rsha.htm

2742. [Unidentified.] *Heinrich Himmler*
http://www.spartacus.schoolnet.co.uk/GERhimmler.htm

2743. [Unidentified.] *Heinrich Himmler*
http://www.isd.net/aswanson/ww2his/himmler.htm

2744. [Unidentified.] *Heinrich Himmler (1900-1945)*
http://www.us-israel.org/jsource/Holocaust/himmler.html

2745. [Unidentified.] *Who Was Heinrich Himmler?*
http://www.holocaust-history.org/short-essays/heinrich-himmler.shtml

2746. van Capelleveen, R. T. *Heinrich Himmler*
http://www.absolutefacts.com/data/himmler.htm

Hirohito

2747. Efron, Soni. *Book Reveals Hirohito the Militarist* (embraces the maximization of his war blame)
http://www.sjwar.org/lat081200.htm

2748. Fisher, Linda, and John Borneman. *Death of the Father: Hirohito and Imperial Japan*
http://cidc.library.cornell.edu/DOF/japan/japan.htm

2749. Gibney, Sr., Frank. *Emperor Hirohito*
http://www.time.com/time/asia/asia/magazine/1999/990823/hirohito1.html

2750. Jensen, Jesper R. *Hirohito*
http://www.ramskov.nu/krih/ww2/personer/hirohito.htm

2751. Simon Wiesenthal Center. *Hirohito, Japanese Emperor, Powerless to Make Peace*
http://motlc.wiesenthal.com/text/x19/xm1900.html

2752. Sugita, Yoneyuki. *The International Military Tribunal of the Far East and Emperor Hirohito: Justice Undone*
http://www.sugita.org/lmtfe.htm

2753. Tsukahira, Toshi G. *Commentary on "Hirohito and the Making of Modern Japan"* (in this book review/rebuttal Tsukahira argues that the emperor had minimal direct responsibility for the war)
http://www.glocom.org/books_and_journals/
book_reviews/20010726_com_hirohito/

2754. [Unidentified.] *Emperor Hirohito*
http://www.angelfire.com/ia/totalwar/Hirohito.html

2755. [Unidentified.] *Japan: The Longest Reign* (obituary; *Time*, January 16, 1989)
http://vikingphoenix.com/public/rongstad/bio-obit/obithito.htm

Hitler, Adolf

2756. Birnbauer, Bill. *The Soviet Secrets on Hitler* (immediate postwar secret Soviet investigation of whether Hitler was actually dead)
http://www.theage.com.au/daily/980102/news/news13.html

2757. Degrelle, Leon. *The Enigma of Hitler* (evaluation of Hitler's essential self by one who knew him)
http://www4.stormfront.org/posterity/ns/enigma.html

2758. Doenitz, [Admiral]. *Admiral Doenitz' Announcement of Hitler's Death (May 1, 1945)*
http://www.sunsite.unc.edu/pha/policy/1945/450501a.html

2759. Federal Bureau of Investigation. *Adolph Hitler Reports* (Freedom of Information Act documents; some pertaining to an early 1930s alleged assassination attempt, others reputed "sightings" of him after the war)
http://foia.fbi.gov/hitler.htm ·

2760. Frey, David S. *Adolph Hitler, 1889-1945*
http://www.geohistory.com/GeoHistory/GHMaps/GeoWorld/hitler.html

2761. Grobman, Gary M. *Adolph Hitler*
http://remember.org/guide/Facts.root.hitler.html

2762. History Place. *Rise of Adolph Hitler* (in 24 chapters)
http://www.historyplace.com/worldwar2/riseofhitler/index.htm

2763. Hitler, Adolph. *Mein Kampf*
http://www.stormfront.org/books/mein_kampf/

2764. Hitler, Adolph. *Private and Political Testaments* (April 29, 1945)
http://www.ibiblio.org/pha/policy/1945/450429a.html

2765. Hitler, Adolph. [*Speeches and Letters*] (with links to specific texts)
http://www.us-israel.org/jsource/Holocaust/hitlertoc.html

2766. Langer, Walter C. *Psychological Profile of Adolph Hitler* (study sponsored by Office of Strategic Services; with links to specific sections)
http://www.ess.uwe.ac.uk/documents/osstitle.htm
http://www2.ca.nizkor.org/hweb/people/h/hitler-adolf/
oss-papers/text/profile-index.html

2767. Office of Strategic Services. *Adolph Hitler* (a lengthy collection of materials collected by the agency, and later declassified, about the life and attitudes of the German leader)
http://www.nizkor.org/hweb/people/h/hitler-adolf/oss-papers/text/

2768. O'Lepp, Wally. *The Propagander* (in depth study of Hitler as a propagandist as well as a large display of war time posters and related materials from various countries)
http://members.tripod.com/~Propagander/index.html

2769. Rempel, Gerhard. *Lectures for the History of Hitler's Germany*
http://mars.acnet.wnec.edu/~grempel/courses/hitler/lectures.html

2770. [Unidentified.] *Did Hitler Knew about the Holocaust? A Psychological Assessment*
http://www.abelard.org/hitler2.htm

2771. [Unidentified.] *The Art of Adolf Hitler*
http://members.tripod.com/~Propagander/index-7.html

2772. [Unidentified.] *The Psychology and Development of Adolph Hitler Schicklgruber*
http://www.abelard.org/hitler/hitler.htm

2773. Wistrich, Robert S. *Adolph Hitler (1889-1945)* (biographical entry from Wistrich's *Who's Who in Nazi Germany*)
http://www.us-israel.org/jsource/Holocaust/hitler.html

King, Ernest J.

2774. Naval Historical Center. *Fleet Admiral Ernest J. King* (biography)
http://www.history.navy.mil/faqs/faq36-3.htm

2775. Naval Historical Center. *Fleet Admiral Ernest J. King* (photograph collection)
http://www.history.navy.mil/photos/pers-us/uspers-k/ej-kng.htm

2776. [Unidentified.] *Ernest King*
http://www.spartacus.schoolnet.co.uk/2WWkingE.htm

2777. [Unidentified.] *King* (biography in connection with a warship named after him)
http://www.hazegray.org/danfs/dl-dlg/dlg10.htm

Kinkaid, Thomas Cassin

2778. [Unidentified.] *Admiral Thomas Cassin Kinkaid* (concise biography)
http://www.microworks.net/pacific/biographies/thomas_kinkaid.htm

2779. [Unidentified.] *Thomas Kinkaid*
http://www.spartacus.schoolnet.co.uk/2WWkinkaid.htm

2780. [Unidentified.] *Vice Admiral Thomas C. Kinkaid*
http://www.battle-of-leyte-gulf.com/Leaders/Americans/Kinkaid/kinkaid.shtml

Kondo, Nobutake

2781. Naval Historical Center. *Vice Admiral Nobutake Kondo, Japanese Navy* (1886-1953) (photograph)
http://www.history.navy.mil/photos/prs-for/japan/japrs-kl/n-kondo.htm

2782. [Unidentified.] *Nobutake Kondo*
http://www.spartacus.schoolnet.co.uk/2WWkondoN.htm

2783. [Unidentified.] *Vice-Admiral Nobutake Kondo*
http://www.geocities.com/dutcheastindies/kondo.html

Kurita, Takeo

2784. Naval Historical Center. *Vice Admiral Takeo Kurita, Japanese Navy (1889-1977)* (brief biography and photo)
http://www.history.navy.mil/photos/prs-for/japan/japrs-kl/t-kurita.htm

2785. [Unidentified.] *Rear-Admiral Takeo Kurita*
http://www.geocities.com/dutcheastindies/kurita.html

2786. [Unidentified.] *Takeo Kurita*
http://www.spartacus.schoolnet.co.uk/2WWkurita.htm

Leahy, William D.

2787. Naval Historical Center. *Fleet Admiral William D. Leahy* (biography)
http://www.history.navy.mil/faqs/faq36-2.htm

2788. [Unidentified.] *William D. Leahy Tribute Page*
http://www.military.com/HomePage/UserCreatedTributePage/
0,10980,713707,00.html

MacArthur, Douglas

2789. Donaldson, Gary A. *Douglas MacArthur (1880-1964)*
http://korea50.army.mil/history/biographies/macarthur.html

2790. Lutz, David W. *The Exercise of Military Judgment: A Philosophical Investigation of the Virtues and Vices of General Douglas MacArthur*
http://www.usafa.af.mil/jscope/JSCOPE97/Lutz97.htm

2791. Patrick, Bethanne K. *Gen. Douglas MacArthur*
http://www.military.com/Content/MoreContent?file=ML_macarthur_bkp

2792. Public Broadcasting System. *MacArthur* (includes transcript of the broadcast)
http://www.pbs.org/wgbh/amex/macarthur/

2793. [Unidentified.] *Douglas MacArthur* (photographs and text of three speeches of the General's)
http://www.homestead.com/douglassmacarthur/start.html

2794. [Unidentified.] *Douglas MacArthur* (audio of one speech and also of his officiating at Japan's surrender)
http://www.jhs.jordan.k12.ut.us/faculty/bcharon/audiomacarthur.html

2795. [Unidentified.] *Douglas MacArthur, General of the Army (1880-1964)*
http://www.wardocuments.com/macarthur.html

2796. [Unidentified.] *General Douglas MacArthur*
http://www.empereur.com/G._Douglas_MacArthur.html

Marshall, George C.

2797. McCarthy, Joe. *America's Restrait from Victory: The Story of George C. Marshall* (controversial Senator McCarthy's vigorous indictment of Marshall; includes first four chapters of book)
http://www.geocities.com/Pentagon/6315/victory.html

2798. Nobel e-Museum. *George Catlett Marshall*
http://www.nobel.se/peace/laureates/1953/marshall-bio.html

2799. Patrick, Bethanne K. *Gen. George C. Marshall*
http://www.military.com/Content/MoreContent?file=ML_marshall_bkp

2800. [Unidentified.] *George Marshall*
http://www.spartacus.schoolnet.co.uk/USAmarshallG.htm

2801. [Unidentified.] *George C. Marshall: Soldier of Peace* (exhibit at the National Portrait Gallery)
http://www.npg.si.edu/exh/marshall/index.htm

2802. [Unidentified.] *Time Man of the Year: George C. Marshall*
http://www.time.com/time/special/moy/1943.html

Montgomery, Bernard L.

2803. Tolppanen, Bradley P. *Field Marshal the Viscount Montgomery of Alamein: An On-line Bibliography* (with chronology of life)
http://www.ux1.eiu.edu/~cfbpt/monty.html

2804. [Unidentified.] *Bernard Montgomery*
http://www.spartacus.schoolnet.co.uk/2WWmontgomery.htm

Mussolini, Benito

2805. B.B.C. *Fascism in Italy* (including how Mussolini changed the nation)
http://ftp.bbc.co.uk/education/modern/fascism/fascihtm.htm

2806. Mussolini, Benito. *Speech Delivered by President Benito Mussolini* (to the Blackshirts, February 23, 1941, describing the progress of the Axis)
http://www.ibiblio.org/pha/policy/1941/410223a.html

2807. Musssolini, Benito. *The Basic Philosophy of Fascism*
http://www.wwnorton.com/college/history/ralph/workbook/ralprs35.htm

2808. Mussolini, Benito. *What is Fascism?* (1932)
http://www.fordham.edu/halsall/mod/mussolini-fascism.html

2809. Pelizza, Simone. *The Illusions of the Duce*
http://www.geocities.com/iturks/html/illusions_duce.html

2810. [Unidentified.] *Benito Mussolini in Pictures* (including pictures of his corpse)
http://www.gvn.net/~lowe/mussolini/

2811. [Unidentified.] *Biography of Benito Mussolini*
http://www.euronet.nl/users/wilfried/ww2/mussolin.htm

2812. [Unidentified.] *The Duce's Musketeers* (his bodyguard troops)
http://freespace.virgin.net/m.roma/

Nagumo, Chuichi

2813. Naval Historical Center. *Vice Admiral Chuichi Nagumo, Japanese Navy (1886-1944)* (short biography and photograph)
http://www.history.navy.mil/photos/prs-for/japan/japrs-n/c-nagmo.htm

2814. [Unidentified.] *Chuichi Nagumo*
http://www.spartacus.schoolnet.co.uk/2WWnagumo.htm

Nimitz, Chester William

2815. Naval Historical Center. *Fleet Admiral Chester W. Nimitz* (biography)
http://www.history.navy.mil/faqs/faq36-4.htm

2816. Naval Historical Center. *Fleet Admiral Chester W. Nimitz, USN (1885-1966)* (photograph collection)
http://www.history.navy.mil/photos/pers-us/uspers-n/c-nimitz.htm

2817. Patrick, Bethanne K. *Fleet Adm. Chester W. Nimitz*
http://www.military.com/Content/MoreContent?file=ML_nimitz_bkp

2818. [Unidentified.] *Chester Nimitz*
http://www.spartacus.schoolnet.co.uk/2WWnimitz.htm

2819. [Unidentified.] *Chester W. Nimitz*
http://www.famoustexans.com/chesternimitz.htm

2820. [Unidentified.] *Chester W. Nimitz Fleet Admiral (1885-1966)*
http://www.wardocuments.com/Nimitz.html

2821. [Unidentified.] *Fleet Admiral Chester William Nimitz* (concise biography)
http://www.microworks.net/pacific/biographies/chester_nimitz.htm

O'Gowan, Dorman

2822. [Unidentified.] *General Dorman O'Gowan* (Acting Chief of Staff to General Auchinleck)
http://www.cavannet.ie/history/people/chink.htm

Patton, George S., Jr.

2823. Ferguson, Paul. *General George S. Patton, Jr. (1885-1945)*
http://www.employees.org/~ferguson/Patton.html

2824. Kay, Michael. *General George S. Patton: Soldier, General, Pilot, Athlete, Father, Gun Owner, Hero, Legend*
http://www.ozemail.com.au/~mickay/patton.htm

2825. Patrick, Bethanne K. *Lt. Gen. George S. Patton, Jr.*
http://www.military.com/Content/MoreContent?file=ML_patton_bkp

2826. Patton, Jr., George S. *Helpful Hints to Hopeful Heroes* (unedited form of what became a chapter in his autobiography, *War As I Knew It*)
http://knox-www.army.mil/museum/helpful.htm

2827. Patton Society. *George S. Patton, Jr., Historical Society*
http://www.geocities.com/pattonhq/homeghq.html

2828. Schmidt, John. *General George S. Patton, Jr., 1885-1945*
http://www.geocities.com/Heartland/Fields/5248/patton.htm

2829. [Unidentified.] *General George S. Patton* (includes text of the speech he typically gave to components of the Third Army)
http://www.1918.com/phil/patton.shtml

2830. [Unidentified.] *My Dad Meets General Patton*
http://members.aol.com/famjustin/Toepan1.html

Pyle, Ernie

2831. Andrews, Allan R. *Ernie Pyle and an Unknown*
http://www.toad.net/~andrews/pyle97.html

2832. Andrews, Allan R. *It's Wise to Remember Ernie Pyle's Words*
http://www.toad.net/~andrews/pyle.html

2833. Greene, Bob. *What I've Been Looking For*
http://texnews.com/opinion97/greene071397.html

2834. McMichael, William H. *"Honoring Ernie Pyle"*
http://www.dtic.mil/soldiers/june95/p50.html

2835. Pyle, Ernie. *Last Column*
http://www.private-art.com/scrapbook/pyle/lastcolumn.html

Rommel, Erwin

2836. Irving David. *The Trail of the Desert Fox: Rommel Revised* (from the *Journal of Historical Review*)
http://vho.org/GB/Journals/JHR/10/4/Irving417-438.html

2837. Parada, George. *Achtung Panzer: Erwin (Johnanes Eugen) Rommel, the Desert Fox* (detailed biography)
http://www.achtungpanzer.com/gen1.htm

2838. [Unidentified.] *Erwin Rommel* (analysis of his strengths; illustrated with photographs)
http://hem2.passagen.se/p47/rommel0.htm

2839. [Unidentified.] *Erwin Rommel* (with internal links to additional material)
http://www.topedge.com/panels/ww2/na/rommel.html

2840. [Unidentified.] *Erwin Rommel, Jr.*
http://houseofice.tripod.com/contents/rommel.html

2841. [Unidentified.] *Field Marshall Erwin Rommel (1891-1944)*
http://www.joric.com/Conspiracy/Rommelb.htm

2842. [Unidentified.] *General Erwin Rommel*
http://www.geocities.com/Pentagon/Quarters/1695/Text/rommel.html

2843. [Unidentified.] *Through Rommel's Eyes* (a defense of Rommel's skills as a general)
http://www.geocities.com/kkh_khan/MobileWar.html

Roosevelt, Franklin D.

2844. Boshoz, Paul. *FDR Cartoon Archive*
http://www.nisk.k12.ny.us/fdr/index.html

2845. Internet Public Library. *Franklin Delano Roosevelt* (election returns and many other materials)
http://www.ipl.org/ref/POTUS/fdroosevelt.html

2846. Mayock, Tom. *FDR: Pacific Warlord* (emphasis on weaknesses and inadequacies of FDR's policies in the Pacific)
http://users.erols.com/tomtud/

2847. Roosevelt, Franklin D. *Fireside Chats of Franklin D. Roosevelt* (1933-1945)
http://www.mhrcc.org/fdr/fdr.html

2848. Roosevelt, Franklin D. *Fourth Inaugural Address (January 1, 1945)*
http://www.yale.edu/lawweb/avalon/presiden/inaug/froos4.htm
http://members.aol.com/forcountry/ww2/fdr7.htm

2849. Roosevelt, Franklin D. *Franklin D. Roosevelt* (selection of speeches)
http://odur.let.rug.nl/~usa/P/fr32/index.htm

2850. Roosevelt, Franklin D. *"Quarantine the Aggressors"* (1937 speech)
http://www.tamu.edu/scom/pres/speeches/fdrquara.html

2851. Roosevelt, Franklin D. *Third Inaugural Address (January 1, 1941)*
http://www.yale.edu/lawweb/avalon/presiden/inaug/froos3.htm
http://members.aol.com/forcountry/ww2/fdr6.htm

2852. [Roosevelt, Franklin D., and others.] *Franklin D. Roosevelt Library
and Digital Archives* (extremely large collection of material)
http://www.fdrlibrary.marist.edu/

2853. Stinett, Robert B. *December 7, 1941: A Setup from the Beginning* (puts
blame for the successful attack on the failures of the Roosevelt Administration)
http://www.independent.org/tii/news/001207Stinnett.html

2854. [Unidentified.] *Debunking the Roosevelt Myth* (vigorous critique of
alleged failures, with links to other materials taking the same approach)
http://www.rooseveltmyth.com/

2855. Willey, Mark. *FDR Scandal Page* (denouncing him as extreme left-
ist with minimal respect for law and fully deserving of impeachment,
with evidence for the accusations)
http://www.geocities.com/Pentagon/6315/fdr.html

2856. Willey, Mark E. *Pearl Harbor: Mother of All Conspiracies* (detailed
argument that the attack was "permitted" as a way to enter the war
against Germany)
http://www.geocities.com/Pentagon/6315/pearl.html

Speer, Albert

2857. Durden, K. K. T. *Albert Speer—Differing Historical Interpretations*
http://www.planetpapers.com/Assets/3612.php

2858. Elson, John. *Twilight Zone: Was Albert Speer a Repentant Nazi or a
Man in Denial?* (book review)
http://www.english.upenn.edu/~afilreis/Holocaust/speer.html

2859. Nuremburg Trials. *Cross-Examination of Albert Speer* (text)
http://www.law.umkc.edu/faculty/projects/ftrials/nuremberg/Speer.html

2860. Sereny, Gitta. *The Albert Speer I Knew: A Personal Assessment*
http://www.fpp.co.uk/Legal/Observer/Sereny/SerenyTimes030981.html

2861. [Unidentified.] *Albert Speer*
http://www.spartacus.schoolnet.co.uk/GERspeer.htm

2862. [Unidentified.] *Albert Speer: Architect, Politician, 1905-1980* (German language site, with key events of his life arranged by the year they occurred)
http://www.dhm.de/lemo/html/biografien/SpeerAlbert/

Spruance, Raymond Ames

2863. Naval Historical Center. *Admiral Raymond Ames Spruance, USN (1886-1969)* (photograph collection)
http://www.history.navy.mil/photos/pers-us/uspers-s/r-sprnc.htm

2864. Patrick, Bethanne K. *Adm. Raymond A. Spruance*
http://www.military.com/Content/MoreContent?file=ML_spruance_bkp

2865. Shultz, Fred. *Overrated and Underrated Admirals* (from *American Heritage*, September 2001 issue; argues Spruance was one of the most underrated admirals in American naval history)
http://www.americanheritage.com/AMHER/2001/06/over-under2.shtml

2866. [Unidentified.] *Admiral Raymond Ames Spruance* (brief biography)
http://www.microworks.net/pacific/biographies/raymond_spruance.htm

2867. [Unidentified.] *Raymond Spruance* (brief biography)
http://www.spartacus.schoolnet.co.uk/2WWspruance.htm

2868. [Unidentified.] *The Battle of the Philippine Sea: 19-20 June 1944— Spruance's Decision* (including the intense debate over whether it was the right one)
http://www.angelfire.com/fm/odyssey/PS_Spruance.htm

Stalin, Joseph

2869. Beach, John B. *Stalin: The Rise of the Beast* (detailed examination of rise to power and consolidation of it over enemies)
http://members.aol.com/redtsar/

2870. Blunden, Andy. *Stalinism: Its Origins and Future* (book length analysis)
http://home.mira.net/~andy/bs/

2871. Jensen, Jesper R. *Joseph Stalin*
http://www.ramskov.nu/krih/ww2/personer/stalin.htm

2872. Martens, Ludo. *Another View of Stalin* (a defense of the man and his policies)
http://www.tiac.net/users/knut/Stalin/book.html

2873. Radzinsky, Edvard. *Stalin: The First In-Depth Biography Based on Explosive New Documents from Russia's Secret Archives* (text of chapter one)
http://www.washingtonpost.com/wp-srv/style/longterm/books/chap1/stalin.htm

2874. Stalin, Joseph. *J. V. Stalin Internet Library* (collection of his writings)
http://www.marx2mao.org//Stalin/Index.html

2875. [Unidentified.] *Joseph Stalin*
http://www.isd.net/aswanson/ww2his/stalin.htm

2876. [Unidentified.] *Joseph Stalin*
http://www.spartacus.schoolnet.co.uk/RUSstalin.htm

2877. [Unidentified.] *Stalin Biographical Chronicle* (including audio of speeches)
http://www.stel.ru/stalin/

Stillwell, Joseph

2878. [Unidentified.] *Joseph Stillwell*
http://www.spartacus.schoolnet.co.uk/2WWstilwell.htm

Tito, Josip Broz

2879. Borneman, John, et al. *Death of the Father: Tito and Yugoslavia* (a favorable evaluation)
http://cidc.library.cornell.edu/dof/yugoslavia/yugo.htm

2880. [Unidentified.] *Josip Broz Tito: Politician, 1892-1980* (German language site; important years in his life and what occurred during them)
http://www.dhm.de/lemo/html/biografien/TitoJosipBroz/

2881. [Unidentified.] *Josip Broz: TITO: Tito's Home Page* (includes speeches and photographs)
http://www.titoville.com/

Tojo Hideki

2882. Simon Wiesenthal Center. *Hideki Tojo* (in two, linked parts)
http://motlc.wiesenthal.com/pages/t078/t07813.html

2883. Thomas, Tony. *The Tanto [= Sword] of General Tojo Hideki*
http://japanesesword.homestead.com/files/tojo.htm

2884. Tojo, Hideki. *Prison Diary of Tojo Hideki* (as translated in the *Journal of Historical Review*)
http://www.vho.org/GB/Journals/JHR/12/1/Tojo31-85.html

2885. [Unidentified.] *Akahata Criticizes the Film Which Hails the War Criminal Tojo* (*Japan Press Weekly*, May 30, 1998)
http://www.gainfo.org/SFPT/Amnesia/AKAHATA_criticizes
_the_film_which_hails_TOJO_Japan_Press_Weekly_30May1998.htm

2886. [Unidentified.] *Biography of Hideki Tojo*
http://www.euronet.nl/users/wilfried/ww2/tojo.htm

2887. [Unidentified.] *Hideki Tojo*
http://www.spartacus.schoolnet.co.uk/2WWtojo.htm

2888. [Unidentified.] *Tojo*
http://www.isd.net/aswanson/ww2his/tojo.htm

Truman, Harry S

2889. McDonald, John W. *10 of Truman's Happiest Years Spent in Senate*
http://www.whistlestop.org/senate/senate1.htm

2890. Truman, Harry S. *Address before a Joint Session of the Congress (April 16, 1945)* (committing himself to the same military victory policy as his predecessor; audio version also available at site)
http://www.trumanlibrary.org/ww2/stofunio.htm

2891. Truman, Harry S. *Letters to Bess* (a collection of letters he wrote to his wife, 1911-1943)
http://www.whistlestop.org/study_collections/personal/large/letters/pff2.htm

2892. Truman, Harry S. *Speech about the German Surrender* (audio version available also)
http://www.trumanlibrary.org/ww2/veday.htm

Turner, Richard Kelly

2893. Dyer, George C. (Vice Admiral). *The Amphibians Came to Conquer: The Story of Admiral Richard Kelly Turner.*
http://www.ibiblio.org/hyperwar/USN/ACTC/index.html

Wingate, Orde

2894. Teicher, Morton I. *Orde Wingate: Soldier for Zion* (book review stressing his ties with Israel)
http://www.jpost.com/Editions/2000/03/16/Books/Books.4143.html

2895. [Unidentified.] *Charles Orde Wingate* (upbringing and early military service in Palestine)
http://www.us-israel.org/jsource/biography/wingate.html

2896. [Unidentified.] *Orde Wingate*
http://members.aol.com/Ocwingate/index.html

2897. [Unidentified.] *Orde Wingate*
http://www.spartacus.schoolnet.co.uk/2WWwingate.htm

Yamamoto Isoroku

2898. Kageyama, Yuri. *Museum Dedicated to Japan's Pearl Harbor Admiral to Open* (*USA Today* article, October 19, 1999)
http://www.usatoday.com/life/travel/leisure/1999/t0414ph.htm

2899. Naval Historical Center. *Admiral Isoroku Yamamoto, Japanese Navy (1884-1943)* (short biography and pictures)
http://www.history.navy.mil/photos/prs-for/japan/japrs-xz/i-yamto.htm

2900. Sherman, Stephen. *Major John W. Mitchell: Leader of the Yamamoto Shoot-Down*
http://www.acepilots.com/usaaf_mitchell.html

2901. [Unidentified.] *The Death of Admiral Yamamoto: America Takes Revenge for Pearl Harbor*
http://www.grunts.net/special/yamamoto.html

2902. [Unidentified.] *Yamamoto v. the Dragon* (from *Time* on-line)
http://www.time.com/time/sampler/article/0,8599,128080-8,00.html

2903. U.S. Air Force Press Release. *Air Force 50th Anniversary: 347th Downs Yamamoto* (dated January 2, 1997)
http://www.af.mil/news/Jan1997/n19970102_970009.html

Zhukov, Georgi

2904. Beckhusen, Robert. *Georgi Zhukov*
http://www.zhukov.org/

2905. [Unidentified.] *Archives* (details on the battles he fought in during his career)
http://web.mitsi.com/zhukov/Archives.htm

2906. [Unidentified.] *Marshall Georgi Zhukov*
http://www.fortunecity.com/victorian/riley/787/Soviet/Zhukov/Zhukov.html

Author Index

References are to entry numbers.

Subject Index

References are to entry numbers.

"Africa Circus" 1894
African-Americans *see*
Black Americans
Air Force and airborne
units (Australia): aces
2506; bombers 2518;
RAF/RAAF Lancaster
Squadrons 2520
Air Force and airborne
units (Belgian) 1300
Air Force and airborne
units (British; specific
units) 4 Parachute
Squadron Royal Engi-
neers 1789; 8th Army
parachute regiment 176;
150 Squadron 1558; 205
Group 1559, 1976; 211
Squadron 536; 358
Squadron 849; 617
Squadron ("Dambusters")
1843; 879 Fleet Air Arm
527; *see also* Royal Air
Force
Air Force and airborne
units (Bulgaria): aces
1326
Air Force and airborne
units (Canadian, by sub-
ject): aces 2018
Air Force and airborne units
(Canadian; specific units):
1st Canadian Parachute
Battallion 178; 421 RCAF
Squadron 1697
Air Force and airborne
units (Finland): aces
1355, 1363; mid-air acci-
dents 1354; planes of
1353, 1359

Air Force and airborne
units (French): aces 1315;
reasons they were defeat-
ed 1309
Air Force and airborne
units (German): Spitfire
hunters 214; *see also* Luft-
wafe
Air Force and airborne
units (Holland): Dutch
East Indies Air Force in
Australia 2151
Air Force and airborne
units (Hungarian): aces
1328
Air Force and airborne
units (Italian): aces 1986;
experimental aircraft
2004
Air Force and airborne
units (Japan): experi-
mental aircraft 2028;
organizational structure
2059; overview 2030;
pre-war western denigra-
tion of its capacities 391
Air Force and airborne
units (Polish): 315 Polish
Fighter Squadron 1267
Air Force and airborne
units (Romanian) 1339
Air Force and airborne
units (Russian) 1630
Air Force and airborne
units (U.S.; specific
units): Air Group 4 524;
2nd Tactical Air Force
1667; 3rd Bombardment
Group 382; 4th Fighter
Group 185; 5th Air Force

380; 7th Bombardment
Group 2629; 8th Air
Force 194, 215, 935, 1536,
1560, 1837; 9th Air Force
1536, 1537; 10th Air
Force 2626; 11th Air
Force 2135; 11th Bom-
bardment Group 2275;
14th Air Force 103, 2616;
33rd Photographic
Reconnaissance
Squadron, 9th U.S. Air
Force 213; 69th of the
8th Air Force (journal-
ists) 192; 82nd Airborne
820, 1639, 1696, 1703,
1817; 100th Bombard-
ment Group 836; 101st
Airborne 175, 850, 1655,
1703, 1801; 303rd Bom-
bardment Group, 8th Air
Force 220, 1446; 306th
Bombardment Group
1548; 308th Bombard-
ment Group 2618; 316th
Fighter Squadron (a/k/a
"Hell's Bells") 228; 325th
Fighter Group 844;
325th Glider Infantry
Regiment 1707; 341st
Bombardment Group
2621; 347th Airdrome
Squadron 2619; 351st
Bombardment Group
203; 379th Fighter
Squadron 210; 404th
Fighter Group 199; 410th
Bomber Group, 9th Air
Force 811, 827, 1552;
452nd Bomber Group

285

Battalion 917, 919; Free-
man Field and black
pilots 897; in Ardennes
898; in European theater
915; in infantry 914; in
Italy 895, 907; in marines
908; in navy 900; in
Pacific 891, 903, 906, 913;
in United Kingdom 892;
integration of military
902, 918; merchant
marine service 924; news-
paper reports on service
925; public war image of
887; quartermaster units
912; race riots 888, 910;
Tuskegee Airmen 885,
886, 889, 893, 896, 905,
921; war involvement of,
World War II and before
894, 899, 904, 911;
wartime movie on 916,
920; women in WACs
981
"Black Sunday": 1343
Black Watch: 2632
Blanchfield, Florence A.
(Lt. Col.): 980
Bletchley Park 1013; *see also*
Enigma/Ultra
bomb disposal 573
Bougainville: firsthand
accounts 2324; Hill 700
2323; overview 2325
Boy Scouts 1036
Boyington, Gregory 373
Bradley, Omar N.: ancestry
2672; bibliography 2671;
overview 2667, 2668,
2669, 2670, 2673
Brisbane Line 2515
Britain *see* Great Britain
Brittany 1307
Bulgaria: air force 1326;
war years 1324, 1325
Burma 98; airfields 2635;
Black Watch 2632;
British Royal Artillery in
554, 2631; Chindits
2632, 2634, 2637, 2641,
2646; chronology 2637;
Death Railway 2644;
firsthand accounts 2631,
2635, 2636, 2640, 2642,
2643; Indian infantry in
Burma 2648; Merrill's

Marauders 2645;
overview 2638, 2639;
Rangers 2636; Stillwell
Road 2633; western pris-
oners taken 859
Bush, George H. W. (pilot;
future president) 488
Butler, McClernand (Lt.
Col.) 1797

Cactus Air Force (Guadal-
canal) 2276, 2305
Caen (France) 1759
Cairo Conference: official
declaration of policy 158;
various documents 157
Cambodia: chronology of
1940s 2653
camouflage: German
bunkers 1212; land based
installations 1150; naval
622
Canada: Bank of Canada
and foreign gold 1023;
Canadian Broadcasting
Corporation 1026; intelligence training activities
1868; international policy
(1921–1939) 160; interna-
tional policy (1939–1945)
161; internment of Japan-
ese 1022, 1024; Labrador
1025; merchant marine
661, 662; military controversies 322; Newfound-
land 1025; role in Battle
of the Atlantic 1496,
1513; sailors 660; women
in the war: *role of Jill
Canuck in advancing
women's military role* 966,
servicewomen 965,
*wartime diaries and remi-
niscences* 1027, 1028
Canada (army): airborne
units, 178, 1647; at Arn-
hem, 1777; Calgary
Highlanders 324; early
stage of the war 323; in
Belgium 1775, 1781; in
Hong Kong 2159, 2160;
involvement in Europe
before German triumph
1305; liberating channel
ports 1782; overseas operations overview, 325; role

in invasion of Sicily 1953;
role in Italian operations
1965; role in Normandy
invasion 1692, 1699, 1714;
role in liberation of
Netherlands 1299; 2nd
Division 1766; solders in
England 1464; SSR
(South Saskatchewan
Regiment) 326, 1737; 3rd
Canadian Infantry Divi-
sion 1783
Canuck, Jill 966
Cape Esperance, Battle of
2262, 2298
Capra, Frank (filmmaker)
Battle of Midway 2215;
film on black war heroes
916, 920
Carlson's Raiders *see*
Marine Raiders
Carney, Robert B. (Rear
Admiral) 459
Carpenter, Eric 554
cartoons (political) 1046
Casablanca Conference
exclusion of General
deGaulle; official com-
munique 125; Roosevelt's
radio address concerning
126
casualties: American proce-
dures to notify nearest of
kin 355; statistical profile
of U.S. personnel 686
CBI *see* China Burma
India Theater of Opera-
tions
Central Intelligence Bureau
997
Chamberlain, Neville: declaration of war 1245;
guarantee of Polish inde-
pendence 1247; "Peace in
Our Time" speech (Sep-
tember 1938) 38; speech-
es on coming of war
1246
Channel Islands: 1143, 1149
Chennault, Claire L. (General): 98, 101, 105, 2674,
2675, 2676, 2677; letters
90
Cherbourg (France) 1679
chaplains: 268, 303, 1643
Cherchell-Mediouna